THE POCKET GUIDE TO THE INTERNET

If you're put off by manuals, thick technical treatises, and high-priced gobbledygook, you're not alone.

Up until now, getting information about the Internet has been like trying to get a glass of water from an open fire hydrant. THE POCKET GUIDE TO THE INTERNET is different. It's designed for the average person, with everything you need to know right here, in one, complete, simple book.

THE POCKET GUIDE TO THE INTERNET is user-friendly because it's based on the most frequently asked questions from hundreds of beginners and new users. It takes you on a personal tour of the Internet, and tells you what the Internet is, how to connect to it, and where the hottest places to go on it are.

This is the one Internet book for everyone. THE POCKET GUIDE TO THE INTERNET will show you how to surf the Web, chart your course, and discover new vistas and horizons on the cyberspace frontier.

Come and join us on-line!
Visit us at http://www.pocketbooks.
com/netguide.html

THE
POCKET GUIDE
TO THE
INTERNET

GARY GACH

Illustrated by Kevin Markowski

POCKET BOOKS

New York   London   Toronto   Sydney   Tokyo   Singapore

First published in Great Britain by Pocket Books, 1996
An imprint of Simon & Schuster Ltd
A Viacom Company

Simon & Schuster Ltd
West Garden Place
Kendal Street
London W2 2AQ

Simon & Schuster of Australia Pty Ltd
Sydney

A CIP catalogue record for this book is available from the British Library

ISBN 0-671-51666-3

Printed and bound in Great Britain by Caledonian International Book
Manufacturing, Glasgow

The Americans have need for the telephone, but we do not. We have plenty of messenger boys.

—SIR WILLIAM PREECE,
Chief Engineer of the British
Post Office, 1876

Contents

TOUR

A THE INTERNET: WHAT IS IT?

B A GUIDED TOUR OF THE INTERNET

C PUTTING IT IN PERSPECTIVE

ALMANAC

Acknowledgments

This book is the product of my teaching basic Internet, several different classes each month, for over three years. I've been most fortunate to have been able to do so. Each time a student might raise a hand and stop me because the logic didn't flow or something wasn't clear, I'd go home, rethink, and, more often than not, reframe the course to incorporate that input, to try out on the next class. So to all the alumni of my classes, for all your questions and comments, from which readers hence can profit, thank you.

In that regard, I'd like to thank Erika Wudtke of Media Alliance, where I first taught, Roseanne Sullivan of The Learning Annex, and Spencer Brucker, UC Berkeley Extension. Special thanks go to Larry Smith, who edited my "Internet Scout" column for a year for *MediaFile,* as well as to *Cyberspace Today, Net Guide, Interactive Age, New Media* (http://www.hyperstand.com), and *Connect!* for publishing my writings about the Net.

While I can't thank the Internet or its pioneers by name, they've been the valuable "without which none of this, of course, would have been possible." Much of my own learning about the Internet came about before the days of trainers, much less books, largely through the generosity and wisdom of two sources. A fellowship from the Washington Research Institute (1989–1991) provided me not only with incomparable technical assistance but, moreover, an unparalleled opportunity to view its dynamic educational and democratic potentials in action. And, for commissioning me to write an Internet manual, and generously providing access and support to do so, Pandora Information Systems deserves equally special acknowledgment and thanks.

I owe a barrelful of ink to Kevin Markowski for the wit and warmth as well as clarity and thrust of his art.

Stellar kudos go to my publisher. Being a part of such a team has been one of my greatest learning experiences. My spotlight falls, first, on Scott Shannon, who listened to my call "out of the blue" and valiantly shepherded it through all the hoops. My editor, Dave Stern, kept me on the page this book wanted to be, from script to print, and, in the process, proved to be like a brother separated from birth. Of the many, many other pairs of eyes and hands at the offices on Publishers' Row that helped craft this book, particular thanks goes to Joann Foster, whose herculean efforts kept this book on track, and to Penny Haynes, Donna O'Neill and Irene Yuss. The unflagging care of my agent, Jack Scovil, stalwart, suave, and sage, was exceptionally critical. Thanks, too, to Rose Nelli, Command Central.

Of my ad hoc Technical Editors, Hank Duderstadt, Dudervision; Ole Jacobsen, Editor-Publisher, *ConneXions;* Prof. Leonard Kleinrock, Computer Sciences, UCLA; and Mike Stein, IGC, words cannot express my gratitude for your patient, cogent clarity, no less from someone whose VCR still blinks 12:00; thank you all. A humble tip of the fedora to DC Jakob for a few drops of comparative morphology. I am particularly grateful to Mark Graham, founder of PeaceNet, now president of Whole Earth Systems at the Well, for his singular vision, generosity, and friendship, over the years.

Additional packets of thanks go to Ed Allendorf; Mike Beach, and Pat Bourne, CERFNet; Howard Frederick; John Jewell, California State Library; the reference desk, Mechanics' Institute; Nancy Moorhead; ProfNet and their numerous associates; Louis Rosenfeld, Argus Associates; Mike Sendall, CERN; May A. and Nasir Naseb, Compu-Tyme; Larry Tuch, Writers Guild of America. Of course, my parents provided essential, tender loving care (TLC) but also much of my skills. Any residual errors are, of course, my own.

All attempts have been made to attribute sources of infor-

mation wherever possible. If any errors or omissions have
been made, they will be corrected in future editions.

Art/charts on pp. 10, 11, 13, 21, 171, and 297 are adapted from U.S.
Report to Congress, "Information Superhighway—Issues Affecting Development," GAO-RCED-94-285; September 1994, Washington, D.C. Vinton Cerf's explanation of packet-switching is taken from his "Computer
Networking: Global infrastructure for the 21st Century," copyright 1995
by Vinton G. Cerf and the Computing Research Association. The quotations from Robert Kahn and John Quarterman on the history of e-mail are
from "The ARPANET Is Twenty" and "The History of the Internet &
The Matrix," *ConneXions*, III:10 and IX:4, respectively. Omar Wasow's
statement about New York Online was taken from "Cyberfuture" by Char-
layne Hunter-Gault, *The MacNeil/Lehrer News Hour*, August 3, 1995. Gay
Crawford's comments about e-mail are from *The NBC Nightly News with
Tom Brokaw*, March 1992. John Seabrook's "E-mail from Bill" was first
published in the January 10, 1994 *New Yorker*. The quotation from Thomas
Wolfe is from *You Can't Go Home Again*, HarperCollins (N.Y., 1940).
Gene Spafford's statement on forums and John S. Quarterman's note on
Usenet are from *ConneXions*, II:10 and X:4 (*op. cit.*). L. M. Boyd's "Grab
Bag" and *Harper's* "Harper's Index" are quoted on pp. 125–6. William
Gibson's definition of cyberspace is from his *Neuromancer*, Ace Books
(N.Y., 1984). Peter Drucker's observations on p. 209 are from "Infoliter-
acy," *Forbes ASAP*, August 29, 1994. Professor Johnson's and Professor
Reddick's observations about electronic journalism are taken from online
forums, with their kind permission. David Rothenberg's epigraph on technology, heading our chapter on science, is from his book *Hand's End*,
University of California Press. George Gilder's quotation in our chapter
on computers is from an interview by Mary Eisenhart in the July 1994
MicroTimes (http://www.microtimes.com). The two quotes from John H.
Fund's article "We Are All Pundits Now" were published in the November 8, 1994 *Wall Street Journal*. Phil Agre's comments on Ralph Reed's
quote have been ongoing in the second series of *The Network Observer*,
1995 (http://communication.ucsd.edu/pagre/tno.html), and are used here
with the author's kind permission. And the quotation from Aung San Suu
Kyi is from her opening keynote address to the NGO Forum on Women,
August 31, 1995, Beijing.

Preface

Welcome!

For those wanting twenty-five words at the very outset as to why they *should* learn the Internet —————:

Fact: Today's computer without a modem is like an amœba—cut off from a vast ocean of resources, both digital and human.

And —————

Fact: In the 21st century, computers can be career-critical technology.

It's as simple as that.

This is basic literacy for the future . . .

. . . today.

Period.

This book is different from the 365 other Internet books on the shelves.

It's the world's first mass-market pocket guide to the Internet. (Hooray for miniaturization of information technology!) Because we're short, we're more complete: we don't go off on so many tangents so that you lose the thread of what's essential.

It's the only book you'll ever need to become Internet literate and to integrate that literacy into your life, for work and play.

The guide's in two halves:

1) A tour. The first half's an ABC, a primer of vocabulary and tools—a definition of the Internet and how to connect, a guided tour of its tools, and directions on how to put it all in perspective for yourself.

2) An almanac. This half spotlights ten major topics where Internet influence is keenly felt. (You'll want to underline or highlight particular compass points for future reference.)

With these as your X- and Y-coordinates, you'll be able to sample the entire Internet and plot your own course.

Some of you may never use a computer (more power to you!), but want to know about the Internet, simply out of human curiosity. Some may be considering getting their first computer just to be able to use the Internet. (Great idea!) Some may have a modem but have not used it yet. Many of you (probably the majority) may be using a portion of the Internet already—at work or at school—and want to know more about it.

Or maybe you have Internet access—from a provider or "in a box"—but they don't explain what you can do with it nor how you can learn more about it yourself.

Maybe you've begun exploring and using it, but are still not sure whether you're using the full Internet yet. This book was written so that you do not have to suffer through what many have endured simply to find out what the big whoop is all about.

The first section includes literal descriptions and How-To that may not apply to you if you're already gotten your feet wet. This was unavoidable; otherwise, this book would have been only for the already-partially-initiated but not the absolute beginner as well.

Readers expecting to jump right in with the world-wide web, Mosaic, or Netscape might be disappointed initially. They will be rewarded, however, for following along our progression of how we arrive there.

The web is last, but not least, in our tour. For sure, the web is the most exciting area of the Internet to date. Its use simplifies much of the Internet. However, as Einstein observed, everything should be made as simple as possible but not simpler. The web pushes on that boundary. (An expert we know recently changed his business card from *Web Consultant* to *Internet Consultant,* because he felt too many were missing much of the Net in all the dazzle of the web.) So, instead, we lay a solid, systemic framework with which to understand and use both the web, and the Net, to their fullest potentials.

It's expected that some of you might hop and skip around, as best you see fit. However, there's a certain sequential logic to this presentation. Here are some notes from my students.

"It's a basic overview." "It makes an amorphous subject quite concrete." "It will get you clear on the concepts—and open your mind." "It will give you confidence and an impetus." "It will help you organize your thoughts about the Internet." "It's a progression." "It's easy."

"It's empowering." "It's inspirational."

And (my favorite): "At last, something for all of us!"

I hope you find that's all true for you, too.

Internet Style

A guide to the Internet necessarily spans two kinds of prose. It combines the descriptive tourism of an automotive travel book and the technical specifications of an automobile parts manual. Something rather surreal inescapably results. (''As you drive through the Rockies, the view of the Pacific fog nestled in the valleys at dawn is breathtaking, especially when the gap between your spark plugs is no greater than three centimeters.'')

I kept tech and jargon down to an utter minimum. I've used only tech and jargon you're likely to hear so you won't stumble over them when you do. Nor did I dwell on PCs vs. Macs. Nor on goodies particular to either America Online, CompuServe, or Prodigy, etc.

Just as there is no common knowledge base for the Internet, there seem to be no common rules of spelling. The creators of archie, I'm told, wanted their name for it to be in all lower case. Usenet, however, prefers to call itself in all caps or with the N uppercase. Tim Berners-Lee originally named his creation WorldWideWeb; now there are spaces between the three *w*'s but no hyphen—which is incorrect, either by the dictionary definition or the *Chicago Manual of Style*.

An early draft of this book tried spelling things as they appear in computer manuals. My editor and I decided all the capital letters strain the eye and seem to shout from the page, preempting the reader's own internal voice.

The Internet abounds in enough three-letter acronyms (TLAs), ''tech talk,'' and hype as it is. My making the page quieter, as it were, is, again, in the interests of minimizing any new-skill jitters and facilitating knowledge-building on the part of the reader. If something's been trademarked or patented (such as NExT, eWorld, Free-Net), then fine. Otherwise, I've preferred to humanize the technical language, and treat it as if conventions of grammar and common usage apply. The majority of people ought not to use conventions established by very bright people who cannot write. Anyone coining a word should respect the language.

I privilege the Internet and treat it as a proper noun—as if it were a place. As to acronyms at first mention, I use the standard spelling. Subsequently, I opt for an initial cap and lower case, or even all lower case. Thus, UNIX = Unix. Similarly, World Wide Web = world-wide web. And ASCII = Ascii = ascii. However, U.S. and U.S.A. remain as is. I've kept the page's noise level down, as it were, so the reader can concentrate. I assume that if the reader wants rock 'n' roll or a cup of coffee while they read, they can help themselves, without the author tasking the Type Department with work wasted, making words pop out at the eye from many directions at once, in boldface, different fonts, garish headlines, etc. Words speak well enough for themselves.

Similarly, the reader can underline and highlight as need be.

When online addresses (such as http://www.bangbang. woofwoof) run over to a new line, I haven't hyphenated them. Just type them as one string, without a space in the middle. That way, you'll know any hyphens are part of the address. However, if they end a sentence, you aren't supposed to type in the final period as part of the address.

Trails change fast in cyberspace. All addresses were good at the time we went to press, but if you try one that's been disconnected, with no forwarding address, not to worry. Just search for the name with one of the web ''spiders'' on page 335, which should take you to the latest version.

And one last item of Internet style: the kangaroo you see in many of the illustrations is the Pocket Books mascot, Gertrude, who illustrator Kevin Markowski and I have ''recruited'' to help illuminate some points discussed in text.

TOUR

This half of the guide is a tour. Not a manual, but a "minds-on." It's more for conceptual knowledge of the medium and an understanding of the tools, rather than "hands-on" skills building.

However, if you have access to the world-wide web and want to get your feet wet first, feel free to peruse one of the online tutorials listed in the Appendix before reading on. Ultimately, learning basic Internet literacy is part conceptual, part practice. In this half of the guide, you'll find out all you'll need to practice for yourself.

THE INTERNET:
WHAT IS IT?

What is the Internet?

Let's define it in two ways: first, using a (hypothetical) real-life example involving networking, and second, with a bit of history.

EVERYDAY NETWORKING AND TELECOMMUNICATIONS

Let's begin with what we can all relate to: everyday life. Let's imagine that, instead of a writer, I'm a researcher at my local branch of Local Global Information, Inc.

Let's say I come into my office one Monday morning. First thing I do, I turn on my computer, and I see that I have an electronic mail message (e-mail) from Gertrude, the Managing Research Officer, entitled TODAY'S MARCHING ORDERS. I call it up to the screen and it reads:

"Mr. Gach: We're about to acquire a new account: widgets. Please prepare a document briefing the CEO about widgets by 5 P.M. Thank you. Gertrude."

NETWORKING

A network is anything that connects two or more people.

The message wound up in my computer from hers because we're a networked office. About 70 percent of PCs today are part of some network.

A network is anything that connects two or more people. It can be a special, common interest, like the PTA, or a gardening club. And a network can be two computers connected by a wire.

It means that after Gertrude typed that message in her computer, she didn't have to print it out, then have our office Mail Clerk route it to my in-box. The "tech talk" for this (which you won't need to remember) is a Local Area Network (or a LAN, pronounced like fan). If my Local Global office was hooked up with a few company branches across town, then our LANs could be part of an even greater network, such as a Wide-Area Network (or a WAN, pronounced like lan). Then a message could travel between different departments of one branch, or several, over computer.

Well, anyway, by the time I clear my desk of last week's mess, it's 10:30 A.M. Time for a quick cappuccino at the cafe across the street! (I live in the Bay Area, where we like our coffee, and strong, please.) I order my cappuccino at the counter and cruise with it on over to my favorite table, the one where there's a computer screen inlaid into the glass tabletop, with a keypad right beside the chair. This cafe is one of twenty that are part of a San Francisco Bay Area network called SF Net. This is a Bulletin Board System, or BBS. It's a kind of a WAN, you could say, only not a corporate application. There are over one hundred eighty thousand in America. They're very easy to set up and can be geared around special interests, like lifestyle, dating, jobs, computer-user groups, sports, genealogy, etc. SF Net is an attraction for people from all walks of life who like strong coffee and who like to engage in some java jive, table-hopping across San Francisco, Berkeley, and Marin for a witty chat, making new friends without worrying about uncomfortable, artificial, or intimidating surroundings. Or maybe to just play chess or solitaire.

So, I put in my quarter for five minutes' time and enter the Community Bulletin Board, where people post messages. I catch up on previous postings from over the weekend about various topics since I last logged in and swapped some gossip—about the big splashy movie that just opened, or about the recent return to the Midwest by a regular of the network to visit their ailing parents, or about The Man with a Pipe, or about The Redhead, and such-like. I also type in a message, entitled TELL ME

ABOUT WIDGETS . . . asking if anybody knows anything and listing my Internet e-mail address. (We'll cover Internet e-mail in just a minute.)

But a coffee break isn't very long. So I'm off to do some work—at the university library. By now, you've probably seen libraries with a computer replacing a card catalog. You press *A* for Author, *T* for Title, or *S* for Subject. If it's a big library, the computer catalog is checking several distinct departments at once, like Periodicals, Records, Special Collections, and Audiovisual, as well as History, Literature, Science, etc. Those individual card catalogs are all cross-referenced together. So I can check all the different departments at one time as one common database—just the way a word processor will search for a key word in a text—looking up "widget" as a subject, say. And if the library is a branch of an interlibrary system, like a state library or a state university library, perhaps the computer might also offer the option of checking the entire state or state university library system at once, including the various departments of each.

Anyway, I gather a bibliography on widgets, and maybe I can print it out right there. And I check out some key source materials. So I head back to the office and collate my research into a report. Maybe, as I'm finishing, I get another e-mail message in my computer. This one's entitled RE: TELL ME ABOUT WIDGETS . . . So I call it up to the screen and it says:

"Hello! My name is Bob T. Widget. I happen to be the only living, direct descendant of Ottmar Q. Assorio III—inventor of the first widget. The family sold the patent long ago, but I'm happy to hear of your interest and am attaching herewith a brief history of the invention. Please feel free to contact me at my address and phone number, below, for more information."

Yesssss! This will be a perfect introduction for my report, and I don't even have to type it up. I download it (pulling it onto my hard disc), delete the cover letter from Bob, and word-process the history he sent me so it matches the same layout as the rest of my report.

This is great. I finish it all up, e-mail it over to the CEO with a copy to Gertrude, under the title RE: MARCHING ORDERS: COMPLETED, and I'm outta here. Time to pay a visit to my bank ATM, then head for dinner in Chinatown.

Okay, let's stop here, hold the picture, and stand back two steps.

The first step back, we see I've just demonstrated a number of different kinds of networks using telecommunications—in the office, in cafes, in the library, and at the bank.

And each of these networks can be networks of smaller networks, internetworked together into a bigger network. The various departments of my office—Administration, Management, Human Resources, etc.—are linked together in a LAN, which, in turn, is part of a network of office branches, called a WAN, composed of various departments of several offices. A computer at one library branch can pool together a number of different department catalogs, and a larger, master catalog can group together various branches, each with all their particular departments. SF Net can be part of a network of BBS's and even participate in something we'll call for the moment international e-mail. And different bank branches can share a common ATM system, just as various banks share a common banking system.

Now, let's take one more step back. Imagine: what if I never had to leave my office. Or, better perhaps, what if I had a work arrangement to telecommute. I could do this if all those networks we've just seen were themselves all internetworked together into one bigger network. Imagine: from a single computer, at home, I'd get my e-mail project description from Management, communicate with my friends at the cafes, post a note that Bob Widget could find, research library catalogs and search through some of the holdings, and (to be futuristic) even do electronic banking.

What would the caption to this picture be? Here, we're *inter*-networking all these networks together—which may themselves be networks of networks, internetworked. We might entitle this conglomeration as one big:

$$\text{I N T E R}$$
$$\text{N E T}$$
$$\text{W O R K}$$

—or

$$\text{I N T E R}$$
$$\text{N E T}$$

for short.

The InterNet.

That's what it is. Simply, a big network of networks.

All kinds of computers—all hooked up together.

Now, to really understand this big network, we'll look at the historical model, the real story, which will yield some very striking insights.

IN THE BEGINNING

Many people helped design and develop the Internet. Indeed, its creation laid down a pattern for its subsequent use up to the present day: a collective, user-oriented, ad hoc, by-your-bootstraps endeavor.

Phase One began midcentury. In 1957, the Soviet Union launched Sputnik, beating the U.S. to outer space. The U.S. had been playing high-stakes poker with the U.S.S.R., and this caught them with their pants down, as it were. So the government created an agency for America to recapture the leading edge in new technology, called ARPA (Advanced Research Projects Association), with J.C.R. Licklider heading up the computer office. Now, when scientists applied for a grant from ARPA for a computer, they'd want one like everybody else's. And so ARPA scientists began asking other ARPA scientists about the resources on each other's computers. Some discussed time sharing and resource sharing with each other's computers. Licklider promoted the idea of linking computers.

Bear in mind that personal computers were still a dream, computers then commonly being dinosaurs with vacuum tubes and punch cards, with names like Eniac, Univac, and Colossus Mark. Interactive meant teletype. A display terminal was a luxury, costing $100,000 (the equivalent of a million today). Yet it looked like computing was getting less expensive much faster than communications. Still, the idea of interlinking computers was high-risk and very visionary.

A CIRCUIT-SWITCHING NETWORK

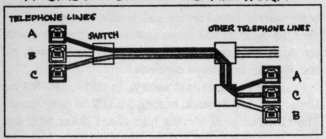

The primary breakthrough was *packet* switching. You don't need to understand it. But it's simple, and you can't help but appreciate the profundity of the innovation. To quote from Vinton Cerf:

> In a packet-switching system, data to be communicated is broken into small chunks [packets] that are labeled to show where they come from and where they are to go, rather like postcards in the postal system. Like postcards, packets have a maximum length and are not necessarily reliable. Packets are forwarded from one computer to another until they arrive at their destination. If any are lost, they are re-sent by the originator [without the whole message having to be re-sent]. The recipient acknowledges receipt of packets to eliminate unnecessary re-transmissions.

The postcards can arrive at their destination in any order. Along the way, however, they can adapt and take different routes from each other if there should be a gang-up or a "road closed." And they intermingle with all the other messages going out (the way postcards mix with letters and parcels). Thus the fabric of the total circuitry over which messages travel is decentralized—and capa-

A PACKET-SWITCHING NETWORK

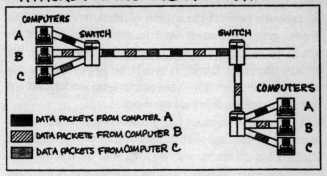

COMPUTERS
A
B
C

SWITCH

SWITCH

COMPUTERS
A
B
C

■ DATA PACKETS FROM COMPUTER A
▨ DATA PACKETS FROM COMPUTER B
▧ DATA PACKETS FROM COMPUTER C

ble of self-healing itself, survivable if any node were injured.

In contrast, in a circuit-switching network (*e.g.*, telephone), a connection is made at a central switching station. That connection, between calling and receiving party, is maintained for the length of the transmission, during which no other transmission can be sent over that circuit. Again, you don't have to think about the concept of movable type to appreciate this book any more than the concept of flexible photographs threaded for 24-frame/second viewing to appreciate movies: but understanding the fundamental bases of such revolutionary media does not detract from, and can even enhance, their use.

Leonard Kleinrock had pioneered the analysis, design, and underlying principles of packet switching in 1959, and published his dissertation in 1962. Making computer networking a reality was further fueled in 1964 when Paul Baran, at the Rand Corporation think tank in Santa Monica, California, published a report on computer networking as a possible means of communication in the eventuality of a nuclear war. His idea was to link a group of computer networks to a mesh of interconnected nodes. If one part of the system were destroyed, communication would be redirected through surviving portions of the widely dispersed fabric. It would be impossible to destroy something with no headquarters, no leader, and not just one machine doing all the work.

Kleinrock's classmate Larry Roberts was made project manager of making such a network, ArpaNet, in 1966. Kleinrock's computer was #1; #2 was at Stanford Research Institute, namely Douglas Engelbart's, inventor of the mouse. Once they got four computers to do it, in 1969, they knew they were onto something.

The Net would prove an excellent incubator for its own refinement as researchers and scientists used it for brainstorming and collaborating on new software applications to enable the Net to do new things. For example, in 1970, Ray Tomlinson and others invented a program that enabled them to send e-mail across ArpaNet, an application that wasn't in the original plans. Robert Kahn, a member of the original planning team, recalls, "One of the vitally important developments was electronic mail, which provided the 'glue' that allowed the research community to interact over the network." Soon someone (Larry Roberts) refined it by creating a program that would list on your screen all the messages you had received, so you could see what mail you had gotten without reading it all sequentially. John S. Quarterman, Internet historian and surveyor, observes the following:

> This new service [e-mail] follows a pattern that will be
> repeated many times: network users see a need; someone

who wants it badly enough and has the technical skills prototypes it; others help develop it; it spreads to others who find it useful; eventually it becomes standardized and everybody uses it.

When the network made its public debut in 1972 at the first International Conference on Computer Communication, e-mail, remote log-in, and file transfer had been developed. Doubters came away converted, and the inventors themselves were all finally convinced. By now, there was serious traffic over the network, as computers could now communicate with computers. And the horizon expanded to include two more networks: a satellite networking researchers in London and Norway with the States, and a packet radio network.

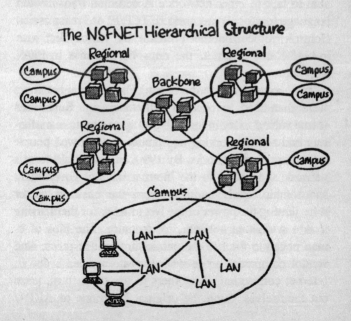

The NSFNET Hierarchical Structure

Along with their overseas counterparts, the Department of Energy and NASA became involved in the mid-1980s, as did the National Science Foundation (NSF). NSF formed a net which augmented ArpaNet as a major backbone. The entire Net further decentralized as NSF-Net fostered the creation of linked regional, or intermediate-level, networks. Now universities and other research institutions could link up more locally to the backbone. (Plug into any part, plug into the whole.)

Phase Two begins around this time, the mid-1980s. This phase was marked by two things. One, it became clear that not only did computers have to be able to communicate with each other, but also networks had to be able to talk to other networks. A common transmission language (protocol) was created: TCP/IP, or Transmission Control Protocol/Internet Protocol, by Vinton Cerf with Robert Kahn. With it, the networks became internetworked.

Two, commercialization began. The regional networks were mandated to become self-sustaining. Businesses (some valued today in the billions) sprang up to manufacture and sell networking equipment that allowed people to build private networks. By 1990, anyone could form a network and link it to the Internet without government sponsorship. Early adopters from the business sector were putting the power of the Net to work for them, using it as a wide-area network, for instance. The idea of e-mail began to filter to the public through the press. And vendor companies arose who'd create and lease out an Internet connection—for others to use or, in turn, lease out themselves. Soon the original backbone of ARPA/

NSF host computers was dwarfed by commercial hosts. The system further decentralized as NSFNet (having augmented ArpaNet) retired, as of April 1995.

From 1995 to 1996, the Internet has gone, to paraphrase Vinton Cerf, from near-invisibility to near-ubiquity.

During Phase One, the number of hosts grew to two thousand; in Phase Two, to one million. In 1987, the National Science Foundation asked the board of National Research Council to investigate the possibilities of high-performance, high-speed networking, at a billion bits per second rather than a million. And their report lent credibility and thrust to Senator Al Gore's proposals for a national information infrastructure.

Since 1988, the Internet has doubled in size every year. Today, the Net interlinks 6.6 million computer hosts, interconnecting over fifty thousand networks, enabling over thirty million people around the planet in over 160 countries to communicate and collaborate. In *Technologies Without Boundaries,* Ithiel de Sola Pool calls the Internet ". . . part of the largest machine that man has ever constructed."

Phase Three is just beginning.

Let's freeze-frame right there and stand back.

What had its origins in a secret, strategic nuclear-war scenario has become one of the greatest potential applications for commerce, education, health, the arts, research, and just plain fun—not to mention possibly peace—in the 21st century.

It's not a given, like TV or a phone line; it's something to be set up, configured, do-it-yourself.

It's not an item you buy in a store, or a number you call. It's not an entity. It's not a thing.

Because the Internet was designed from the very start to *not* have any central computer, there really is no "central Internet."

It evolved with relatively little planning.

It's simply all these computers all hooked up. As new networks get internetworked and applications get added, it gets ever more powerful and capable.

There *is* an international group, the Internet Society (http://www.isoc.org) based in Reston, Virginia, that represents major concerns and acts as an international forum for the exchange of information about the further evolution and use of Internet technology. And there are the Internet Engineering Task Force (IETF) and Network Information Centers (NICs). But the Internet itself is like the wind. It's a concept, just like the international postal or banking systems.

So: you don't get in your car to visit Highway 180—you get in your car and head out on Highway 180 in order to reach specific people and places. Similarly, you don't get online and visit the Internet. Rather, the Internet connects you to particular resources, both digital and human. Or—like the Butch Hancock song says, it's a wave, not the ocean.

Up until recently, the core, or backbone, of the Internet has been academic- and research-oriented. We can expect to locate a healthy, collegial culture within it. But, too, there's now a newer, commercial culture—of business use and the Internet itself as a business.

The caption to the picture: *The Internet Is Not Just a Community of Networks—It's Also a Network of Communities*. To say this simpler, *Networking Builds Communities*. This is very important to realize and to learn more about. In our real-life example we saw corporate culture, cafe society, library research, and finance. Each has its own culture, or shared outlook.

So the Internet's not just a matter of learning technology, which is being made easier and easier. It's also about understanding and respecting the various cultures out there. It's people sharing things. It's all do-it-yourself, with no one "in charge," so what constitutes being on your best behavior has been likewise evolving in a do-it-yourself way. These customs, largely unwritten, go to make up a culture—everything from a whole philosophy of use, to rules of etiquette.

So that's what the Internet is.
Decentralized.
Heterogeneous.
The network of networks, internetworked into one.
Connect to a part and you can connect to the whole.
Do-it-yourself. Autonomous.
It builds communities.
And it has a culture.

To sum up with the words of Anthony-Michael Rutkowski, Executive Director of the Internet Society, ". . . a world of shared minds that transcends the accidental boundaries of history, the distance of geography, the machinations of institutions, and the mischief of manipulation is potentially one filled with discovery, fulfillment, and fascination for all peoples—individually and collectively.''

Now that we've defined the Internet, let's refine our knowledge a bit more. Let's regard it from a second perspective.

Access.

HOW TO CONNECT

Those already connected and running might want to skip ahead, to Part B. For those of you uninitiated, as yet "unwired," we'll answer your most frequently asked questions. Be prepared to hear some basic jargon and technical terminology (tech talk), which just comes with the terrain.

Having a good, general picture of what the Internet is, we'll bring that picture into sharper focus by addressing the question of how to connect to it. First we'll look at the gear. Then we'll differentiate types of access (direct vs. dial-up, online services vs. Internet service providers, partial vs. full Internet) as well as explore key criteria (interface, culture, and rates).

First, there's the gear.

GEAR

You need five things:

- a phone
- a computer
- a modem
- telecommunications software
- an Internet service provider (connectivity)

You don't need to understand how your computer works, much less your *phone,* in order to use them. (They're magic.) But—to aid your comprehension: you need a modem to enable your phone to talk to your computer and your computer to talk to your phone.

Why?

1) Computers speak a language composed of electricity passing across their circuits. It's a vocabulary of two words: *on* and *off.* This is a *binary*-base system, as opposed to, say, decimal. It's also called *digital* because its vocabulary is just two digits, 1 and 0.

2) Phones are *analog.* If digital is like particles, analog is like waves. When you talk louder, the waves get bigger. When you whisper, the waves get smaller.

So: in order for your computer to talk to your phone, and your phone to talk to your computer, you need something to modulate and demodulate, back and forth, between digital and analog. That's what a *modem* does. It

M O D u l a t e s /
D E M o d u l a t e s

between computer and phone, and phone and computer. It turns digital information into sound, and sound into digital stuff.

TELECOMMUNICATION

You need a modem to enable your phone to talk to your computer, and your computer to talk to your phone.

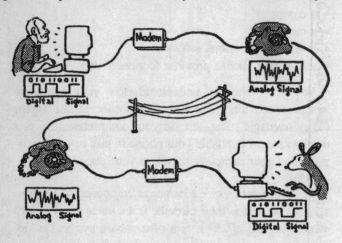

A modem can come built into your computer (an internal modem). Or you can buy an external modem and attach it to your computer's serial port with the cable that probably came with it. If you've never seen a modem, they can be the size of this book.

The important thing is speed. It's measured by the number of signals (or bits) sent per second (bps). Speed gets faster all the time. As of this writing, a 14,400-bps modem is the standard, and under $100. If you're using the world-wide web, it will run faster if you are connected at 28,800. Sending a 50,000-word text at 1200 baud could take about an hour. Sending the same text at 14,400 baud takes about a minute. Enough said.

MEDIUM	ADVANTAGES	DISADVANTAGES
Copper Twisted Pair Wire	• Is used extensively in residential telephone systems • Is inexpensive • Is widespread	• Has low information capacity • Is susceptible to electronic interference
Coaxial Cable	• Accessible to 95 percent of U.S. households • Is used extensively for cable TV • Has sufficient capacity to handle most advanced telecommunications applications likely to be used	• Is used primarily in one-way TV networks • Will require additional switching equipment in most cable TV networks to permit two-way communication
Fiberoptic Cable	• Has very high information capacity • Is relatively secure • Is not susceptible to electronic interference	• Is expensive to install supporting equipment • Not installed in most residential areas
Over-the-Air	• Enhances mobility • Does not require wire conduits	• Is relatively insecure • Requires allocation of the frequency spectrum, a finite resource • Is susceptible to electronic interference

PIPELINE AND BANDWIDTH

As of this writing, the telephone companies are the primary Internet transmission medium (*pipeline*). A word often used in association with pipeline is *bandwidth*. It's the equivalent of how wide a pipe is, and thus how fast it can transmit stuff flowing through it—in this case, data/information. You can fill a bucket faster with a wide hose than a drinking straw. More bandwidth is thus called higher speed, because with greater bandwidth it takes less time for information-intensive things like pictures, not to mention video and sounds, to transmit. Users of the world-wide web, even with a high-speed modem, often want more speed, through greater bandwidth, to further quicken their use of the web, or be able to access super-high bandwidth things like multimedia events. A new transmission medium which the phone companies have in addition to narrow, twisted, copper wire is known as ISDN (Integrated Services Digital Network), with much more bandwidth. Another pipeline with more bandwidth is fiber-optic cable.

Two possible pipelines of the future are coaxial cable, as in cable TV, and wireless/over-the-air, as in radio.

QUESTION: *Do I need a separate phone line for my modem?*

It is an option, for a few dollars more per month. But it's hardly a necessity. You can use the same phone line you use for your phone and/or fax. But if people are likely to phone you when you're telecommunicating, they will get a busy signal. A slightly less expensive option to a separate phone line are phone company message centers. They not only replace your personal answering machine (which will eventually need repair), but will also take messages when you're on the phone, whether you're talking, faxing, or on the Internet.

Note: if you have call waiting, when you go online, you need to have your modem enter *70 to disable it. (You might type the letters ATDT, which allow you to enter commands from your keyboard, followed by *70.)

You can use any *computer.*

If you want to use the world-wide web, here's a short shopping list. You'll want eight megabytes of RAM. If you have a PC, you'll want Windows and at least a 486. Mac-sters will want at least System 7 and an LC II or better.

You need *telecommunications software.* Telecommunications is communication over a distance, computer to computer. If you aren't familiar with them yet, a computer is considered literal *hardware,* like a hammer or a saw. Actually, it's more like a robot, an inert mechanical box, that will hear and obey if you tell it what to do today, and *software* is its intelligence, its marching orders. Software programs enable your computer's hardware to do various useful things (utilities) and functions (applications), such as play games, make spreadsheets, wordprocess, spell check, etc. In our case, we want telecommunications software to tell our computer how to communicate with other computers (which also have telecommunications software).

Internet service providers and online services may furnish you with their own telecommunications software. They used to charge $50, now they can give it away. It's convenient to have your own telecommunications software, too, in case you want to just use your computer to call resources not on the Internet, like some BBS's or local libraries. Inexpensive telecommunications software for IBM are things like WinComm or ProComm; for Mac, Microphone or Z-Term.

SAVE YOUR EYES

Telecommunications software usually allows you to change the size of the letters displayed on your screen. I recommend you consider trying a larger type size, to see how you like it. Z-Term, for example, is set for 9-point, which is roughly the size of the extracts in this book. But it's less easy to read on a screen. And today's health standards recommend staying one whole arm's length away from the computer screen. So 9-point can strain the eyes for lengthy sessions. Try upping the point size of the type to, say, 14- or 18-point. Even 24-!

9-point type
18-point type
24-point type

I suggest trying this to ease eye strain. I also recommend it, where appropriate, when making a presentation from your screen; the drawback is that some things, such as text menus, might not align. Try it out for yourself.

Besides a phone, a computer, a modem, and software, the final thing we need is an *Internet service provider*. An Internet service provider is connected to the Internet—or, in turn, to another Internet service provider connected to the Internet, such as a regional network.

However they themselves get connected, they *provide* the service of letting you connect to them and their connection to the Internet. They furnish the connectivity factor.

If you want the world-wide web, you need a provider who can offer a SLIP or PPP connection, or something equivalent. SLIP stands for Serial Line Internet Protocol, and PPP for Point-to-Point Protocol, which double-checks for errors.

In any event, we come now to the jackpot, quiz-show question: *Which is the best way to get connected to the Internet?*

There's no one correct answer. There are several.

Also, there's so much competition, affording so many options—the best way to make an informed choice is to consider the variables.

But bear in mind this is just an aspect of the Internet, not the thing itself. Whether we get there by stretch limo or skateboard, the Internet remains exactly the same.

▶ *Direct vs. dial-up*

The big question about connectivity is "Whose?"

You can get connectivity two ways:

1) You can buy your own, direct connection to the Internet. This involves buying a computer (server), configuring it, and leasing some fiberoptic cable or similar transmission media. In this case, your computer becomes a node on the network. You'd become part of the Internet by being a permanent domain *on* the Internet (a domain is the site of a host computer). Unless this is part of your company or job description, most readers won't have the need, or the budget, to do this. As of this writing, a direct

connection costs about $5,000 for equipment, plus at least $500 per month for the pipeline, plus additional expenses for custom interface design, and maintenance.

2) In addition to a direct connection, there's a dial-up connection. Here, you dial up someone who already has a direct connection and is renting use of their connection. (Connect to any part of the Internet and you can connect to the whole.) We mentioned this when we talked about the historical evolution of the Internet: in Phase Two a market developed as Internet service providers started renting use of their access.

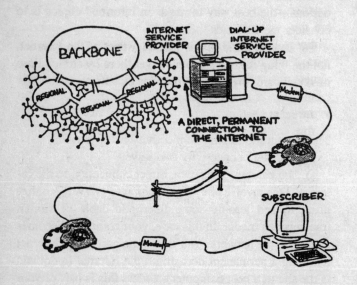

Think of the Internet as if it were a restaurant. Would you buy a restaurant in order to go dining there? Or would you rather pay them to buy the groceries, hire a chef to prepare the produce, etc.?

Most people choose connectivity through some dial-up arrangement: (again) to have their phone dial up someone who *is* on the Internet and connect to it, through them.

Note: this way our computer doesn't have to be *on* all the time, the way it would if we make the investment to actually be a node of the Internet.

Widely known examples of dial-ups are America On-line (currently 3 million users), and H&R Block's CompuServe (the oldest) and Sears's/IBM's Prodigy (with another 3 million users currently between them). These are the big three. Prodigy, CompuServe, and America Online's computers are on twenty-four hours a day; not ours. Thus, for example, e-mail sent to us across the Internet lands in their mail room, where it sits until we dial them up there to pick it up, instead of it coming directly to our computer.

You might also have heard of General Electric's GEnie, MCI Mail, Netcom, Delphi, etc. Apple runs eWorld, and now Microsoft has the Microsoft Network (MSN). All these kinds of commercial services have been the source of the big boom in the Internet population. As of this writing, hundreds of thousands of new Internet users go online through them every month.

▶ *User interface: graphical & text*

QUESTION: *If I connect to any part of the Internet and connect to the whole, then what's the difference whether I connect to the Internet through one provider or another?*

The answer brings us to the next important variability, *interface*. Interface, in general, refers to how information is presented for you, and how you interact with it. A radio's interface is its volume and tuning dials. A TV has dials plus a hand-held zapper. The interface between you and me right now is the way this text follows on numbered pages, with a table of contents, an index, and pictures. And you can use it wherever you go. Popular modifications of this interface include underlining, highlighting, and writing in margins. And a bookmark can return you instantly to anywhere you want.

With computers, we speak of user interface. A user is the person served by the information system. A user interface refers to how information is displayed on the screen for you to access, manipulate, and interact with, from your keyboard and/or mouse (a small mobile tool attached to the keyboard, manipulated by hand). The information itself doesn't vary, but the way it's presented can.

There are two common types of computer interface (each the product of some particular telecommunications software):

• graphical
• text (menu or command)

Graphical is the same as what Microsoft named Windows and that Mac calls its desktop—with folders, files, a trash can, etc. Someone dubbed it Graphical User Interface, abbreviated *gui* (pronounced "gooey"). This kind of interface offers pictures representing the functions desired. We simply move our cursor (a movable pointer on the computer screen) to the image or symbol (icon) of what we want. E-mail might be depicted as a big postage stamp showing the globe. We'd move our cursor to it, click on it, and we're ready to send and receive e-mail. Similarly, if we select a picture of a Roman forum, we can communicate with a group of people. We read by merely seeing. A no-brainer.

Point and click.

Voilà!

A major reason for the world-wide web's popularity, by the way, is thus its use as a gui interface to the Internet.

The other kind of interface is text. Text interfaces can be menu or command. In a menu interface, we can read and choose items displayed in a list (the menu), such as the following:

```
1  Mail
2  Forums
3  File transfer
4  Remote log-ins, etc.
```

We can either select the item by number or just move our cursor to the line it's on. The only trick in navigating menus is that there may be menus within menus until we get to the file we want. It can be like the frustration we experience when we call a computerized phone system that puts us through ten minutes of voice-mail hell. We want the electronic media to work fast, but the interface can become cumbersome. Nevertheless, menu interfaces are still fairly simple. And, being standard, there's little or no learning curve.

The other text interface mode is by commands. The same menu of options might look like this:

```
A  (M)AIL
B  (F)ORUMS
C  FILE (T)RANSFER
D  (R)EMOTE LOG-INS
```

Here we press the letter in parentheses, as our command—just like the library's "A" for (A)uthors, "T" for (T)itles, and "S" for (S)ubject. But with commands, entering an *S* in one interface might mean (S)ave, whereas in another it could mean (S)end. Two opposite ideas. Or, *E* in one interface might mean (E)nter, but (E)xit in another, and (E)dit in yet another. There's no universal, standard command language.

BBS's are easy to maintain, but they require a certain learning curve of their users—and they vary widely.

Unix (pronounced "you-knicks") is the basic Internet command language. I'd estimate that as many as 20 percent of Internet users today have a Unix command interface (a shell account). However, that number is shrinking as more and more people are using standardized or universal interfaces which "sit on top of" the Unix shell.

Selecting an option sends out a Unix command which you never see or know about.

Gui or text, there's usually never one single interface in any given system. Any one can shade into another. This is true, for example, in Windows, as it is in the Internet. You start out in a gui, but a few levels deeper into the system you may find a menu environment, and further down you're moving through a command environment (such as DOS).

ENTERING COMMANDS

Command interfaces can vary by whether or not the commands must be followed by the ENTER or RETURN key. That is, sometimes, we might tap the letter of a command and then the ENTER or RETURN key. Other times, we just tap the letter—in which case the ENTER or RETURN key would mean "Take us back to the previous menu." This is why online services' support people commonly field calls from somewhat frantic subscribers who call up and say, "Help! I'm in a loop!"

Develop the Internet touch: slow and light, one step at a time, and watch what happens.

Pictures are easy. Menus are universal. Commands vary. Generally, there's been a migration "up"—from command to menu, and menu to gui. BBS's, such as the coffee-house network, usually start out with command interfaces, and later graduate to a menu or a gui. (Takes all kinds, though. Some people say they prefer Unix to gui.)

▶ *Online services vs. dedicated Internet service providers*

QUESTION: *How do I know whether something I see on-line is the Internet or not? And if I see something at Prodigy, can I get it while I'm in CompuServe?*

The big three (CompuServe, America Online [AOL], and Prodigy) began as essentially big BBS's. As they grew, and as the Internet became more and more popular, they stayed competitive and added popular features of the Internet, such as e-mail and ftp. (As of this writing, AOL and Prodigy still do not have what was the third most popular Internet resource, telnet.) They've been called *online services*—as opposed to *dedicated Internet providers* (like Netcom, Pipeline, Portal, or Psi), offering just Internet connectivity alone. Internet service providers are dedicated to giving us the Internet; that's all, that's a lot, and, as we'll see, once we know how to use that, that can be enough.

Some online services, such as Dialog and Lexis/Nexis, which furnish information databases, don't have the Internet at all. Others may have the Internet, too. Because an online service might offer an array of preselected links to popular Internet sites (such as the Smithsonian Institution), people often think these are proprietary exclusives of the service, available there only. But the Smithsonian is on the Internet. Anybody can access it on the Internet. The online service has just set it up so that it might automatically come up as an option, without your having to go out and find it. But if we're Internet literate, we can find these things ourselves. (As we'll see, a central outlook of Internet literacy is do-it-yourself.)

Now, if I'm connected to the Internet through, say, America Online (AOL) as my provider, I can access the Internet (e-mail, Internet-wide forums over Usenet, gopher, the web, etc.). Plus, I can access services with which AOL makes proprietary arrangements, like *The New York Times* and *Weekly World News*. And my subscription also entitles me to participate in AOL's exclusive forums amongst subscribers, such as their popular live chat rooms. If, on the other hand, I'm connected to the Internet through the Well (Whole Earth 'Lectronic Link)—I can access the same Internet features as people on America Online (e-mail, Internet-wide forums over Usenet, gopher, the web, etc.), but I can't access AOL's *The New York Times* or *Weekly World News* areas, their

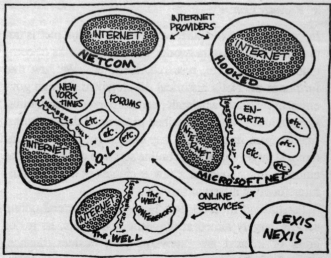

ONLINE SERVICES vs. DEDICATED INTERNET PROVIDERS

live chat rooms, their Mighty Morphin' Power Rangers for kids, or any other of their proprietary features. Instead I can access all the special, exclusive forums that the Well hosts, for *their* subscribers only. And someone on AOL can't access these Well forums.

Each has members-only stuff, plus the Internet. But through our mutual Internet portholes, as it were, we can send each other e-mail, participate in forums together over Internet-wide forums, etc.

In addition to interface, direct vs. dial-up, and online service vs. dedicated Internet service providers, let's look at how else connections can differ: by culture, by rates, and by other criteria.

▶ *Provider culture*

In our real-life examples, we saw that the Internet is not just communities of networks. It's also networks of communities—corporate, research, BBS, etc. We saw that further in the Net's historical development through government research, academic, and corporate communities. Communities can be described in terms of their cultures. Just as there isn't exactly one culture for the whole Internet at large, so, too, can online services offer particular cultures. Let's consider a few examples of different cultures found at different services.

Established in 1988, Prodigy is a commercial online service largely aimed at domestic consumers. Its major areas of interest are "news/weather, business/finance, sports/ESPNet, communications, entertainment, reference, shopping, computers, travel, and home/family/

kids." Up until recently it has routinely monitored the incoming and outgoing e-mail of its subscribers to censor out obscenity, to ensure "safe screens." That way, little kids won't log-in to their parents' accounts and learn to read by practicing an adult vocabulary that might make even a marine blush.

Established in 1986, Institute for Global Communication (IGC), on the other hand, is a nonprofit organization. It is a network of networks (PeaceNet, EcoNet, ConflictNet, LaborNet, and WomensNet) that provides full Internet access, and is thus: "a world-wide community of activists using computer networking tools to create progressive change in the fields of human rights, social justice, environmental sustainability, conflict resolution, women's empowerment, and the equitable treatment of workers." In addition to the thousands of conferences, special interest groups, and nongovernmental organizations (NGOs) involved, it has also sponsored free access to the events, documents, and NGOs of the UN Conference on Environment and Development in Rio in 1980, the UN Conference on Human Rights in Vienna in 1993, and the UN World Conference on Women in Beijing in 1995. And it is the only major North American Internet provider affiliated with the Association of Progressive Communicators (APC), whose mission is to get relatively out-of-the-way countries hooked up to the Internet. IGC had connections in the Socialist Bloc long before the collapse of communism opened up channels of communication there. Economically developing continents such as South America and Africa are beginning to get online, and APC is helping them make the transition.

Of course, family values and a progressive social outlook are not mutually exclusive. But IGC and Prodigy offer different cultures. In other words, what's trivial to some people may be important to others, and vice versa.

Incidentally, as I'm basically reporting facts, rather than trying to editorialize upon them (it would be a judgment call for me to label Prodigy as conservative), I should state that there are no conservative Internet providers, but there are BBS's: chiefly, The Freedom Network (formerly AIMNet) and the Town Hall forum. (Several conservative web sites are mentioned in the chapter on politics in our almanac, in back.)

Let's consider two more examples. Founded in 1985, the Well began as a nonprofit BBS for its telecommunication forums in Sausalito, California, originally as part of another nonprofit organization that produces *Whole Earth Review*. It grew to a commercial online service specializing in forums, and along the way it provided the full Internet too. We'll soon discuss forums separately, but, for now, here's what one Massachusetts Well subscriber said about the time he turned to his virtual community at the Well, when he experienced anxiety over his two-year-old daughter's illness:

> I found it [the parenting conference] full of 24-hour compassionate ears and souls. They not only listened, they talked back. They helped. I found myself keeping a kind of online journal in the company of these people I'd never laid eyes on. It seemed kind of miraculous, really, this communion late at night in front of the screen.

The Well can be as lively as any late-night cafe or bar. A perpetual salon, its topics ranging from spirituality to politics; cooking to business; arts, computers, and health.

To reinforce true community, they have open office parties monthly and periodic barbecues for local subscribers. Their success has inspired the creation of other online cultures—such as EchoNyc (East Coast Hang Out) and *HotWired* (*Wired* magazine's online sister). At the Well, the culture is not of content (sources of information) but community (people)—convivial, collective, and interactive.

At our book's conclusion, we'll explore two community networks, designed for their local population. But, let's mention one here. New York Online's community is multicultural—about 50 percent people of color. Subscribers often deal with issues of race. Omar Wasow, its twenty-four-year-old founder, says of its logo, a subway token:

> People are talking to each other who had never talked to each other in real life. And like the subway, we're a network; it links up the whole city. Unlike the subway, people are talking to each other. Even when there's disagreement, there's a kind of connection and communication that's quite valuable. Most people have a sort of fixed circle of friends that's work and neighborhood and friends. What's happening online is that all of a sudden you're mingling in a much broader world, and you're doing it in a way that's still very comfortable and convenient but that sort of undermines a lot of the cleavages in society.

Thus, online services can have different cultures. You might want to consider that when deciding if one's right for you.

▶ *Rates*

For some, Internet access is free. As we've already mentioned, some people may have Internet access through work. Full-time students and faculty at many major colleges have an Internet account as part of their tuition or tenure. And, as we'll see later, some cities have Free-Nets.

QUESTION: *Are there toll calls? And, if not, then what am I paying for?*

If you're connected to the Internet through a dial-up account to a local number, the cost of an Internet session will be the cost of the local phone call, plus whatever your provider charges. In other words, you can be online and communicate anywhere in the world for no extra toll. How? For one thing, it would be too complex to set up a mechanism to track packets. And everyone has paid for their own gateway, so when you're part of the Internet, you're part of something akin to a big switchboard, like one great big 800-number (though the Internet is not the same as the phone).

So if you're online through a local, dial-up, Internet provider for five minutes, you'll get a phone bill for a five-minute local call (or a flat-rate fee) in addition to the provider's bill at the end of the month, regardless of whether or not you communicated down the street or across the planet, with a person or with a robot computer, etc.

One more example: if a long-distance fax is a toll call, sending the same document by Internet is not: it's the cost of the call to the dial-up provider, wherever it goes from there.

The cost of a provider's infrastructure and maintenance is either absorbed by its engineer (as with academic access and access at work) or passed along in some nominal form. Because this is a highly competitive marketplace, the pricing varies widely.

Some variables include:

- sign-up fees
- minimum fees
- a per-hour connect rate
- peak and off-peak rates
- special rates for heavy-volume usage
- à la carte fees for premium items
- special training costs

Peak/off-peak rates affect you if you're likely to call from a particular time of day or night. Premium services refer to the proprietary features an online service provider may feature exclusively, and can vary within the service; CompuServe dropped this kind of pricing in 1995, but Microsoft is adopting it. It *can* get complicated, but rates average $20–40 per month. More and more Internet providers are springing up offering a flat fee, as low as $15 per month. With a flat fee, of course, you're not constrained from trying something unknown, but you may also spend more time if the system is hard to learn.

Now you can evaluate a provider in terms of important criteria not always spelled out in the ads.

- How do you like their interface?
     How steep is the learning curve?
- What is their culture like?
     What proprietary, special features do they offer? Is

political, social, or professional climate of importance to you?

- How long does it take to connect?

  If they take a half hour to get a free line in to them,
  even with automatic dialing, then you're on hold
  more than online.

- How are their support services?

  Do they answer within 24 hours? Online or by
  phone? (Prodigy has the best phone support, AOL
  the best online.) If there is a manual, is it clear to
  you?

- If you plan to have your own domain or online services, what are their rates for that?

There's no *Consumer Reports*-type survey of the
major providers. Unlike cars, providers have no standard
dashboard; each interface takes time to learn. The field is
constantly evolving, changing as you read. Two books
out thus far are *Connecting to the Internet* and *Infosurf-
ing*. Eric Braun's book *Internet Directory* has Internet
providers for all area codes. And a list exists online as
well: ftp thelist.com.

Bottom line: One day, you may be able to get Internet
access from a toy inside a cereal box. Meanwhile, if you
don't have access yet and want to try the Internet, pick a
service offering a free trial period, just so you can try the
Internet out. As of this writing, Prodigy offers five free
hours, CompuServe and America Online ten, PSI and
Portal seven free days, Hooked ten free days. If you find
you like the provider, then stay put. But if you're watching your budget and you plan to be online for more than
ten hours a month, then a dedicated Internet service provider will save you money.

Perhaps by seeing some variables of access, you've gained a clearer picture of the basic essence of the Internet itself. But our primary subject here is the road, not whether you're driving a car or a bus, walking or biking, or if your car has a CD-player. Let's finish our survey of connecting with just one more frequently asked question.

▶ *Partial vs. full Internet*

QUESTION: *Why don't all the services have full Internet access? After all, connect to a part, connect to the whole. And what makes the difference between partial Internet and full Internet?*

As we've seen, the various applications of the Internet evolved, one by one, over time. And for each application, the host domain must have it at their end, as well as it being at the site we're connected to.

They may not have all the newest accouterments and gimmicks (bells and whistles). If they offer the five major functions we're about to cover—e-mail, forums, file transfer, remote log-ins, and information resources like gopher and world-wide web—they're a full Internet provider. There are six hundred full-service Internet providers.

To get the whole picture, next we'll tour the full Internet step by step.

A GUIDED TOUR
OF THE INTERNET

Let's put theory into practice. Having reached the gates,
let's now cross the threshold.

We've seen how the Internet is decentralized. Just as
we don't get into our car to visit Highway 180, so too we
don't get online to visit the Internet. Rather, we log on,
then go to particular places and do specific things. The
general, full range of Internet possibilities is defined by
five specific things. They can be memorized on the fingers of one hand. E-mail . . . forums . . . file transfer . . .
remote log-ins . . . and information resources, such as
gopher and the world-wide web. Consider them your essential destinations or sites:

- basic vocabulary elements
- primary software applications
- regions to visit, reasons to use the Net

Although the Internet seems amorphous, its potentials
can be grasped in a logical, step-by-step progression.
Here's a quick run-through:

E-mail is from you to me, and me to you (*point-to-point*). It also has the possibility of going from one person to many (*point-to-mass*), as in a broadcast, and from many people to one (*mass-to-point*), as in, say, a petition.

That variability as to number of people brings us to *forums,* where we participate in group communication, many to many (*mass-within-mass*). This has two modes of presentation: one is via e-mail, called *lists,* and the other has its own mode, called *conferencing.*

Next, we might want to check archives of a conference, to catch up on what was said before we joined. Storehouses of archival material are available via something known as *file transfer protocol* or *ftp.* (A protocol is simply a common language enabling two computers to transmit data.) Here, it isn't a matter of the number of people

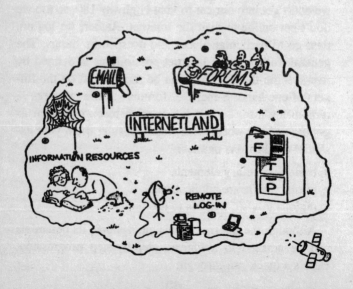

but the *number of files:* big files, and many of them—stored at big warehouses, like libraries. Ftp libraries contain many kinds of cool things like back issues of magazines and gigabytes of software, yours free for the asking.

When we access one of these libraries, we can post files to it or take files from it. To do so, we're operating another computer from our computer, much as we might operate a computerized library catalog remotely from our home or office. This is called *remote log-in (telnet)*. We log in remotely, from a distance, to another computer, from ours. The essential thing here is the number of different kinds of computers—using many different kinds of softwares, dedicated to *offering many different resources* to run. Besides library catalogs and archival warehouses, we can tap in to real-time multi-user games, medical databases, weather satellites, etc.

Finally, with all these resources, how can we find our way through it all? At first glance, it looks like getting information from the Internet can be like trying to fill a glass of water off an open fire hydrant. This is where *information resources* come in. They help us *organize and search* for information, as well as to *customize and personalize* the Internet. For example, to search ftp files by words in their titles, there's an information resource called archie (archive without the v). Saving the best for last: the climax of our tour will be a discussion of the two newest, most useful and incredible information resources: gopher and the world-wide web.

That's our roadmap: 1) e-mail, 2) forums, 3) ftp, 4) remote log-in, and 5) information resources. Currently, the three most popular are e-mail, forums, and the web.

Afterward, we'll put it all into perspective so you can apply these tools for fun and profit, however you like—and even use the Internet as a medium with which you can create.

E-MAIL

We'll start with mail for the following reasons:

- it's initially the most like the real world
- it's the most commonly available Internet feature
- it's the lifeblood of Internet communication
- its use entails basic skills reflected throughout the Internet

Once upon a time the skies of America darkened with the passage of carrier pigeons. Today over 50 million people worldwide send each other messages invisibly through their computers. As they do so, they're erasing geographical borders and time zones.

E-mail is ubiquitous.

It's a new window on the world for people who might have been too lazy, busy, or shy to write. For people in remote regions, it's a vital link, like the pony express. Like penpals, people now have keypals, even if they've never met. And e-mail is becoming an essential tool for business associates to keep in touch and collaborate.

Gay Crawford, a volunteer with her local branch of the Cancer Society, has keypals at the newspaper. She says, "It's so immediate, and it's so easy to use. You don't have to be a very formal letter writer, you don't have to address this person, you don't have to fill out an envelope and do the stamp, you just do your casual little 'hello' and 'this is what I think,' and sign your name and it's done.''

Plus, this most popular Internet feature proves very handy for the new user (newbie, a nonperjorative term which means a new user) learning how to ask. E-mail helps you learn everything there is to know about the Internet, because you can always use it to ask some friendly, knowledgeable person online a question. As the Internet doubles in size every year, 50 percent of people online are always newbies. Everyone else was once a newbie, too.

For people with very low-tech set-ups, where e-mail is the only application they have, all the other Internet applications can be run by mail alone.

Note: As with access, our tour of e-mail will be geared for totally new users: those who may not even use computers yet or do but haven't logged online yet.

There's no common knowledge base for the Internet. If you're already familiar with e-mail, you might want to skip ahead to the end of this chapter, *Culture,* where we talk about integrating e-mail into your daily life. But you might want to skim along. We dwell on skills here, because they can acclimatize new users to some of the basic concepts behind them, and we build upon them as we proceed.

▶ *Crossing the threshold*

Let's start from Square One.

First, we turn on our modem and computer. (Our computer doesn't have to be on all the time. Instead, we're going to dial our provider, where computers are on all the time, holding our mail for us until we log on to them.)

Next, we go into our telecommunications software.

Then we use it to call our provider. (We might type the number or, more likely, as a frequently called number, we've already programmed it, and pull it down from a menu bar.) We might hear our modem make the same electronic musical interlude we hear when sending a fax.

We're at the gates of our domain.

Like a sentry, our provider asks us for two things: our i.d. and our password.

▶ *I.D.*

Your i.d. (user name, log-in name, account name, screen name) is like a glow-in-the-dark sticker that says "Hi! My name is . . ." wherever you go on the Internet. When you register to use their services, if your provider gives you a choice, you can be anyone or anything. You can use your first name alone, if you're the first one to ask for it. You can use initials. You might pick your profession, or a key word associated with your craft or field. If you're in business for yourself, you might incorporate your company name—excellent for your business card:

> Jane Doe, President
> IRS—Information Research Services
> irs@trinity.com

Or you might want to be truth. Or beauty. Or fastfood. For our learning purposes, here, let's pick "Newbie."

Note: If we have more than one provider, we can register the same i.d. at each of them, if it's available. In other

words, if we want, we can be value@ukans.edu, value@
pentagon.mil, and value@hairnet.net. Or we can have a
different i.d. at each.

Meanwhile, back at the prompt—
We've typed in our i.d.

Second, it asks for our password. When we registered,
we were either assigned a password or we picked one
ourselves. If you're concerned about security, use a password that combines upper and lower case and nonalpha-
betic characters. If you're ultracautious—maybe you
negotiate high-stakes business deals, for example—you
might wish to change your password periodically. You
can change your password at any time.

The computer checks, and *bingo!* We've crossed the
threshold.

We're online.

We see our provider's welcome mat, like the home
plate in baseball.

We're connected to our provider—connected, in turn,
to the Internet. But, just as we don't get in our car to visit
Highway 180, so too do we have to specify where we
want to go in InternetLand.

To begin with, let's start with mail.

▶ *Sending mail*

Getting started, e-mail is just as at a post office or mail
room. We can do either of two things: send mail or pick
up mail from our box.

Let's walk through the steps to send a quick, test message. Keep in mind that the next five or so pages would

take about five seconds online. (Again—skip ahead if you've been here and done this already.)

First, we address the letter.

▶ *@ = address in Internet*

If we're in, say, Prodigy and we want to address our e-mail to someone else in Prodigy (in the same domain), we just type their i.d. But if we're addressing anyone outside the domain where we're writing from, then we need to use their full Internet address.

Here's how that works. An Internet address is made up of two things, an i.d. and a domain name, separated by the @ sign. (The @ sign is the shifted 2 on standard keyboards.)

In your own Internet address, everything to the left of @ is the i.d.—who you are—and everything to the right of it is the domain—the Internet access point where you're writing from. So:

I.d. + @ + Domain = Address

For example: President@whitehouse.gov. Research@ logloinfo.com. Teacher@abc.edu. Man_with_pipe@sf cafe.sf.ca.us.

A domain name has a number of phrases, and they work just the same way an address on a letter does: from specific to general. Right now, I am writing this book from Suite 727 (the exact room), at 1528 (very specific) Corkscrew Avenue (more general), San Francisco (still more general), California (even still more general).

The last part of the domain, being the most general, can tell us who an addressee is affiliated with:

Edu = an educational institution
Com = a company or commercial enterprise
Org = an organization, often nonprofit
Gov = the government
Mil = the military

Domains can also reflect geographical region. Se is Sweden. Cn is China.

If the domain were igor.frisco.abc.edu, then igor might be the name of the computer on the San Francisco campus of ABC University that handles telecommunications (within networks, computers are assigned names).

QUESTION: *Can I pick my domain name?*

Yes, if you're directly connected to the Net. Or, for a fee, many commercial providers can register your personalized domain name on their system. No one need ever know that you're not directly connected.

Can anyone pick any domain name they want? Well, a teenager in New England registered the names of a hundred Fortune 500 companies for himself. When a company like McDonald's would then get around to trying to register mcdonalds.com as their domain name, it was already taken—and they would have to buy it from this very unethical cyberpreneur. As of September 1995, a minimal registration fee is being charged, partly to help screen for authenticity, as well as to make the service self-sufficient and assure timely processing.

▶ *A few rules*

Addresses have to be duplicated exactly.

There are no spaces in an address. If you want an i.d.

that combines phrases or syllables, you might use upper and lower case, as in LoGloInfo, or you might use the underline, the hyphen, the period, or the tilde, such as Lo_Glo-Info.Inc~.

An i.d. might be *case* sensitive (but not a domain). If so, if you tried it in upper case it wouldn't work. Otherwise, it doesn't matter if you use UpPeR oR 1OwEr case in any combination.

Be careful when reading an address to differentiate between the number 1 and the letter l.

And now you know how to address others and be addressed in the Internet.

▶ Subject

Next, we give our message a subject. This is like the subject line in memos. It's wise to insert something. Anything. If nothing comes to mind, INFORMATION EXCHANGE is a good, all-purpose subject.

If we really want to catch the recipient's attention, we might try a teaser line, like "THE SECRET OF LIFE IS . . ." Or "ABOUT LAST NIGHT . . ." We might also use an eye-catching combination of type styles, as in "I*M*P*O*R-*T*A*N*T: OPEN IMMEDIATELY—>" (In which case, it'd better be good!)

▶ Sending the message

Let's say we've addressed our envelope to gary@pocket guide.com, and entitled it TEST 123 TEST 456. We have two options as to how we want to send a message. Do we want to type a message right now, from our keyboard? Or do we want to send a previously prepared file?

Well, being online is like being at a post office or at a mailroom. At a post office, we might write a postcard on a ledge by a window, but we wouldn't write a ten-page business contract there. Similarly, online, we might compose a brief message, but something needing to be composed more carefully we'd create offline, at our leisure, to send when online.

So if it's a brief message, we might type it in, such as this: "This is just a test. Let me know if you *don't* get this message." (We've added the illogic just to see if they're awake as well as online.)

If you're using a gui, the next thing is to *send* it; if you're using a text-based interface, you *upload* it. Same difference. Upload means send, download means receive. Either way, these are basic processes used in other Internet applications.

Sent or uploaded (same difference)—our message goes out into cyberspace—*shazam!* How long will it take to reach its address? If we're sending a message to someone in the same domain as us—say, if we have the same provider or work in the same company—then it appears in their mailbox in *<snap of the fingers>* a split second. Even if we're sending it from Moscow, and they're in Rio.

If it has to go from one domain to another, then it gets passed along through what are called gateways, which are like borders or portals. Sometimes that can take a matter of minutes, or seconds. Or it might take as long as an hour, if it gets held up in, say, a packet jam up. Either way, it's relatively fast, which is why the online world calls the postal service "snail-mail" or "turtle."

Let's say we didn't type a message in while online.

Say we'd composed a beautiful love letter while off-line, now smoldering in our hard disk as a file called LOVE. Or maybe a hot business proposal called WIDGET.NET ONE.

First, we want to create our file in Ascii.

You'll never need to know it but *Ascii* (pronounced "askey") stands for American Standard Code for Information Interchange. Technically, it can be an adjective or an adverb. As an adverb, it can be a mode for sending e-mail, as in a text-based interface.

Much, much more importantly, Ascii is an adjective.

As an adjective, Ascii signifies text that will wind up in a *nonproportional* font. A proportional font, like the one you're reading, is made up of letters of different widths. As you can see, an M is wider than an N, which, in turn, is wider than an m, n, or i. And so on. In a standard typewriter font like Courier, however, each letter is the same width or proportion, and so is called nonproportional.

Internauts all use Ascii as a universal font. See the chart opposite, which I found while doing research on Internet AIDS resources. It's from an AIDS conference on the Internet, sci.med.aids. It's quite detailed and concise. To you it looks just as it looked when I saw it on the Net, just as it looked when it was sent by its creator. Ascii is a universal format—used so things will look the same on the screen for all of us.

We might print out in a nonproportional font too. Many people still use typewriters as their printers, with no option but a nonproportional font.

To save a file in Ascii: When you select Save As—your word-processing software has a number of File Type op-

```
+--- Estimated total number of people who read the group, worldwide.
|   +--- Actual number of readers in sampled population
|   |    +--- Propagation: how many sites receive this group at all
|   |    |    +--- Recent traffic (messages per month)
|   |    |    |    +--- Recent traffic (kilobytes per month)
|   |    |    |    |     +--- Crossposting percentage
|   |    |    |    |     |   +--- Cost ratio: $US/month/rdr
|   |    |    |    |     |   |    +--- Share: % of newsreaders
|   |    |    |    |     |   |    |    who read this group.
v   v    v    v    v     v   v    v
```

39	110000	1700	76%	3845	6418.0	6%	0.07	3.6% soc.motss*
77	96000	1420	67%	1885	3541.1	11%	0.04	3.0% alt.drugs
131	81000	1203	80%	1571	4064.6	13%	0.06	2.6% sci.med
231	6500	961	61%	1269	2863.5	6%	0.04	2.0% [alt.politics.homosexuality
558	44000	647	66%	282	760.5	38%	0.02	1.4% talk.politics.drugs
605	41000	615	78%	383	1556.0	2%	0.05	1.3% sci.med.aids
724	37000	545	68%	512	1053.6	12%	0.03	1.2% sci.med.nutrition
729	37000	542	77%	53	96.0	12%	0.00	1.2% sci.med.physics
880	32000	481	43%	436	1033.5	8%	0.02	1.0% alt.homosexual
1202	25000	370	41%	326	529.6	9%	0.01	0.8% alt.drugs.caffeine
1320	22000	332	21%	27	62.4	4%	0.00	0.7% alt.sex.homosexual
1343	22000	326	66%	48	99.1	7%	0.00	0.7% sci.med.occupational
1398	21000	314	35%	182	2557.2	0%	0.07	0.7% bit.listserv.gaynet
1412	21000	310	56%	145	510.1	0%	0.02	0.7% sci.med.telemedicine
1425	21000	307	59%	97	353.2	0%	0.02	0.7% sci.med.dentistry
1559	19000	276	48%	99	138.4	8%	0.01	0.6% sci.med.pharmacy
1685	17000	254	42%	235	378.1	0%	0.02	0.5% alt.med.cfs
1888	14000	213	13%	12	29.3	100%	0.00	0.5% clari.news.law.drugs
1916	14000	207	38%	5	19.7	20%	0.00	0.4% bionet.molbio.hiv
2449	3500	52	11%	55	97.5	6%	0.01	0.1% de.sci.medizin

* (Motss = members of the same sex)

tions. You don't notice them usually. The default is Normal. But there's also Text Only, Text Only with Line Breaks, etc. To save a file as Ascii, select *Text Only with Line Breaks*.

First, do three things.

1) Make sure it's in a nonproportional, 12-point typeface, such as Courier, on a line length no longer than 60 characters.

2) Ascii is the standard keyboard. Plain vanilla. No curly quotes or apostrophes (" vs. " and ' vs. '). No dashes. No rule lines, bold, italics, underlining. No pointsize or font changes. Not even any discretionary hyphens.

3) Instead of paragraphing with indents (like this book), people often use two hard line-returns instead, in between each paragraph. (You'll see why in a minute.)

Non-Ascii (binary): Everything else—Greek math signs, font and point-size changes, bold, italics, a graphical insert and so forth—is called *binary.* (It's in the digital, binary language of computers.) For binary to work, the person on the receiving end will have the same software on their computer as we created the file in. If you e-mail me a business proposal in WordPerfect, and I have WordPerfect, I'll be able to read it exactly as it looked on your screen when you'd created it, after I leave my telecom software and go into my WordPerfect. But if Romeo composed a love letter in MicroSoft Word and Juliet only has WordPerfect, she'd get a message that would read like something from Mars:

```
a8@m•ß∂n  v∂d/k  w²20∫  +4≤9ß3@ßá-œl&√ ∫mm

≥©πµd_∂søm  ds3[y80ykjm.,  weu9vkml

vco˙dm²,x©xwe  .mc˜µd  v=poiw{}elkm#fcxva

0we9u39∆283ur  0-9wefi23
```

<Sigh!>

Tip for text-based uploading: If you're offered a choice of modes, usually Z-modem is the best: it's the fastest and it double-checks for errors. (Maybe a squirrel jumped on a telephone pole and a packet of bytes got some static in 'em.)

Bingo! You're on your way to becoming an Internet e-mail expert.

EXERCISE:

If you've never sent e-mail before and you want to try it out, e-mail my *infobot*. Infobot? That's an information robot, also known as a mailbot. It sends back an automatic reply. You can find mine on the inside front cover of this book. You can leave the subject line and message body blank. It's as simple as that.

▶ *Reading mail*

Having sent e-mail, let's read e-mail. Mail addressed to us is waiting for us at our domain, as with a mail room or at a post-office box.

We've seen how e-mail evolved out of users' need for it—and how it was refined so that, for example, a program was created to list incoming mail, so you don't have to read it all in one long batch. That list may vary in format, but here's the general concept. In a text-based interface, it might look like this:

```
1—  Happy New Year!       Jan 1   1:34   (35)    joe@day.com
2—  Re: About Last Night  Jan 1   4:20   (247)   sue@kis.com
3—  I*M*P*O*R*T*A*N*T      Jan 2   2:04   (46)    hal@uc.edu
4—                        Jan 2   10:36  (728)   99+@aol.com
5—  Re: Widget-Net        Jan 4   5:26   (42)    jah@lsfmt.net
```

We see the titles (except for #4, untitled). We can tell the date and time received. And we can see how many lines they are and who sent them. Gui mail software (such as Eudora, Pegasus, and Claris Mail) give us additional options.

Once our mail is saved or downloaded to our hard disc or floppy, then we can do whatever we like with it.

REFORMATTING AN ASCII FILE

When an ascii file is created (saved as Text Only with Line Breaks), a hard return gets placed automatically at the end of each line, breaking it down into tiny packets, ready for the voyage out into cyberspace. Windows users can open ascii files and eliminate those returns by specifying soft line returns. But Mac users have to use another method to eliminate those hard returns. Here's how to do it:

Say we've downloaded the following from the Internet, and opened it in our word processing software (I've used ¶ to indicate a hard line return):

TO: Newbie@Abc.Edu
FROM: Thomas Wolfe
SUBJECT: From "You Can't Go Home Again"

Some things will never change. Some things will always be the same.¶
Lean down your ear upon the earth, and listen.¶
¶
The voice of forest water in the light, a woman's laughter in the¶
dark, the clean, hard rattle of raked gravel, the cricketing stitch of¶
midday in hot meadows, the delicate web of children's voice in bright¶
air—these things will never change.¶
¶
The glitter of sunlight on roughened water, the glory of the stars,¶
the innocence of morning, the smell of the sea in harbors, the¶
feathery blur and smoky buddings of young boughs, and something there¶
that comes and goes and never can be captured, the thorn of spring,¶
the sharp and tongueless cry—these things will always be the same.¶
¶
¶

Now we'll do the following three things:

1. Search and replace the double hard returns (¶¶) with an unused character, such as ##.
2. Search and replace the single hard returns (¶) with a single space or no space. (Here, we'd replace with a single space. Other times, the word-processing software that saved the text might put a hard return after a space. It varies. You just have to look and see how it came out.)
3. Replace ## with two hard returns again (¶¶) (you may need to look up the code for hard returns in your word-processing manual.)

This way, we've 1) kept paragraphs intact, by sheltering them with an anomalous character set, 2) eliminated the hard returns, 3) then put the paragraphs back. Now you can format the document as you wish.

> SOME THINGS WILL NEVER CHANGE. *Some things will always be the same. Lean down your ear upon the earth, and listen.*
> *The voice of forest water in the light, a woman's laughter in the dark, the clean, hard rattle of raked gravel, the cricketing stitch of midday in hot meadows, the delicate web of children's voice in bright air— these things will never change.*
> *The glitter of sunlight on roughened water, the glory of the stars, the innocence of morning, the smell of the sea in harbors, the feathery blur and smoky buddings of young boughs, . . . etc.*

▶ *Refining our skills*

We've crossed the threshold to the online world, and we've seen how we can send and read mail. Next we'll look at how we can forward and reply to mail.

We can send multiple copies of the same message, much as we can with cc's (courtesy copies, aka carbon copies). Only all the copies will go out at the same time, without our having to wait for each one to be dialed individually. We can send one message to a hundred people, with just a few keystrokes. Because it's digital, e-mail can be forwarded along to a couple or several dozen other people with just a few keystrokes. *Consider:* would you rather that I sent you a hard copy or e-mail, if you might be inclined to forward something I sent you to other people? With hard copy, you'd have to Xerox it, address envelopes, buy postage, and find a mailbox. With a digital version, it can be forwarded along in five seconds.

(Personally, I spend a small fraction of my e-mail time just forwarding things I see on the Net to others I know will be interested, and who will probably forward or publicize them to others. It's part of my way of repaying the Net for all the good things I get. Balancing the karma.)

It's the same for replying: E-Z! Here, the subject and the sender's address is automatically copied, for our quick response. Five seconds, total.

Replying is recommended for another reason. An acknowledgment is practical, because e-mail is still just slightly less reliable than paper mail. (Or, more accurately, the gateway process can be fallible.) An acknowledgment reassures the other person their message in a bottle arrived across the seas of cyberspace. That reassurance builds a bridge of trust, across the anonymity, to reassure the other person that we're there, this is real, and we care. We don't always have the opportunity to acknowledge all our phone calls or mail, but it's real easy with e-mail, and useful—if only to send back a one-word reply, "Thanks." Sometimes it's nice just to be nice, and this is an opportunity.

This brings us to something called Netiquette.

▶ *Netiquette*

> I sh'n't always answer your letters, and you may do just
> as you please.
> —HERMAN MELVILLE, a letter to Nathaniel Hawthorne, 1851

Etiquette is the code of behavior and manners reflecting the culture of shared experience. Miss Manners says, "The great art of etiquette was invented to translate the incoherent jumble of human feelings to which we are all subject into something more presentable." Internet etiquette is known as Netiquette, discussed in books such as Virginia Shea's *Netiquette*. To get S. Hambridge's *Netiquette Guidelines*, e-mail rfc-info@isi.edu. Leave the subject blank. In the body, put two lines, just like this:

```
Retrieve: FYI
DOC-ID: FYI0028
```

The best rule of e-mail Netiquette I know is *Where appropriate, quote what you're replying to.*

It works like this: some e-mail software has a feature that will automatically copy the message you're replying to. The original message reappears with >'s (the "greater-than" sign) in the left-hand margin:

```
> Hiya, Gary!
> This is just a test.
> Let me know if you *don't* get this.
> Thanx.

> —An Internet newbie.
```

The original message here, of course, seems intentionally illogical—to test if we're awake?—on which we might comment. Our text won't have any >'s in the margin:

```
> Hiya, Gary!
Yo! Gary ain't here! This is Abner speakin'.
> This is just a test.
Will I get graded? Pass/fail?
> Let me know if you *don't* get this.
Huh?!?!?!?!
> Thanx.
You bet.
Now let me know if you don't get *this*.
```

(*Note:* I edited out the sender's signature. That's another bit of Netiquette: KISS, or Keep It Short & Sweet.)

This can lead to more gears-meshing kind of dialog. Talking with, instead of talking at, someone. Moreover, it reproduces the "thread" (the original idea plus its continuation).

Why is this so important? Well, you can write and send more e-mail than snail-mail in the same amount of time. E-mail can fly back and forth several passes in one day. It's very easy to (R)eply, dash off a quick reply and send it off without quoting the context. And context is very important, too.

For example, if I get an e-mail message saying:

```
Sure. 10 p.m.
```

I might have forgotten what my original question was. Maybe I'd asked, "Do you want to meet me for dinner next Wednesday at 10 P.M., or Thursday at 9 P.M.?" But maybe now I'm reading my e-mail from my laptop, on the road, without my appointment book or my PIM (Personal Information Manager). Was 10 P.M. Wednesday or Thursday?

Going a bit deeper, between two people, one-on-one, a message may accumulate a few layers of quotes. I might reply to the above:

```
Hiya. You wrote to me:
> Sure. 10 p.m.
But I forgot: was this for Wednesday or Thursday?
Sorry. (Hurriedly,) Thanx!
```

And I might receive a reply, in turn, like this:

```
>> Sure. 10 p.m.
> I forgot: was this for Wednesday or Thursday?
> Sorry. (Hurriedly.) Thanx!

Wednesday. You must be on the road. Sorry. Am looking
forward.
```

That's about as many levels as it might go before starting anew. Like uploading and downloading, we'll see this process of quoting what's being replied to is reflected elsewhere on the Internet.

Of course, use as appropriate. Sometimes it may not even be necessary. And, on the other hand, don't reproduce a lengthy letter and then at the bottom place a one-sentence answer. Put your response on the top and edit quoted material freely.

One more tip to keep in mind when using the automatic reply feature: differentiate between replying to a single sender and to everyone else. That is, mail can come to you along with others as part of a cc. If you don't specify that you're replying only to the sender, your reply will go to everyone else on the cc-line—and some messages can carry one hundred people on the cc-line. Even if there are only two or three other people on the cc-line, don't forget they're "in the loop."

▶ *Sigs & emoticons*

I have a confession to make. I'm a bit dyslexic about people's names. I easily remember faces and associate them with the places where I've met them. But names often go through my head.

If remembering names is a problem, the Internet has a fine convention for you. It's the equivalent of a letter-head, except in the topsy-turvy Internet it occurs at the bottom instead of the top. (Go figure.) This way I can remember who 99+@aol.com is, or 7667,823@Compu Serve.Com, or dkih27jj@prodigy.com.

An Internet letterhead is called a "sig" for signature. For example:

```
                                          _\|/_
                                          [o o]
 ( __ )=-=-=-=-=-=-=-=-=-=-=-=-=-=-=-=-=-=-=-w=U=w-=-=-=-( __ )
  |  | Howard H. Frederick, Ph.D.        Associate Professor  | |
  |  | Division of Mass Communication           Emerson College | |
  |  | 100 Beacon Street              Boston, MA 02116-1596 USA  | |
  |  | +1-617-578-8875 (voice mail)        +1-617-578-8804 (fax) | |
  |  | hfrederick@igc.apc.org      cyberprof@emerson.edu (email) | |
 (____)=-=-=-=-=-=-=-=-=-=-=-=-=-=-=-=-=-=-=-=-=-=-=-=-=-=-=-(____)
```

Or:

```
        gary gach  |_|_|_|_|  generalist
  528 corkscrew ave |_|  _|_|  & internet trainer
san francisco, calif |_|_ _|_|  <gach@uclink3.berkeley.edu>
        94101-1508  | |  | |  415.808.50.00 ext.7301
```

That's me. In addition to name, e-mail address, snail-mail address, phone, and fax, a sig can include title and company. If company is listed, it may be accompanied by a disclaimer, that ideas expressed are those of the author and not the company—disclaimers varying in degrees of irreverence.

Two other optional sig items are quotes and art. For example, E. Carter Brooks, editor of a free online newsletter called *Carter's E-Reader,* (bookmarks@manoman. com), signs off with the following:

```
In theory, there's no difference between theory
and practice. . . . But in practice, there is.
```

Here's one I created:

```
When Elvis Presley died in 1977 there were 37 Elvis
impersonators in the world.
   Today there are 48,000 Elvis impersonators in the
world.
   If the current trend continues, by the year 2010
one out of every three people in the world will be an
Elvis impersonator.
```

Some e-mail setups keep your sig on-hand for you, automatically; otherwise, you have to keep it on your computer and upload as needed.

Sigs can include pictures, too. A new breed of artist has emerged in the online world, equivalent to the anonymous medieval scribes who'd illuminate manuscripts they were copying, but using ascii. (For them to work, on your screen or printed out, you have to use a nonproportional font, like Courier.) One example may remind you of the graffiti that, like "KILROY WAS HERE," has been around for about a century:

```
                          .`.
                        :     :
                    o (O-O) o
-------ooO----v(_)v---Ooo-----
                        vvv
```

Another reminds me of someone's self-portrait drawn from the point of view of the person's computer:

```
        _____

   |     { { { { {        |
   |    ( @ @ )      |
   |     | U |         |
   |      ~          |
   |    ~~~~~        |

        _____
```

Others can be for special days. One Halloween, I saw this one:

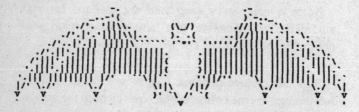

That's a tough act to follow. But it gives you an idea of how some people are overcoming a drawback inherent to the Internet: plain text doesn't reflect the sender's facial or vocal nuance.

I should qualify that. The Internet is not exactly plain text. It's plain text—electrified. Excitement can be amplified. And any shadow of a doubt or possible negativity can multiply at the other end and be interpreted as downright hostility: people have reported seeing words that are merely in all-caps online as shouting at them. Some refrain from using the Internet for anything possibly negative, whether intentional or not.

Returning to one of our examples above: ''Please let me know if you *don't* get this,'' had asterisks at either end of one word for emphasis. Similarly, one can indicate italics with _underline_ signs.

How else to convey subtle shades of meaning?

Another mode shows the sender's intended emotion through little faces, called emoticons (or smileys). One slight drawback: they have to be viewed sideways (by tilting your head). The above example might have included a wink, like this:

```
Please let me know if you *don't* get this.
;-)
```

:-) is the standard happy-face. Here are some others:

:-(or :(	an unhapppy face
8-)	someone wearing glasses
:-P	someone sticking out their tongue
>:-O	someone screaming in fright, their hair standing on end
:->	a sarcastic remark
:-@	a scream
:-&	tongue-tied
:-)#	a face with a beard

There are dozens of these simple icons, and you can find them all online. They've found their way into typewritten correspondence now, too. (There are at least two books in print that are just compendiums of smileys.)

Plus, like FYI (for your information), there are short-hand verbal equivalents: BTW, by the way; IMHO, in my humble opinion; ROTFL, rolling on the floor laughing.

▶ *Bells & whistles*

Now we know the rudiments of sending and reading e-mail—plus, we've learned a little Netiquette and some cultural niceties like emoticons and sigs. Here are a few bells and whistles (little accouterments, neat features).

If you're going to be on vacation, you can set your mailbox so that all your incoming mail will automatically receive a notice, such as your schedule, until you return.

If you don't want to have your e-mail i.d. posted, you can arrange to be anonymous. Your mail might be routed via an intermediary, such as in Denmark, that will vow not to reveal your identity. A bunch of journalists recently set up an online mail forum with inner-city juvenile gang members, giving them anonymity. E-mail can be somewhat anonymous, in and of itself, but shy participants might feel more bold if they use a pseudonym or remain anonymous.

And if you're sending a love letter or a business proposal, time may be of the essence. If you're both in the same domain, some e-mail softwares allow you to check and see if the recipient of your letter has read your message yet—and, if so, whether or not they've downloaded and/or forwarded it.

A commonly asked question is this: "How can I find somebody's e-mail address?" There are a couple of applications, such as WhoIs and NetFind, though they only search a fraction of this vast matrix. (*See Appendix.*) Of course, where possible there's always writing or phoning someone to ask an e-mail address.

With the Internet's phenomenal growth, the need to filter out information (info glut) becomes bigger, and there are softwares designed for those purposes, such as a "bozofilter," which blocks mail from specified people or on specific topics, and automatically files your incoming mail into organized folders.

Last, but not least, some systems introduce something called *chat* or *talk*. This enables you to communicate live with somebody else on the Internet (if their system also has this program). A common writing area opens up on each of your screens, wherein you both see whatever either of you type, in real-time. It is still fairly slow—but intriguing. And there's no toll. Another development is the Internet phone, enabling people to hear and send live voice messages. For more info, e-mail voice-faq-request @northcoast.com. As the subject, put the word "archive." In the body, write: send voice-faq.

Eventually "live" Internet mail might be a videoteleconference; videotelephone (telephony). As of right now, for under a hundred dollars, you can get a mini-videocamera, the size of a silver dollar, to sit on top of your screen. With that, plus the right software—such as CU-SeeMe—you can use your computer as a videophone. To download CU-SeeMe, ftp://cu-seeme.cornell.edu/pub/video.

▶ *E-mail culture*

Initially, we compared Internet e-mail to mail in a post office. (Internauts sometimes refer to the realm of flesh and blood by the initials RL, for real life—as opposed to VR, virtual reality, which is like real life, but different.) The more we've learned, the more we've seen e-mail also has unique features, as well as resemblances to post-office mail.

In addition to all the gadgets, there's also culture—which includes the Netiquette, if you will—of how to best use e-mail. As we saw with, say, quoting what you're replying to, and with sigs and emoticons—appropriate use of culture can play just as much a part as any technology in shaping the Internet as a useful tool. Besides becoming proficient at sending and receiving mail, it's important to learn the culture.

You'll learn by doing, but here's some background about e-mail culture.

I once wrote an article about telecommunications in China and a proposal for it, then submitted a query letter

The Internet erases boundaries of time and space.

online to about five or ten editors whose e-mail addresses I had. Via e-mail, the *Whole Earth Review* asked to see the proposal, then the article, then asked for some revisions, and somewhere in there I asked about payment— and by the end of the day, the production department was pasting it up, direct from my e-mail transmission. If this was real life (RL), the process of query and reply would typically take weeks, perhaps even months. The Internet virtually erased temporal boundaries. And it made no difference where the publisher was—in Sausalito or in St. Petersburg, since we both could hook up in cyberspace. Spatial boundaries were of little importance—in fact, their erasure was part of the subject of my article.

It no longer felt like a cat-and-mouse game or a lonely fishing expedition, as the dance of getting published can be. Instead, I felt empowered. Jazzed. This was fun, all the way.

I was able to begin my hunt by being able to query the editor-in-chief directly, thanks to the decentralized nature of the Internet. It's an open system. Every node on the Internet is equally accessible. That structure can shape the communication it mediates. For instance, the network structure doesn't repeat the traditional top-down vertical hierarchy, the pyramid—where a CEO's gates are guarded by an Executive Secretary, who's intimate with Management who, in turn, liaisons between Administration and the general workplace, etc. Instead, if everybody in a corporation has e-mail, anyone can be written to directly, regardless of title or job description. There can be more sense of autonomy. Every individual, for example, is responsible to upload and download their own mail.

Eventually, Very Important People (VIPs) may delegate authority as to the reading and answering of their e-mail just as they do with snail-mail. If you have the e-mail address of your favorite rock star, or CEO, or whomever—and you have something to tell them you think might interest them, go for it. You never know: you just might get a personal reply.

Now here's another. A young journalist named John Seabrook, Reporter at Large for *The New Yorker,* once wrote a portrait of Bill Gates in which the culture of e-mail became an integral part of the story. In "E-Mail from Bill," Mr. Seabrook tells us, at the very beginning, that, having been assigned by *The New Yorker* to profile Mr. Gates, the founder of Microsoft and the world's richest man ($14 billion at last count), he was given Mr. Gates's e-mail, and so he tried it. He reproduces the message he e-mailed to Gates, "out of the blue," and a reply came quickly from Bill. A correspondence ensued, and a great deal of the article is composed of the author's reproducing the e-mail, back and forth, and commenting on it. It has the present-tense quality of e-mail to it, and rather than a one-shot interview one-on-one with a highly busy man, it gives a fuller, more dimensional portrait. And so there formed a better sense of how Gates works as an individual—how he organizes his time, energy, and attention—and that which he values. Seabrook is able to show us what kind of mind Gates is driving online.

Had Seabrook used only the traditional modes, in addition to a press kit, he would have had an interview maybe an hour or two long, and maybe a chance to follow the Busy Man around his business for a few hours. Of course, Gates understood that a CEO must be able to use information technology himself, not just delegate it. In this instance, he was able to create and micromanage his own press releases on demand and directly collaborate with the author.

Just as I was able to go back and forth between an editor in one day, several times, so can any e-mail correspondents go back and forth several times in one day. Even though there's a *lag* which the phone doesn't have, you can go back and forth more times than if you were on the phone, because it's always mutually convenient. If you and a friend were calling each other up on the phone, back and forth all day, eventually you'll be reluctant to make yet another call in the same day because you know that eventually they might be eating, etc. There's a different kind of distance online—through which you might gain insights—maybe even a common language, sometimes even a certain bond of intimacy.

▶ *Fit it in to the ecology of your communication*

The more you use e-mail, the more you'll start seeing ways in which it's like media you've already known and ways in which it's not. As such, let's put it into some kind of perspective. It has its own place in context with other forms of communication.

For example, let's return to how I placed my article on China in print. This was an ordinary business proposition, not much different than applying for a job, or trying to sell anybody something. Normally, such a process might involve one or all of the following modes: phone, fax, letter, and a personal visit.

The unwritten etiquette is to orchestrate these media

together, using each appropriately, with the sequence remaining up to the user. That is, you can write someone out of the blue, follow up with a phone call, and have lunch to seal a deal. Or you can start with a phone call.

But only a bumpkin phones a stranger at midnight to propose business. Or drops in unannounced—or submits a 250-page manuscript by fax.

In whatever order, each media should be appropriately used, according to its own merits and drawbacks.

Meeting face-to-face is ideal: nuanced, immediate, interactive, one-on-one, and vital. You want to make the best of it—perhaps by preparing the ground with a letter first.

A letter allows you to create something to think about—to reread and possibly circulate. And the recipient(s) can read it whenever and however he or she likes—say, while wearing a bathrobe and cozy slippers. But it's also slow—a day to a week's lag. And, especially in business situations, you might never know if someone's actually read it or delegated it to someone else.

The phone is faster, more immediate, more direct. But it can be intrusive. The person might be doing something else when you call, whereas five minutes later they'd be free: you never know. Its spontaneity means a conversation can go in any direction. You have less opportunity to think through and refine everything you're going to say on the phone, as you do with a letter.

A fax can be a compromise. You can revise and polish it before you send it. It's about as fast as a phone call. And the person can read it when it is convenient for them.

Enter e-mail into the ecology of communication. E-mail has those potentials of a fax: speed, convenience, and polish. But a fax is a fixed document. If you want to edit it or include it in anything else, you have to re-keyboard or scan it. And toll charges can mount up to hundreds of dollars a month.

With e-mail, on the other hand, you don't have to re-key text or scan pictures: they're all right there, fluid, to be used as you wish. You can forward e-mail along, as is or edited, to anyone else with a tap of the finger. There's no toll charge. And some people privilege it, the way the fax can be a priority; some people check their e-mail before their voice-mail.

Of course, like fax, phone, or post, e-mail is always more impersonal than face-to-face (f2f), as noted with emoticons. Trying out new media, don't let them substitute for human contact. (Another good rule of Netiquette!) Never forget the human at the other side you're communicating with. If someone has your letter on their desk, your phoning them a week or two later might help them express their reply if they're too busy to write back; it can be the same with e-mail, too. It's not a magic bullet.

E-mail is the Internet's most common denominator. Does this mean that if you've only been using your computer once or twice a week that now you'll have to turn it on every day just to check your e-mail? Perhaps. As you become proficient at it, you'll want to explore its virtues and vices, test it, play with it, and find how e-mail best suits your own ecology of correspondence and communication.

In fact, you'll want to do this—thinking through and putting in perspective—with each aspect of the Internet, as well as the Internet itself. The variety of possibilities during a revolutionary shift such as this can become confusing until a new pattern gets set. Until then, those who use new technologies best won't necessarily be those with the most expensive toys with the most bells or whistles—but those who know their ecology.

E-mail addresses can be found throughout the Internet, in the other four areas we're about to tour. If you need special assistance or information, you can ask most of the people attached to them. Some may be busy. But most everyone in the Internet is friendly.

And remember—because the Internet has been doubling every year, 50 percent of the people online are new, at any given time. Don't be afraid to e-mail someone for Internet help. The First Law of the Internet is:

Ask.

Having toured e-mail and learned about its basic culture, two last things:

1) Even though you can get e-mail on Sundays and holidays, you can give it a day of rest.
2) I mentioned that you can cc a letter to a hundred people at once.

QUESTION: *What if each one of the one hundred addressees in a cc had a different list of a thousand people, and each forwarded the letter to everybody on their list, all at once—like in a telephone tree, where one person calls an announcement to twenty-five people, each of whom will relay it to twenty-five other people?*

Can do. The Internet can streamline, automate, and refine the process. Just as we can communicate one-to-many (and many-to-one), so too can we communicate many-to-and-with-many, which is what we'll explore next. It's one of the Net's most popular and exciting attractions.

FORUMS

We've seen how the Internet can facilitate communication from one person to another, and between one person and several. Next we'll see how it mediates between several people as members of a group—from thirty to thirty thousand people.

If e-mail is the life blood of the Internet, here is its nervous system. We'll see how forums can work in two ways—as *list* and as *newsgroup*. Either way, you're likely to find them your favorite Internet discovery.

MAILING LISTS

Who hasn't come home from work and found mail saying, "Congratulations! You're a Grand Prize Finalist in our TEN MILLION DOLLAR sweepstakes!"? (And this on top of mail announcing a check is being cut in our name for a million, and another asking if we want our booty in bullion, cash, or bond.) Isn't our reaction to ask ourselves, "Now what did I buy? Who got my name and address? What did I subscribe to? How did I get on *this* list?"

We're about to look at some mailing lists that may not award you ten million dollars but are very, very good to be on.

To return to our example from the previous chapter: what if there were over two hundred thousand names, total, in our e-mail version of a telephone tree? What if we could put the list of all the names in a computer? And what if we could send forty messages for that computer to route, via e-mail, to everyone on the list? Well, good news: we can.

It's called a mailing list, or just a *list*. Sometimes they're known by their software. The most common is Listserv, plus there are newer ones like Majordomo, Listproc, and Mailbase. (When you hear people refer to aliases or reflectors, these too are similar to lists.)

▶ *Custom newspapers & newsletters*

A list can serve a number of purposes. To begin, let's consider custom newspapers or newsletters—produced by and for special-interest groups.

A special-interest-group custom newspaper—voted one of the Top Ten Lists of the Internet—is *China News Digest (CND)*. It was started by some students and scholars in Canada and the U.S. in March 1989. The staff has grown to fifty volunteers, servicing a list of sixty thousand subscribers at last count, on every continent.

It was conceived as an online daily newspaper, with five feature articles and five or more brief articles about China. In one way, it's no different than if a group of people had taken all the daily newspaper and magazine articles about China, laid them side by side, and sent them out, every day.

That alone is a pretty neat accomplishment. After all, most newspapers usually publish only one or two articles a week about China—out of the dozen or so stories they get from wire services. Many wire services are online, and their stories can be forwarded to others; just not reproduced for profit. So *CND* can call from both domestic and foreign wire services, such as Agence France, Kyoda (Japan), Xinhua (China), etc. Plus, Boston *Globe*, Chicago *Sun*, *South China Morning Post* (Hong Kong), *Globe and Mail* (Toronto), etc., all have special correspondents in China. So if any member thinks an article in a local paper might be worthy of sharing with the group, they can upload it to the editor, so it might get added into the mix.

China News Digest even has five different editions: global news, U.S. regional news, Canada regional news, Europe and Pacific regional news, and a weekly magazine in Chinese by members of the group. If you need software to read Chinese on your computer, they furnish that, too. And it's all absolutely free.

But that's not all. This kind of mailing list helps form communities. Articles not only have the headlines and the authors' bylines, as they appeared in the originals, but also articles can have the name of the person who submitted them. So, after a while, you might notice that, say, a Mr. Chan frequently posts articles about Christians in China, whereas a Ms. Liu seems to have an ongoing interest in computers in China, and Mr. Kuo regularly posts articles about tariffs. So, if suddenly you acquire a personal interest in any one of these topics, now you know to whom you might send an e-mail query.

For example: if, say, you're interested in marketing computers in China, you might send some e-mail to Ms. Liu and Mr. Kuo. Or if your church wondered if there might be BBS's or computer networks yet for Christians in China, you might ask Mr. Chan and Ms. Liu. Would anybody throw a fit and write back in a huff, saying, "Why are you asking *me* this? Who told you I was interested in this, and why would you think I'd care about a stranger's interest anyway?" No, not necessarily. Not if you properly identify yourself as a regular reader of the *China News Digest* and what *your* interest is. After all, here they've already publicly identified their special interests, frequently, to a group of some sixty thousand.

(*Note:* you won't want to send your query to the whole group. You'd e-mail the individual directly.)

Compare this custom newspaper to the newspaper that hits your doorstep. Of the one or two articles published about China a week, any of those could be bumped by some hotter news front; in *CND*, the news is constant and in-depth. The newspaper has no community; *CND* builds community. Consider how close you come to connecting with anyone at the newspaper. For example, how many times have you matched wits with a particular movie reviewer? Let's say you've just seen a film they loved—which you hated! You might think to youself, *Darn it! This is the sixth time I've been burned by that reviewer.* But are you going to write a Letter to the Editor? Naw, probably not. Maybe they already get enough of them, already.

In a forum about movies, on the other hand, conducted via a list on the Internet, everyone is a moviegoer *and* a movie reviewer, and even a commentator on other people's movie reviews. It's as if you could hear what people are saying when they walk out of the movie theater, and they could hear each other—and you could all talk about the movie for days. And a community, with its own culture, evolves. For example, as Netiquette, people will put in their subject lines the word "Spoiler" if their message might spoil the film for someone who hasn't seen it yet.

▶ *Mailing list culture*

A custom newspaper/newsletter is basically one-way. We receive it, but don't reply to it. A movie forum is two-way: a full-on, interactive group.

Lists can assume their own kinds of landscape and process. If they're one-way (post only), not only can they be like newspapers or newsletters, but they can also provide action updates, a thought for the day, a weekly summary, correspondence courses, etc.

If they're two-way (post and reply), they can be like twenty-four-hour cafes, where you can sit in at any table (like the bar in the classic TV-series "Cheers," "where everybody knows your name").

Or: talk shows where nobody's put on hold . . . with multiple topics under discussion at once . . . nonstop, around-the-clock. (*Note:* as they're not happening in real time, you can pick up the threads any time you want. And you can deal only with those subject lines or e-mail addresses you like.)

They can also take the form of support groups, user groups, focus groups, rap sessions, organizing committees, debating clubs, fan clubs, brainstorms, book clubs, round robins, etc.

Eugene Spafford, a longtime active participant in Internet forums, says the following:

> When you're relating to other people [online] . . . *all* you know about them is what they *say*, in a very positive sense. You have no inherent way of knowing if they're

young, old, male, female, short, tall, Jewish, Gentile, Muslim, physically or sensory handicapped, etc. And that can be an intriguing, enabling concept. It provides a unique forum for shared discussion and development.

Just as e-mail enables a gears-meshing kind of close dialog, so can forums, even more so.

One user of forums says of them, "The quality of the minds behind the words must be experienced to be understood." Indeed, if we were to print out all the postings we read in a forum during a week, they'd seem as lifeless as reading rather than seeing a movie or a play. As they say, "You would've had to have been there."

Forums can be unmoderated (free-for-alls), or moderated (hosted, edited, or filtered). If seven people all sent the same joke on the same day, a moderator might hold back six of them and release just one to the group. Or a moderator might not publish something if it was felt to be irrelevant to the group. And a moderator can help keep the discussion moving.

Another variable is that a forum can be public or private. Maybe there might be a fee. Or maybe the special-interest group just wants to filter out extraneous noise. People in a recovery program might want anonymity. A journalist's list might require that members be associated with an accredited news source. An African-American list might be only for African-Americans. Maybe the interest group wants to feel assured their list is a haven, a safe house, a private retreat.

▶ *Netiquette*

> To do is to be. —*Thomas Dewey*
> TO BE IS TO DO. —JEAN-PAUL SARTRE
> . . . DOOBEY-DOOBEY-DOO! . . . —Frank Sinatra
> —GRAFFITI, 20th century

The Netiquette we learned regarding mail applies to mailing lists, too. Indeed, here the importance of considering the other person, quoting what you're replying to, etc., is magnified exponentially.

Here are two more items of forum Netiquette:

1) See if the group is right for you.

See how much traffic there is—how many messages posted per month, week, or day. See how many topics of interest there are. See how many postings are of interest to you. Sometimes a list posts thirty or forty messages all month that may seem very trivial to you, and then, once a month, *bingo*, it comes up with some real jewels. (The techie equivalent for this is "determining the signal-to-noise ratio.")

Even though it's easier to delete e-mail than to throw away paper, you'll want to make sure your incoming mailbox isn't clogged with more e-mail than you can comfortably handle.

And you don't want to barge in like a bull in a china shop. It's customary to monitor a group for two weeks without jumping in. It's called "lurking," like sitting on a bench in a dugout. Lurk before you leap.

2) Sometimes you might want to call upon the opinions or expertise of the group without taking up the group's time as a whole. In that case, you might post your question and state that you wish members to e-mail

their replies to you directly. Afterward, you might write up a summary and post it to the entire group, as a single message.

Again, at other times, you might want to send a message to an individual member of the group, and not take up the group's time at all.

▶ *Topics*

Lists are created around thousands of topics and affinities. Often there are dozens of lists for each topic. A random sampling of lists for topics beginning A, B, and C includes:

    Accounting, advertising, agriculture, animals, ani-
    mation, anthropology, archaeology, art, astronomy,
    automotive, aviation, biking, biology, birds, boat-
    ing, books, business, cats, cinema, collectibles,
    comics, commercial, communications, computers,
    crafts, cultural . . .

[*Note:* The last item shows an Internet idiosyncrasy. On the Net, culture often refers to special-interest groups, such as by lifestyle or nationality (Argentines, Bosnians, Croatians, gay, et al.) as well as the arts (which can also include martial arts). Sometimes, as here, combinations of the two might be found, too, such as the Australian Rave list and the Middle Eastern Music list. The Swiss Watch list is categorized here, too.]

There are lists about the Internet, and there are lists on the subject of mailing lists.

There's a phenomenon known as *cross-posting*. This means a message has been posted to a number of related forums to help spread the word or generate more wind.

This requires being savvy with the culture of each list before doing so.

(There's a corresponding negative phenomenon known as spamming. This means a message has been indiscriminately posted to as many different forums as possible, as where merchants stick flyers under car windshield wipers. The Internet thus has its equivalent of junk mail, chain mail, and Ponzi schemes—make easy money fast—carpetbaggers tramping on the Information Superhighway.)

There are *tens* of thousands of lists.

But is there *one* master list of *all* the lists?

In our Appendix, you'll find at least three. This question also brings us to an important, general Internet phenomenon.

Who would be in charge of compiling, maintaining, and distributing a list-of-lists-of-lists? Volunteers. And wouldn't they have to update it quite frequently, as new lists spring up and others grow dormant? But even if they could get credit for it at school, eventually they'd graduate. So it might be expected that there could also be lulls when volunteers went off to raise a family, before other volunteers come to fill in the gap.

Meanwhile, there are ways that we can get this information ourselves. There are books that are like Internet yellow pages, with lists arranged by subject. Each different list software has a function that will tell us the names of the lists it is currently hosting. From there, we'll find at least one list that interests us. And on that list, we'll hear backfence gossip about other lists of interest.

So there are two different approaches to information.

One is top-down, where one or two people hand a master list down to everyone else. The other is bottom-up, where people do it themselves, and spread the word, laterally. This is a prime characteristic trait of the Net.

▶ *From broadcast to narrowcast: tuning the dial*

> You have no idea how difficult it is to rule a country that has 242 different kinds of cheese.
>
> —CHARLES DE GAULLE

The Internet has a bad reputation among some folk who haven't taken the time to survey the terrain for themselves. One common gripe among the impatient, misinformed goes something like this: "It's just a bunch of Grateful Dead fans." Or "There's only a whole lot of trivia out there." Well, if you were to turn on a media source with a two-hundred-and-fifty-thousand-channel dial, expecting it to be like TV or radio, you'd probably say the same thing, too. Blaming the Internet for its wealth of variety is shirking the responsibility it puts on each individual to tune their own dial.

The Internet is a whole different mode of communication. Consider for a moment my publisher, Pocket Books.

Besides publishing mass-market best-sellers like *Forrest Gump* and *The Road Not Traveled*, Pocket Books has special divisions that publish just the Star Trek books . . . and the Fear Street series by R. L. Stine, for kids . . . books of gay interest, African-American interest, and bilingual books. *Narrowcasting*. But it's just a token of the winds of change blowing in the media worlds, from Publisher's Row to Hollywood. As Al Jolson said in the first big "talkie" motion picture, "You ain't seen nothing yet!"

Today, it's already as commonplace for people to make their own compilation tapes of favorite music as it is to have their own movie library on VCR.

Now, on the Internet, anyone can be a publisher.

Anyone can host their own talk show.

Anyone can find something just for them—or make their own. It takes understanding the culture. Taking a bit of time to tune the dial as to the capabilities of what's out there.

There's no *TV Guide* to the Internet. It's more like radio—for which there's no *Radio Guide*. Yet we know when our favorite show airs, be it Larry King, "Computers with Gina Smith," or old radio theater. How? From word of mouth. Notice in a paper. Or just . . . tuning the dial. Except, here, the dial has over fifty thousand channels—each an individual affinity niche, large or small.

But the Internet is not broadcast. With *TV Guide*, we either have to be at our TV set, at one particular point in time and space. Or we have the show taped. And if two shows we like are on at the same time, we might have a tough decision to make. The Internet, on the other hand, not only has a vaster menu of options to choose from, they're always at our convenience. Here, information can exist simultaneously, in as many places as needed. And it can be more participatory, if we like. But we have to put out the extra effort to scout out what we want and stay abreast of what's new. That's part of the culture.

We can expect to devote up to 15 percent of our time online at just this. Some people call it surfing the Net. I call it tuning the dial. Imagine you're in a strange foreign city and you turn on the radio. You might turn the dial from left to right—just listening to what's out there. You may not care for most of it, but you might really like one or two stations. Except here it's a dial a block long . . . and keeps changing!

At this point in our tour, before we move on, we can say five things that are true for the whole Internet:

1) The Internet is pull rather than push. It's not pushed at us, and we're not being pushed at it. We pull the information in ourselves.

2) The Internet is the alternative channel for mainstream culture, and a main channel for alternative cultures.

3) Point your arm, follow your shoulder, and see where that takes you. (Like Vespucci, discover for yourself.)

4) Remember: getting information about or from the Internet can be like trying to fill a glass of water off an open fire hydrant. (Expect to find a wheelbarrowful—so accept a thimbleful at a time.)

5) Information literacy is not just being fed facts. It's also identifying information, knowing where to get it and where it goes.

▶ *Fine-tuning lists*

To return to our discussion of mailing lists, if you've just joined a great list, and it's been going on for fifteen years prior to your discovery of it, you may be glad to hear it has an archives where you can look up previous postings, by topic. Mailing lists provide other amenities as well, like turning your list off when you go on vacation. And setting a list to Digest mode will give you all messages in a list each day in one packet, with a table of contents.

Here are some important things to know:

• A list has two addresses. To one you send your address, to subscribe or unsubscribe. To the other you send your messages, to be distributed to the group.

A classic newbie blooper is to forget this. One way this can happen is to send a request to unsubscribe to the list owner: then everybody on the list will see your futile message, which can be as annoying as getting a wrong-number phone call.

Let's get clear on this. If we're sending *command* requests (administrivia) like subscribing or unsubscribing to the Internet pocketbooks List or putting our subscription on Vacation mode, we'd e-mail our command to listserv@domain, or pocketbooks-request@domain (called the *list server* or the *list address*).

If we're sending a *message* to the subscribers of the list, we'd e-mail pocketbooks-1@domain or pocketbooks@domain (called *the list* or the *list owner*).

• Listserv doesn't have an e at the end. This is useful to remember when the word occurs in an e-mail address (which has to be typed exactly).

• When you've joined a list, you'll get an initial form message welcoming you and giving you instructions on the basics and the amenities. Save this message. If nothing else, it may come in handy if you forget how to unsubscribe and can't get out of there. Keep all these introductory messages in one folder, for easy reference.

- Again, as with e-mail, where appropriate quote what you're replying to. (Forums are where the practice first evolved on the Net.)

EXERCISE:

NewbieNewz is a list for getting started with the Internet. It hosts periodical tutorials as well as a group discussion forum. To subscribe, e-mail majordomo@io.com. Leave the subject line blank. In the body of the message put one line: Subscribe Newbienewz <Your e-mail address>. Within a few hours, you'll be e-mailed your first reply, an introductory message to save in your lists folder.

Help-Net is an unmoderated question and answer list for help with Internet functions. To subscribe, e-mail listserv@vm.temple.edu. In the body of the message, put on one line: Subscribe Help-Net <Your e-mail address>.

▶ *Grow your own*

This year, I'll be starting a list or two of my own. For information, see the inside front cover.

If you want a presence on the Internet, having your own mailing list might not be a bad thing to consider. After all, e-mail is the Net's most common feature; everybody has it (unlike the web). It's very easy and inexpensive to have a provider or solutions person set up a list for you. All they have to do is just set aside a small amount of their disc space and run a mailing list software there.

If this is for your business, you'll want to brush up on the Netiquette of using lists for ads or sales. It's okay if it's information the group would want to know about. After all, if you treat them right, the subscribers have become part of a qualified mailing list that you own. (But this can be tricky.) Maybe you may just want to use the list as an ongoing focus group, as to what your clients are thinking (and maybe your competition, too) about your product or service.

Or maybe you just want to generate a little conversation over by the virtual water cooler. Perhaps you've always dreamed of hosting your own radio show or perpetual garden party. Now it is easy.

▶ *Synergy*

Before we move on to another kind of forum, let's pause just to marvel a moment at an essential phenomenon that makes mailing lists and e-mail possible: *synergy*. Synergy is when two work together to do something neither could have done alone.

When differing human and computer skill-sets fit together, like the teeth of cogs coming together, the mesh can be marvelous.

James Brooks, a professor of the University of North Carolina, has created the phrase Intelligence Amplification (IA) for a general instance of this. Basically, he says that machines are good for certain things (mass storage, linear thinking) and bad at others (pattern recognition, leaps of logic) and that humans are also good at some things and bad at others. The good news is that the things humans are bad at, computers are good at, and vice versa (which only makes sense when you think why humans created computers to begin with).

E-mail is one example of IA. Lists are another. The computer can store and keep track of a massive subscription list plus automate delivery of messages to its members—beyond what any human could. And, recognizing the advantages such technology affords, people are forming affinity groups, observing Netiquette, cross-posting, etc.

CONFERENCES • NEWSGROUPS

Nobody expected e-mail would be a part of the original Net. But there it came, out of synergy its early users saw between capabilities and needs. Out of e-mail came mail lists. Then in 1979 (way back when the round, yellow Happy Face logo said "Have a nice day"; when people sported crushed-velvet bell bottoms and wi-i-i-ide shirt collars; and when the human immune system was a new field of physiology) Tom Truscott and Steve Bellovin invented Usenet (Users' Network). They wanted to imitate mailing lists, because their respective schools (Duke University and University of North Carolina) were not then on the Net. According to Internet historian Quarterman:

> Necessity was the mother of invention. . . . Instead of sending a copy of each message to every person that wanted to read it, which would have required sending multiple copies to each participating machine, Usenet sends one copy to each machine and only that one copy is stored on that machine, rather than multiple copies in mailboxes for each user.

The next step was developing the equivalent of the incoming e-mail list. It depends on the software used (called a reader). The following is a typical model.

Messages get grouped according to their subject line. So instead of appearing as separate mail messages, the first message in that subject appears, and all the subsequent ones get threaded up after it, one after the other—much like individual sheets of bathroom tissue.

Consider our mailing list for readers of this book. (*See inside cover.*) When you subscribe, the first thing you might be asked to do is send a message to the group entitled Introduction, telling everyone who you are, etc. People reading each other's introductions could then begin topics of discussion on their own. If you were one of the first twelve people to join, you'd get a dozen messages in your mailbox, each entitled Introduction.

Here's how such a list might be threaded up as a news group:

1 - 11	Introduction	July 7 1:34	(35)	ggg@rgpl.com
2 - 3	Internet Videos	July 7 4:20	(155)	joe@day.com
3 - 3	Internet for Profit	July 8 2:04	(64)	gog@gill.cn
4 - 11	Community Internet	July 8 10:36	(12)	hal@uc.edu
5 - 8	Internet for Fun	July 9 5:26	(24)	99+@aol.com

Notice the number in between the subject and the rank on the menu. That indicates how many additional messages are there, one after another, following the one posted by the initiator indicated, in this case me. If you clicked on the first, you'd get my initial introduction, followed by eleven others, all stitched together into one long scroll. In the second, Joe started the first post, about Internet videos, and there are three more posts—maybe three other people each contributing the title of a different video, or Joe and someone else having a dialog about one video, back and forth. Hal's initial post about community Internet resulted in eleven messages posted. So the fifth topic may have eight people commenting on Internet for fun, two people discussing it four times, or any combination thereof.

If we read through each, the numbers indicating the number of posts will vanish. (Or we could mark them as read, without reading them all.) Then, when we'd check back again—say, a week later—and there were more numbers in the margin, that would mean additional postings have been added.

(Incidentally, mailing lists can be threaded up in this way for you. Ask your Internet service provider if they offer this service.)

The art, opposite, depicts variabilities of people-to-people telecommunication. First, Bob e-mails Flo, who replies (point-to-point). Next, Bob e-mails Flo, with cc's to Dan and Jan (point-to-mass). Jan forwards Bob's file to Lou, Jim, and Pat (again, point-to-mass). What Jan's doing is a model for a mailing list, which automates mass delivery and opens up communication mass-within-mass. In our last example, Bob's posting (and Viv's and Flo's, etc.) are there for all to read and, as Pat is doing, to comment upon.

QUESTION: *Are there real-time conferences?*

No, like e-mail and mail lists, these aren't real-time.

There *is* an area on the Internet called IRC, Internet Real-time or Relay Chat, with about five hundred separate "rooms." It's still more of a subculture, but some of them are beginning to be used for things like talk shows with guest celebrities. Some online services, such as AOL, have their own real-time chat rooms. That's a different kind of conferencing, which we won't get into here. (Intermediate-level users might wish to try a recent software enabling any seven people on the Internet to hold a real-time conference, exchange files, and browse the world-wide web together, just by knowing each other's e-mail. It's called Pow-Wow and it can be downloaded for free at the world-wide web site of Tribal Voice, an organization of Native Americans: http://www. indigenous.com.)

▶ *Usenet*

We've grouped mailing lists and conferences together, generically, calling them forums. We've seen how the conference interface differs from lists. Next, we'll see how the culture can differ as well.

Online services have their own conferences, with varying cultures. However, it's the Internet-wide conferences, Usenet, that concern us here. Having evolved parallel with the Internet, from way back in Late Phase One, Usenet has evolved a rich, unique, diverse population and culture.

Conferences in Usenet are called net news, or newsgroups. Think of them as a cork bulletin board with push pins in a public space—or an electronic newspaper of Op-Eds. *Case in point:* In 1994, *The Middlesex News* ran two Op-Ed pieces on the recent Israel/PLO accords side by side. One was by a Jewish settler in the West Bank, the other by a Dutch woman living with Palestinians in Gaza; both were taken direct from daily Usenet postings. Although the word ''newsgroups'' has become ubiquitous, it has its definite downside for brand-new users. Many Internet service providers and online services have an icon of the front page of a daily newspaper, with the word *News* underneath it: the uninitiated would never think to look there for forums of people talking.

If you subscribe to an online service that has Usenet's news groups, that service has *subscribed* to them. Techies can set up their own software (called readers) to subscribe to them themselves.

How many are there? The total may be near fifty thousand by now. All but a third of that is research-related, scientific specialties. Of the remaining fifteen thousand or so that might interest lay people like us, there's a large degree of subtopics within topics, such as twenty to thirty conferences about aviation, another twenty to thirty about Star Trek, etc. If you have access to five thousand to seven thousand of them, that's plenty.

Usenet conference names have their own hierarchy. They're arranged (in the reverse of Internet domain names) from general to specific. Thus the prefixes tell us the general category. Main prefixes are the following:

- Alt—alternative topics
- Clari—for the ClariNet news services (UPI/AP—etc.)
- Comp—computers and communications, for professionals and hobbyists
- Misc—miscellaneous, not easily classified, or multiple categories
- News—Usenet itself
- Rec—arts, hobbies, and recreational activities
- Sci—sciences
- Soc—groups primarily addressing social issues and socializing
- Talk—debate-oriented

There are fifty-five other prefixes—including regional conferences specific to state and city. To learn more about the prefix categories, for example, there's a conference called news.groups, with copious information on just that.

The Usenet spectrum spans a wide rainbow of interests. The more mainstream topics include algebra, Algeria, alumni, and alchemy . . . antiques, autos, and aviation . . . bicycles, birds, boats, and books . . . cinema, climbing, comics . . . fine arts, federal jobs, filmmaking, financial aid, fitness . . . music . . . sports . . . zymurgy (beer-making) . . . in short, a dizzying array that tempts any commentator to give up and just add, ". . . and much, much more!"

On any given day, Usenet generates more words than an entire encyclopedia.

Here are some tips: The ClariNet newsfeeds are not discussion areas; they simply post news clips, according to over a hundred separate topics. There are thousands of conferences on computer-related questions. In the soc. culture group, every nationality and sexual persuasion has their online conference—from Asian-Americans to Bosnians and Herzegovinians, feminism, men's issues, singles, and gays (given their own Internet name—an acronym, of course—MOTSS, members of the same sex). In Usenet, you can read and write with others in French, Spanish, Finnish, Chinese, Russian, Urdu, etc. You can find cyberpunks, Mormons, pagans, and activists. You can discuss economics, debate about abortion, or just chew the fat. People talk about scripture, pursue personal ads, and join clubs. Like lists, they can be moderated or unmoderated. As in lists, people often cross-post to reach overlapping interests.

Some Usenet groups of interest for new Internet and Usenet users are news.announce.newusers, alt.culture. internet, alt.internet.services, and, for a taste of the weird side, alt.usenet.kooks.

Lists tend to be more focused than Usenet groups. They take place in the most intimate area of your Internet domain, your mailbox. Usenet is more anonymous. It's easier to subscribe and unsubscribe. Though there are many serious topics, there is a tendency for Usenet groups to be more diffuse than lists might be.

For example, take China as a topic. As to lists, there's the *China News Digest* newspapers and newsletters. Another group discusses computing in China. And there are lists for people to just hang out—"Over a Cup of Tea" is one, for example, and Chinese Community Forum is another.

On the other hand, there are more Usenet conferences. Talk.politics.China is a debating forum. Soc.culture.china is more of a hangout, representing a larger, greater cross-section than "Over a Cup of Tea," including mainlanders, Taiwanese, and Hongkongers. There are specific hangouts, too, for soc.culture.taiwan and soc.culture.hongkong. Clari.news.china has news feeds that might not appear in *CND*. There are three separate groups for film buffs: rec.arts.movies.Asian, rec.arts.movies.hong.kong, alt.fan.jacky.chan.

If Usenetters think there's enough valid interest in a certain topic, they can petition and lobby the Usenet administration to add a new group. Already existent groups can, likewise, petition and splinter out into subgroups. For example, rec.pets.cats was getting a thousand posts per day (!). So the members voted on what they felt were the most frequently discussed topics, and new sub-groups were formed: rec.pets.cats.breeds, rec.pets.cats.veterinarians, rec.pets.cats.feeding, etc.

With such a huge array, you'll find not only what's important, but also what seems trivial. One person's trivia is somebody else's meat and potatoes . . . and vice versa! Remember: the Internet is an alternative channel for mainstream culture and a main channel for alternative cultures.

This brings us to three primary cultural curiosities of Usenet: flames, democracy, and faqs.

▶ *Flames*

With millions of people all rubbing elbows at a global watering hole, there's bound to be some friction. Not to worry. The Net has evolved its own code of ethics, and the vocabulary to go with it. A *flame* is when one person takes exception to something in another person's post. A *flame war* ensues when members of the whole group take sides, flame others who try to maintain order, everybody flames everybody else, etc. It can be over in an instant . . . but some have been known to last over a year. Again, not to worry. Remember: it's easier to ignore something on the Internet than it is to tear up a piece of paper and throw it away. The delete key only takes a touch of a finger. *Blink!* . . . gone!

Well, this may be fine when it comes to ignoring other people's flames. What if you, dear reader, happen to get flamed? That is, what if someone reposts some of your words to the group with strident or abusive comments about them (such as "the author of these words is so clueless he wouldn't have a clue if someone rubbed clue oil all over him—you should get a life!'')? Ignore it, unless . . . maybe you have something at stake.

Say that this is happening in a conference that touches upon your economic livelihood. Now, if you can write a good defense, then go for it, post it. You'll win the confidence and support of potential clients or customers in the group—maybe thousands or tens of thousands of them—who'd all see that you know your stuff and aren't afraid to say so.

Again, flames are the exception, but if you want to expose yourself to the phenomenon, in and of itself, visit the conference dedicated to the topic: alt.flames.

The bottom line: some people say flames are the price of freedom.

▶ *Netiquette (democracy)*

The difference of interpretations as to flames' being malignant or harmless is kind of like the difference between anarchy and anarchism. Anarchy is degenerate lawlessness; anarchism is a self-governing utopia.

Flames come with the freedom of the Internet. They call attention not only to Netiquette but the politics that have evolved, ad hoc, among users. Its culture is, of course, an outgrowth of the Net: decentralized, do-it-yourself, democratic.

▶ *FAQs*

A very remarkable and useful feature of Usenet is the group of documents posted periodically in many groups, called FAQs (Frequently Asked Questions), pronounced either F.A.Q., or "fack." They list the questions, then answer them. Here's the beginning of one for the group alt.meditation:

```
              >                          >
        >            >   >
     >            >              >
       /\   /\  /\   meditation-faq       /\
  /\  / \/\/ \/\ /  /\  /\ /\      /\   /\ /\   /\
/ \ /   \    \ /  \/  \/\_/  \/\ /\ /\ / \ /
/ \ ----------------- /_____\  --------___/  \/
```

The FAQ (Frequently Asked Questions) for alt.
meditation is posted at the beginning of each month.
Comments and suggestions are welcome; please send e-
mail to jeffjc@binkley.cs.mcgill.ca

CONTENTS

1.0 Charter [About alt.meditation]
1.1 Comment on the faq
1.2 Other meditation resources on Internet

2.0 What is meditation?
2.1 How is meditation different from relaxation,
     thinking, concentration, or self-hypnosis?
2.2 What are the different meditation techniques?
2.3 Which is right for me?
2.4 What are the abc's of meditation?

3.0 Is there any religious implication or affilia-
     tion with meditation?
3.1 Does meditation have any ethical implications?

4.0 What is the best time of day to meditate?
4.1 Why do some people use music while meditating?
4.2 Should I meditate with my eyes open or with my
     eyes closed?
4.3 What are the physiological effects of medita-
     tion?
4.4 When I meditate I experience physical pain in my
     body. What should I do?
4.5 How long should I meditate?
4.6 Do I need a teacher?

After the header, it says it's posted once a month. So
if you've just joined a conference of interest, hang around

and lurk for a while and see if a faq gets posted. A faq can have both very useful information about the topic as well as guidelines for what is and isn't discussed in the particular conference. So they can act as the group's Netiquette guide as well as a general information resource about the topic.

They can range in length from a dozen to dozens of pages. Some are so big as to be broken into separate files. If you want to climb up a learning curve or sharpen your knowledge about golf, beer-making, AIDS research, legal resources on the Net, directories of bookstores, movie trivia, Ascii art—there are hundreds of faq files.

Like everything else, they're available for free—to download, print out, file, forward along to your family and friends, and so on.

The charm is that anybody can contribute additions, deletions, corrections, or revisions. So it's a group document, evolving over time. It's unlike any other form of literature. It's the *ne plus ultra* of Usenet culture.

There's a Usenet news group that just posts faqs: news.answers. There are also ftp, gopher, and world-wide web archives of faqs. (*See Appendix.*)

Similarly, there are library-like archives of forums, as there are of mailing lists. Usenet keeps postings current for anywhere from a week to a month, depending on the group, and then they get swept clean and start all over again—but many are archived.

How we might access these archives—and transmit and receive other large amounts of data—is what we're going to cover next.

FILE TRANSFER (FTP)

The next two stops on our Internet tour, ftp and remote log-in, are essentially mechanical processes, rather than human. Until very recently, they were two of the Internet's most popular resources. They've since been eclipsed, but their former glory is not diminished.

We've seen how the Internet facilitates communication among people one-on-one—and one-to-many/many-to-one—via e-mail; and many-to-many, via forums (mail lists and conferences). The next feature, *ftp,* concerns not the number of people communicating but the bulk of the files—big ones, and sometimes lots of them—and how to transmit, store, and access them.

Ftp was created circa April 1971 when advanced research folk were mailing each other huge bundles of computer tapes. Very icky. And slow. With the Net, they could send the files instead of the tapes. Easier. And faster.

And they could send something to one place everyone could access.

File transfer protocol (ftp) essentially does two things:

1) It transmits large files. If you've ever tried sending or receiving many-paged documents by fax, you'll know how sometimes a page in the middle won't get there, or it falls on the floor out of order, etc. Ftp, on the other hand, is the equivalent of taking the entire document and hand-delivering it.

2) It hand-delivers it right to the file folder in the file cabinet at the destination where you want it kept in. This

way, you can tell anyone else where it is. And they can access it, in the reverse—by a messenger who could pick it up and hand-deliver it to their computer. Just as in a posting to a conference, any number of people could inspect it and, if they liked, download a copy.

A protocol is like a program or language enabling two or more computers to transmit data to each other.

(As you've probably noticed by now, many of the Internet's applications can be used as a noun and a verb. A thing and an act. Software and what it can do. You can e-mail me your e-mail. And you can ftp to an ftp site.)

Having an image of the verb *ftp,* now let's look at the noun. Imagine the *p* in ftp stands for place. File transfer places. In our analogy, the equivalent of the filing cabinets are portions of a mainframe or hard-disc dedicated to being a repository. An archive. A warehouse. It might even be a cd-rom. (A cd-rom looks like a music cd, although some allow you to write to as well as read from it. Small and light, a cd-rom can hold quite a large amount of stuff, at least by 20th-century standards. I've put this entire book on a floppy disc; a cd-rom contains the equivalent of 450 floppy discs.) Let's consider two types of examples of ftp sites: business and noncommercial.

Let's say Local Global Information, Inc.'s already using the Internet internally, as our office network, but we want to use it now as a window of exposure to the outside world.

Take our quarterly report, for example. In order to be edited and printed, it had, at some point, to be converted to a digital textstream. Once it's a digital textstream, it

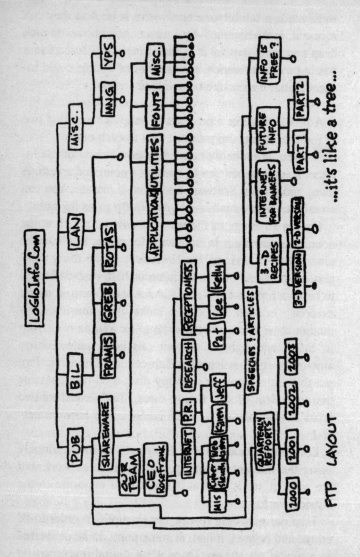

...it's like a tree...

FTP LAYOUT

can be made available to anyone who wants to access it. From our computer to theirs, direct. Maybe the public doesn't want to wait for it by snail-mail, or maybe they want to be able to search it for key words.

We might also make available a list of our clients, biographies of our team, articles our administrators have published during the year, and so forth.

To add value, we might also make available some neat software applications that help people with information.

And so we put all of this into one big folder, marked "Pub," for public. Maybe we'll build what's called a firewall around everything else, so that the public won't read our inter-office mail. Now we're directly accessible to the outer Internet. In our ads and brochures, we can invite people to ftp: LoGloInfo.Com.

If LoGloInfo.Com is our domain, that might be the name of our ftp site, or it might add a prefix: ftp.loglo info.com.

It would be like a public Information Desk (or public virtual server). Open twenty-four hours a day. Able to handle multiple requests at once.

Currently, there are probably over 1500 active public ftp sites. Universities on the Internet often have an ftp site. In addition, however, to course catalogs and campus information, they might also have ftp sites in individual departments. And they might be two-way, as well as one-way.

That is, in keeping with a university's active culture of information exchange, people might upload as well as download to some ftp sites. For example, someone might announce in the soc.culture.patagonia conference, to all the Patagonians and Patagonia fans, that they've just returned from Patagonia and uploaded their best snapshots (taken maybe with digital camera, whose pix wouldn't need to be scanned). And they'll tell people what folder they're at on the Patagonia ftp site, which some university has, for people to download and look at. (Next season, another traveler might add more.)

One way ftp began to be used over the Internet, in the early days, was for collaboration. Research could be shared by all. Someone might ftp a prototype model of some software they were developing to an open site for people to try out. (And they could discuss it via mail or a forum.)

Today, in the beginning of Internet, Phase Three, there are so many ftp sites, with so much Net stuff, people download far more than they upload. But if you take something—the "original" stays there on the shelf, for the next person to copy!

And it's all free—although some software can be *shareware*. Shareware is honor-system software. You can copy it and share it, with a relative or friend. But anyone using it for more than thirty days is on their honor to send the author a nominal fee (typically $5–$35). Sometimes, the shareware fee will entitle you to a user's manual, and an updated or fuller version. Or there may be a "nag screen," which goes away only after you've paid the fee. There's freeware, too, which of course is 100 percent free.

There are gigabytes of free stuff on ftp sites. Text as well as graphics, sounds, and software. Text can be archives of forums (mail lists and Usenet groups) . . . back issues of periodicals . . . databases on particular topics (music lyrics, recipes, lifestyle, Star Trek info, genealogy, etc.). Software can be fonts . . . personal information managers (PIMs) . . . video players . . . games . . . utilities and applications for your computer, PC or Mac, virus protection, etc.

Like forums, some sites may be private, Members Only, such as for employees of a certain company. Many public sites have become known as "anonymous ftp," because you can log-in directly, identify yourself with the word anonymous, then give your e-mail address as the password.

Two interesting recent software tools for accessing ftp are Win Ftp for PC and Fetch for Mac. For users of a Unix shell account without any additional ftp software, I have listed the half-dozen chief ftp Unix commands in the Information Resources appendix.

► *Examples*

To learn by doing, here are a few sites you might want to visit. Lest you think that ftp sites are only software, ftp to wiretap.spies.com and check in at Library (rather than the usual, Pub). For example, you'll find articles about:

```
aeronautics and space, backcountry and outdoors,
civil rights and liberties, cryptography, elec-
tronic publishing, food and drink, gambling and
oddsmaking, journeys and travels, language, legal
and criminal matters, mathematics, religion and
philosophy, science, sex, sociological issues, and
sports,
```

and assorted documents, such as:

> civic and historical documents, classics (about 500
> texts), cyberspace, weird areas called ''fringes of
> reason,'' humor, mass media, music, religion (An-
> glican, the Bible, Catholic, Christian, Coptic,
> Fringe, Jainism, Mormon, Presbyterian, and the
> Quran)

and so on.

And there are ftp equivalents of boxes of three-by-five
recipe cards: ftp gatekeeper.dec.com/pub/recipes has
over five hundred of them, from advokaat, African stew,
and apple pie, to ginger zucchini, zuccoto, and zwetsch-
gend.

Five major sites bulging at the seams with software
are ftp.csusm.edu/pub/winworld (for windows), ftp.
csusm.edu/pub/macworld (for macs), archive.umich.edu,
sumex-aim.stanford.edu, oak.oakland.edu, and, one of
the oldest (seventeen years), SimTel, at ftp.coast.net. To
give you an idea of what we're talking about here, the
MsDos directory at SimTel begins like this:

Name	Description
astrnomy	Astronomy-related programs and utilities
bbs	Bulletin board (BBS) programs and utilities
bible	On-line versions of the Bible
cad	Computer Assisted Design programs
calculat	Calculators
cdrom	CD-ROM utilities
clock	On-screen clocks and clock utilities
compress	MS-DOS ports of Unix compress, gzip, etc.
database	Database management programs and utilities

Name	Description
decode	encoding/decoding and other encode/decode programs
editor	Text editors
educatin	Educational programs
entertn	Entertainment, various
fileutil	Utilities for maintaining and handling files
finance	Finance and money-management programs and utilities
genealgy	Genealogy/family history programs and utilities
graphics	Programs for viewing and handling graphics/images

▶ Finding your way around

With even the niftiest ftp software, it pays to understand the way ftp sites are organized, to take full advantage of all they have to offer. This will teach us an essential Internet skill, sometimes known as surfing. And on the way, we'll bump into an information resource, named archie, to help us find things.

First, the layout of an ftp site. Anyone who's used computers knows that files can be put in folders, which can be nested in larger folders, ad infinitum. An ftp site arranges files in a hierarchy of folders within folders—main directories, with subdirectories, and subsubdirectories, etc. As you can see from our illustration on page 106, it's like a tree, with a trunk branching out into twigs, at the ends of which are leaves and fruit.

As an ftp user, we usually go to Pub, first. This Public area is divided into directories. In a gui, they'll be fold-

ers; in a text-based interface, the names of menu items
are followed by a slash, such as this:

```
Software/
Text/
```

So it goes, as we cruise our way through directory and
subdirectory until we reach a file. If we like it, we can
download/save it.

This is rudimentary surfing. When you surf, you im-
merse yourself in a big ocean and paddle along until you
find a wave you like. (This particular kind of surfing is
also called navigating menus.)

▶ *Paths & archie*

The route along the tree to get to a specific file is its *path*.
It's the series of menus you navigate to get there.

Specifying for someone else the exact location—in
this case the site, and the path—is called a Universal Resource Locator (*url*, pronounced as initials or as ''earl'').

Let's say I want to let someone know about a speech I
delivered about the Internet for brokers, which is archived at the ftp site where I work. I might give them an
url that includes the ftp site and the path on its menu tree,
like this:

```
Ftp:LoGloInfo.Com
Path:  /  Pub  /  Speeches  /  Net.for.Brokers
```

Knowing that, an ftp-user can go directly to the file, without navigating menus.

QUESTION: *How do we find files and ftp sites for stuff we're looking for?*

There's a software application available to the Internet called archie—archive without the *v*. If we enter the word or syllable we're looking for, within ten to fifteen seconds, archie will give us a list of the file names with urls including path names. (If your provider doesn't have archie, our Information Resource list in the back shows you how else you might be able to find it.) More sophisticated software will even bring you the files direct.

▶ *Compression/decompression*

The only other thing you need to know about ftp is that many files are stored in a format called compression. It's the Internet equivalent of shrinking, or folding up, for storage, to take up less space at the site, and to take less time to be downloaded. So, after we've downloaded/ saved a compressed file, we decompress it, to unshrink or unfold it, like adding water to the freeze-dried crystals of instant coffee.

There are a number of commonly used decompression softwares. If a file has been compressed with Zip, for example, the file name will carry that information as a suffix: say, Net.for.Bankers.Zip. Then it has to be opened with the UnZip decompression software. Zip/UnZip is common for PCs, and StuffIt/UnStuffIt for Macs.

Some other common suffixes are these: .Z (for Unix), .hqx (for Binhex), and .sea (for self-extracting).

These days, online services and Internet providers

offer the latest models, if you can't find them on the Internet, so you don't have to hunt for them. (You might find an archive of decompression tools, but it might take some time to track down the latest version.) Usually, these can be downloaded and transformed into working tools with a mere click, in a format called "self-extracting." Decompression tools don't take up much disc space, are fairly easy to master, and take relatively little time to operate.

▶ *Ftp netiquette*

Many if not most ftp sites often contain material of use to people associated with that site, which those people felt the rest of the Internet community might wish to access as well. To return the favor, access ftp sites during nonbusiness hours (relative to the time zone where the site is): between 7 P.M. and 7 A.M. They can handle only a certain number of people using them at once, so let the community associated with the host site use them during prime time without our causing a busy signal.

(*Tip:* The Internet can use odd language, like "Nothing is available," to say a line is busy.)

It's also considered polite not to ask for more than ten files in one ftp session.

Next, we'll explore more about the *process* of accessing an ftp site. As we've just seen, this entails entering into another computer's domain. This can open up into a whole other world, one where computers hold far more for us to use . . . including the opportunity to interact live with other Netizens.

REMOTE LOG-INS (TELNET)

Mail evolved spontaneously, as messages accompanying file transfers. Forums grew out of mail. And ftp, in a way, evolved out of remote log-ins. Here's how. One of *the* initial rationales the government had for funding the development of the Internet was to make computer resources freely available to federal researchers in as many different sites as possible. It was thus maximizing return on the taxpayers' investment in the computers: researchers in remote locations could log-in to some supercomputer, say, as if they were a user actually there, running programs at that computer. From their computer. By remote control, as it were.

This process was called remote log-in.

The original users of the Net saw it as a system of distributed resources.

In the Early Days, pioneer Netizens sent each other bound directories about all the computers on the Net. They'd keep the directory by their computer, as a guide to the resources available to them.

This was not a matter of how-many-people or how-big-a-file—but of the number of different things available and do-able, on many different computers, running many different software programs.

▶ *Telnet culture*

The Internet jargon for remote log-in is *telnet*. It's used as both a noun and a verb. If we have telnet at our domain, then we can telnet to any other domain that has telnet, too.

One author has described it as if he were astrally projecting to some distant computer. It's not really so esoteric. Another has used an even starker metaphor: the master-slave relationship—a distant computer becoming a slave to our computer, which we now operate from our keys. This may be true, if overdramatic. Simply, we log-in to a portion of the distant computer and interact with a program it's running, by typing commands from our keyboard. While we're logged in, tapping an A on our keys is just like tapping an A on its keys, and our screen shows us what we'd see on its terminal (a process called terminal emulation). Again, the process can cover many different purposes—which is what entitles it to a chapter of its own.

With ftp, a distant computer allows us to download/save large files from its storage area. With remote logins, we can actually run programs on distant computers. They might let us browse information—library catalogs, for example—as if we were there, real-time. No waiting for a librarian.

Or an entire book may be online, and we can search it for key words. A Webster's dictionary, Roget's thesaurus, and a book of quotations are on-hand whenever we need them, online, freeing up our personal working space. At present there are about eight hundred books available online.

Or, we might conduct a search through pools of information (databases) such as law citations, medical diagnoses, consumer product evaluations, agricultural market prices, or employment information. We might track and also order stocks and bonds. (A few iconoclastic Netizens have asked, "If we can do home banking, why can't we print our own money?")

If you don't have certain Internet resources at your disposal, but you can telnet—no problem! Just telnet to a site that does. The Information Resources appendix has some examples.

Uses can be immediate. Say you're planning a trip and want to know the weather. You can access the weather satellite and get an instant peek of what's out there.

Other telnet sites connect people together across the Internet as multi-users of the same telnet site, to play such classic board games as backgammon, chess, and the Chinese game of *wei chi,* also known as *go* in Japanese. You can play with whoever's online, or rendezvous with a friend, or maybe just sit in on the sidelines and discuss the game.

Interface becomes critical here: with so many machines to tap into, loaded with so many different kinds of softwares dedicated to do so many different things, the interface—usually command-oriented—varies from system to system. (Remember our tip about entering commands, from our first mention of interface. It comes in handy here.)

Tip: A common question when inside a new software program is "How do I get outta here?!" Two common exit commands are Control C or Control] (written on-screen as ^C and ^], respectively). The word quit sometimes works, too.

▶ *MUDs, MOOs & MUSHes*

Besides chess and such, there are multi-user (MU) telnets that are unique to the Internet. They're called MUDs, MOOs, MUCKs, and MUSHes. MUDs, for example (Multi-User Dimensions), tend to resemble the role-playing dungeons-and-dragons games so many game fans are into. You're given a fictional identity, cast into a strange new realm, and given objects with which you can interact with that environment and with other players logged in the same time as you. Part of the object of the game is to figure out the rules. Or else. (They can get violent.)

Here's how to play some of the more popular ones:

- Hidden Worlds, telnet csns.com:4000
- Lost Realms, telnet iguana.voknor.edu:6666
- Tazmania, telnet ukko.rowan.edu:5000.

Because these are like theatrical spaces, they can have more serious applications, such as a business conference (making presentation materials available for all remote attendees to pick up and inspect). A MOO (a MUD that's Object-Oriented) can take people on a guided tour that interacts with its environment, for example. Or they can conduct a Sunday service. Or an interactive performance piece. Some are beginning to add graphics, giving users not only a fictional name but also a cartoon persona and pictures of objects to interact with. Eventually, they may support 3-D spaces (like *Myst*) and even virtual reality. In short, they're ripe for killer applications. (For more information, there's Sean Carton's *Internet Virtual Worlds,* in the *Quick Tour* series, among other books about MUDs, MOOs, and MUSHes.)

MicroMuse is a popular site, for kids of all ages, enabling people to build an environmentally sound, socially just 24th-century city. Telnet michael.ai.mit.edu (home of some other neat MUDs, too). To be the tropical animal of your dreams, visit Brazilian Dreams, telnet red_panda.tbyte.com 4201. For a more cyberpunk experience, visit The Sprawl, telnet chiba.picosf.com 7777; or Abacus, telnet abacus.hgs.se 4000. And to see what the best and the brightest in new media are up to, visit MediaMoo, telnet purple-crayon.media.mit.edu 8888.

EXERCISE:

Urls for telnet sites are simple domain names. Here are two to try:

1) Telnet: library.wustl.edu.
2) Telnet: nessie.cc.wwu.edu. Log in as Libs.

The first is the library at Washington State University, St. Louis. The second is Western Washington University.

Logging in to either is exactly as if you were on campus. You're logged in there and interact with the computer in real-time, just as if you were there, in the lobby.

After you've familiarized yourself with the telnet process, there's a second exercise to make you an Internet expert:

▶ *Teleportation (interconnectivity)*

Besides local campus information, the above sites have links to other telnet sites on the Internet. One word for this, teleportation, comes from science fiction. *Teleporting* (the act of teleportation) is where a person can project from one site to another instantly—the way they do in "Star Trek." We go from here to over there, *shazam!*, without having to cross over. In the Internet, the process is similar, plus it can involve leapfrogging.

Let's say we've logged in to the LIBS program at Western Washington University (nessie.cc.wwu.edu). Besides campus information, we see a directory of libraries in the U.S., plus another directory of foreign libraries. They're links we can remotely log-in to, from Libs. When we log out of any of them, we return to the Libs menu at WWU, from which we can telnet to another library site. The Libs menu thus acts as our home base, home plate—or, as it's called, too, our home page.

Another example of this can be found at the library at Washington University. If we telnet to this site (telnet: library.wustl.edu), we'd see on our computers exactly

TELEPORTATION

what we'd see if we were to hop on a plane right now and fly there and go to the computer in the lobby of the library. The menu offers us resources at Washington University, but also offers a program called WorldWindow, which links to other Internet sites, including online Internet tutorials—which we can teleport to, and come back to its menu for more options.

EXERCISE:

Teleporting can be dizzying, especially when you're doing it while also having a goal, such as researching a particular topic. So I recommend that you practice doing it, in and of itself, just to get the hang of it.

Log into one of those sites above. Familiarize yourself with the main menu. Then hop from there to some other site, and cruise around that menu. Then hop back.

Once you've hopped one level out (counting your home page as home, or ground zero), your next exercise is to try hopping two levels out. For example, you might be remotely logged in, from your New York computer, to Paris, from which you've logged in to another remote host, at a library, say, in Cairo.

Your final test is to log-out and get back home all in one piece. You'll log out from Cairo and still be at Paris. You'll exit Paris and return to New York, complete with the resources you acquired at those other sites, and ready to teleport to your next location.

Teleportation and *selective* linking to other sites can allow you to create your *own* home pages of resources and thus customize the Internet for *you*. To prepare the ground for that, we'll conclude with one of the fundamental processes that make it possible.

▶ *The client-server relationship*

Let's take two steps back. Underlying remote log-ins is *the client-server relationship*. Think back to the real-life example when I left the LoGloInfo office, went into a cafe across the street, and ordered a cappuccino at the counter. I was the client, and the person behind the counter was the server. If I'd ask, "Can I please have a cappuccino?" the server would reply, "Yes, here it is."

Similarly, with telnet, we are the *client*. The remote host we are logged-in to is the *server*. Our computer asks the server, "Do you have a library catalog?" and if the server does, it answers, "Yes, I do. Here it is." We type an A, asking, "Can I see the search prompt for (A)uthors?" and it shows us the prompt. We input William Faulkner, and it shows us what it has by Faulkner.

Note: Now, here's the beautiful part. What if we are asking the catalog to search for Faulkner not just at that library but, say, throughout an interlibrary system, such as different campus branches? If it can, it will. If so, at the same time it was our server, it would become a client to another server to answer our request. This is the beauty of the client-server relationship, as we shall see in a moment. As the Net adds more and more powerful, intelligent systems to the pool, interlinked—the answers to our questions become that much better and easier.

This client-server relationship pervades networked telecommunication. An Internet service provider, for instance, is really a server, providing the user (the client) the Internet. Their Internet server may be a big mainframe or a server-farm of hard discs, all hooked up with multiple phone lines and modems. We remotely log-in to them, and our first question is, "Can I see your Internet interface?" Then, "Can I see your e-mail interface?" Then, "Can I see my incoming mail?" Etc. When there is a glitch, and they tell us, "Our server was down," that simply means that their computer, to which we connect, had a problem.

Or, when companies advertise new media things like five hundred TV channels and interactive games, they'll probably talk tech about their "server." Now you'll know what the tech they're talking about.

For a guide to what's out there in TelnetLand, our Information Resource guide, in the Appendix, points you to Hytelnet, which acts as a kind of directory.

Tip: Telnet is one way to log-in to remote BBS's and Internet service providers who only have local numbers. This is extremely useful to Internauts when they're on the road.

INFORMATION RESOURCES

Now we understand the Internet and how to connect to it. We've seen the four major applications for which it can be used: e-mail, forums, ftp, and remote log-ins. We are amazed. Dazzled. Nay, dizzy, even. It can seem daunting Anarchic. Overwhelming. It's as if we'd discovered a library far larger than anybody had ever dreamed of in human history. But, too, it's as if there'd been a major earthquake and all the books and papers in that library had been scattered everywhere.

Information resources are what can help us organize

and find things on the Internet. Our discussion of these resources will climax all we've learned thus far, and complete the conceptual framework we've been building.

Some call them resource guides: guides to the resources on the Net.

Others call them information resources.

Either way, they can do three things: search, interface, and link.

WAIS

We've seen how we can search for things by key words, as with whois, for e-mail addresses, and archie for ftp files. The term for these applications is *search engines.*

Here's another: Wais (pronounced "ways," or "wayce"—short for Wide Area Information Server).

QUESTION: *What if we're searching for the word* Vulcan, *but it appears in a file entitled "Star Trek FAQs"? Can we find it?*

Answer: Wais searches for words within documents.

Archie is like a table of contents—it deals with headings. Wais is like an index—it deals with words within the text itself.

A Wais search has three simultaneous criteria: how often does the word occur, how close the word occurs to itself, and how close the word is to the top of the text. Averaging between those three criteria, a Wais search turns up a list ranked best to worst. It's a hot list: the items are linked directly to the files it finds and will remain hot during that search session. That is, from the list you can go directly to the files it's found, back to the list for other files, etc. The links remain active until you're through with that search session.

And it can search multiple databases at once.

For a sample session, telnet to the Wais site in our Information Resources appendix.

▶ *Interfaces are information*

An information resource isn't only a search engine.

Interfaces organize things for us to interact with. As such, that's an information resource, too.

By way of example, let's compare two trivia lists. In my Sunday paper, there's a syndicated column, by L. M. Boyd, called "The Grab Bag." It tells us:

- Ant blood is without color.
- If the researchers have it right, more than a third of the world's people still eat with chopsticks, but only about a twelfth eat with hands only.
- That giant wave called the tsunami can move across the open ocean as speedily as a jet plane above it, say the experts.
- Mouse mating is a five-second affair.
- Historians claim to know that Hannibal, even while he crossed the Alps, always wore his wig.

It's a stream of factoids, without any discernible organization or pattern (unless you're a student of Chaos Theory or have drunk many, many cups of very strong coffee).

On the other hand, *Harper's* magazine publishes something entitled "Harper's Index," where part of the draw is to see how the factoids have been arranged. Sometimes juxtaposition creates meaning, sometimes not. Connect the dots. For example, a recent one begins:

- Average value of a merger or acquisition among major U.S. hospital chains this year: +$833,000,000.
- Portion of all for-profit hospitals now owned by the two largest hospital chains: ¾.
- Ratio of the price of an ounce of gold to that of an ounce of Zofran, a new anti-nausea drug: 1:292.
- Hours of psychotherapy California's Contra Costa County exchanged for each handgun turned in this year: 3.
- Rank of "bad communication" among the most common reasons cited by the LAPD for "errors in shooting" by its officers: 1.

Here we see the original meaning of the word information, as Aristotle meant it:

$$IN$$
$$FORMATION$$

Information is the meaning we place upon data—how we put it in formation, such as through the design of a particular interface.

▶ *Links*

A third kind of information resource is *linking*. In the previous example, if "Harper's Index" and L. M. Boyd's "The Grab Bag" had the same fact—and that fact served as a porthole to teleport between the two lists—that would be a link.

Gopher and the world-wide web are two applications that are both information resources. They 1) act as interfaces to organize the Net's resources for us, 2) provide search engines to sift through those resources, and 3) link those resources together.

GOPHER

Gopher can be used as a noun or a verb. It's named after the mascot of the university where it was developed, in April 1991, at the University of Minnesota. (It would have been called surfer if it had been developed at the University of California at Santa Barbara.)

▶ *Interface*

Gopher's interface organizes information in two ways: tree and crystal.

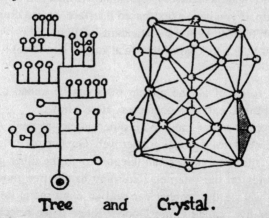

Gopher's interface organizes information in two ways:

Tree and Crystal.

▶ *Tree*

Gopher's basic interface is a menu, which is like a tree. This, again, is the hierarchy of directories and subdirectories and subsubdirectories, etc. Things *branch* out from a central trunk, and the files are at the ends of the twigs, as it were, like leaves, flowers, or fruits.

Any site that has gopher running there will have a menu interface. So many but not all ftp sites have come to adopt it. When I began teaching the Internet, I had to spend about ten minutes drilling the class in the ten basic Unix commands for ftp, and then show them where the other fifty commands could be found.

For example, on page 106—using a standard ftp command interface—if you were at *Framis,* and you wanted to go to *Yps,* you'd have to enter the command "cdup" ("change directory up") twice, and then "ls," to display the new directory, then "cdmisc," then "get yps."

Now, instead, if you can gopher to an ftp site, then you either navigate with arrow keys, numbers on a list, or just U for up, if you have a text-based interface, or just cruise through folders. Universal, standard, easy.

That's the first kind of interface gopher has. Tree.

The forest of all the gopher trees can be joined at a central trunk, called gopherspace. Here's how:

A gopher server links to all other gopher servers. All these links form a global gopher web. Gopherspace.

Any site with gopher can teleport to all the other gopher sites on the Internet. Returning to our tree model again, we see that gopher can add an extra menu item, number five, called Other Gopher Sites. If we selected that, we'd get a menu with options for going to other gopher sites—by country, by name, or by seeing an alphabetical listing of all the gopher sites in the world, A–Z, and so forth.

EXERCISE:

If you have ten to twenty minutes, try cruising through the menu of All the Gopher Sites in the World. Tuning the dial. Speed-reading the names. It will help acquaint you with the kinds of cultures that are part of the gopher totality. You can expect to find university domain names there, research organizations, and big corporate ones, but you might also be surprised to find *Academe This Week*, a magazine listing news and job openings in higher education; the African National Congress; Arts & Farces, an Internet training organization; the Grateful Dead's humongous archives; etc. However, there are probably four times as many gopher sites as you will see in this list—currently over 2500—because some university gophers contain others within them, and because there are others that aren't registered here.

Current gopher sites all interconnect—forming one, big gopherspace; pooling into one, big, main gopher menu.

▶ *Crystal*

The second type of gopher interface is crystal.

We've seen how files are at the ends of branches, which radiate off a central trunk. In crystal formation, the same files might be at the interstices of the facets of a crystal. In our picture of such a crystal, if we shine a beam of light at it, the light will be reflected by all the facets at once. And each facet will also reflect the light reflected in all the other facets.

You'll note, too, that the crystal in our picture is currently resting on a particular facet. But it can rest on any facet. There's no top or bottom. We could flip it onto another facet, such as the shaded area, and then that would be the bottom. (*Note:* it's not important whether the crystal is symmetrical or asymmetrical.)

Gopher is crystalline in the following way. Any item in any gopher site can be linked to any item in any other gopher site, throughout gopherspace. Files and directories can be linked across gopher space. And going from one to another can happen *within* one gopher site without having to log-in to any other (thanks to the client-server relationship).

From the user's point of view, items presented on a gopher menu appear to come from the same place. But, thanks to the client-server relationship, we can be hopping around gopherspace. (It's like teleporting—but without having to log on and off, back and forth, or even know that we're doing it. No matter whether an item is a specific directory, subdirectory, or file—if one site forms a link to it, we can get there from that site, wherever or whatever it is.)

For example, imagine we have a domain tree which has only one file for Libraries. But if the domain has gopher, we can write links to some other gopher's menu of library resources, which will automatically teleport the user there, without ever leaving our site.

If a user visits Libraries in our revised model, they will teleport to the other domain, can download/save any of the files, and move instantly back anywhere else in our gopher.

Plus, imported or mirrored gopher stuff may itself carry within it other links. It's just as if someone dug up some earth in China and planted it in their backyard, and now had gopher holes that led to China—and maybe some that already led to Norway, and some that also lead to Minnesota—all those tunnels in one shovelful, now transplanted in one backyard.

This ability to mirror and link led people to build gopher *subject trees:* menus linking to other menus and files, by topic; much like a list of lists. We'll discuss this phenomenon at greater length later.

For now, consider that gopherspace forms one big tree and one big crystal.

▶ *Practical examples*

Since the best way of learning is by seeing for yourself and doing: gopher to www.library.ucsb.edu. Here, along with library information for UC Santa Barbara and online reference tools and electronic journals, you'll find a Subject Collections option, with over fifty topics, from art to women's studies. That's their subject tree, hot-linked to other sites on the Internet, which librarian Andrea Duda puts together, and keeps adding to. Point your arm and follow your shoulder. See where that takes you.

Next, try the gopher at UC Irvine, peg.cwis. uci.edu:7000. (The number at the end refers to "port," which is usually 70. Actually, the seventy is not really necessary, but anything other than 70 has to be added along with the domain.) Here, you'll find PEG, a Peripatetic Eclectic Gopher. Under the topic Internet Assistance, you'll find nearly 100 links alone. (No wonder this gopher was used over 4 million times in 1994, alone.)

Another good avenue for beginners is to try the gophers at Internet providers and online services, such as Netcom, the Pipeline, EchoNyc, and the Well: gopher. netcom.com, gopher.nycpipeline.com, gopher.echonyc. com, and gopher.well.com. Each has a big folder of Internet resources, as well as ones for business, arts, fun . . .

Some ftp sites are also gopher sites: they may (or may not) add the word gopher as a prefix to their domain names; and gopher may simplify the paths to the files.

The ftp site we mentioned with all the recipes, however, does not have a gopher correlative: you can only ftp there. Yet a gopher site that might make that robust site pale by comparison does not have an ftp equivalent. The site in question is at the home of gopher, the University of Minnesota: gopher spinaltap.micro.umn.edu. Its recipe database is under Fun, arranged by food groups, and searchable by key word(s).

Moral: it's good to know both ftp and gopher.

▶ *Veronica, the search engine*

Besides interface, there are two other ways gopher is an information resource. The first is an actual search engine. It's called veronica, which stands for Very Easy Rodent-Oriented Net-wide Index to Computerized Archives (which you'll never be tested on). You can find it on the

Other Gophers menu. (There are about six sites in the world that run it.)

In veronica, we type in a key word or words to search for. In seconds, it will come up with a menu of where that word or words occur in menus and names of files throughout gopherspace.

And those links remain hot.

That is, if we searched for the word gull we might get this (in a text-based interface):

```
1. Gulliver's Travels <?>
2. Seagulls of Southern States
3. Seagull Travel Agency/
4. Gulls & Terns: Bird Watchers' Alert <Tel>
5. Gulliver's Travels <?>
6. Jonathan Livingston Seagull
                                        1/6
```

(Note the number at the bottom: that means there are five more screenfuls, or *pages,* of options.)

If we select number two, we'd go directly to the file and see it on our screen (from whatever gopher site it might be). If we liked it we could download/save it. And when we exit the file, we'll be returned to the menu of all the previous options, with the links still active, or hot. Select number four, and we'll go to a telnet site. We can operate its software program, navigate back to the list, and browse some more.

(Note the repetition, between number one and number five: it looks like another site has copied—linked—that item to theirs.)

Getting information from the Internet can be like getting a glass of water off an open fire hydrant: sometimes we need to just get the glass half full, bring it back home, and examine what we have under a microscope. Maybe we'll find micro-organisms we can farm into algae.

For example, perhaps the file Seagulls of Southern States had the e-mail address of the person who posted it, whom we can e-mail for further assistance. And if we check and see the domain where it's housed, we can log-in to it and cruise through its menus to see what other related things might be there. Tuning the dial. Hacking around. Surfing.

I'm always amazed at what turns up in a veronica search. When I was trying out for my position teaching at the University of California, Berkeley Extension, and doing my demonstration of the Internet for the future boss I was seeking to hire—when we came to veronica, I asked him what word he would like us to search for. He said, "Iroquois constitution." <*Gulp!*> I crossed my fingers under the keyboard, very carefully typed the two words in correctly, and, *bingo!*, up came the constitution, posted at many sites. (A popular item, it turned out!)

Veronica searches come up with things we aren't looking for as well. (Searching for robins, and finding Mrs. Robinson.) We can sharpen our skills and learn how to refine our search. For example, if we want to search for Star Trek, we'd enter "star and trek." And if we wanted only the television series, we might specify "star and trek not movie." And a wild card will search for everything containing a certain syllable—such as Wom*, to search for woman, women, woman's, women's, womb, etc. To get up to speed on this, there are often documents posted on the gopher branch, alongside veronica.

▶ *Bookmarks—custom links*

Gopher is an information resource by virtue of its two interfaces (crystal and tree), and veronica, its search engine. The third, and most powerful way in which gopher is an information resource, I've saved for last.

We've seen how gopher creates a menu out of an idiosyncratic or even unruly command interface, but also how a gopher menu can sometimes have complicated paths of subsubsubsubdirectories. Plus, some of those paths might even be links to other sites—like chutes and ladders in asymmetrical and interlocking crystals. This could get complicated. Like voice-mail hell. Or forgetting which street you parked your car, late one night.

Well, gopher has a feature which is similar to the way Hansel and Gretel left a trail of bread crumbs when they went out into the forest. (And here the birds won't eat them.)

In any gopher session (including veronica), whenever we're at an item we like, we can form a link to it. In gopher, these personal links are called *bookmarks;* Microsoft Network has its own name for them: shortcuts. If you're in a text-based interface, just tap the (lower-case) letter *a;* in a gui, just select "bookmark," and click.

For instance: let's say we have an academic degree and we're interested in a job in North Carolina. Let's say we've just found the *Chronicle of Higher Education* online. It had some good job postings for the week, which we've downloaded/saved, and we want to check the site again next week. If we go to the North Carolina directory/folder and tap the letter *a,* or clicked on the bookmark, we've *added* that directory to our own "home page" of gopher links.

Now, whenever we're back at our gopher launch pad, we just tap the letter *v*, for *view*, to view our customized links; in a gui, we just click on our bookmarks directory. We'd see the directory/folder North Carolina. And it would be a hot link. Click on the bookmarked item, and we're there!

(*For text-based interface users:* To refine our control, if we tapped a capital letter *A*, we'd add the directory on the level *"above"* where we are. For example: let's say we weren't sure if we wanted to work in North or South Carolina. With our cursor at North Carolina, we could tap a capital *A*, to add the directory/folder marked States. When we'd view that link in our custom list, we'd get States, under which would be fifty-two options. By now, the idea of a directory/folder "above" the one we're at should be familiar—or will be from practice.)

Bookmarks are like the tracers people can buy to put on frequently misplaced things. Another analogy might be the speed-dial option on some phones, for frequently called numbers—except this automatically enters the frequently called number while you're talking to someone at that number. It's another example of the client-server relationship. The bonus is that now you don't have to know computer programming to form links—it's automatically built into gopher software!

With this, we can make our own home page. The Best of Gopherspace. What's cool and what's hot. Something that may be a subsubsubsubdirectory, a folder within a folder within a folder, somewhere out there can be number one on our own personal gopher tree. What was maybe looking blurry, as if through the wrong end of a telescope, is now coming into focus for us. Now we can really begin to imagine big possibilities for creating with this medium. We can see how we can make a way for ourselves in this big, huge ball of wax. (In the second half of this book, for example, we'll explore further how some dedicated, generous folks started creating Subject Trees for us to cruise.)

In 1992, the first year of its emergence in the Internet, gopher traffic increased about 600%. Many saw in it the ultimate Internet interface.

The same year, however, saw the invention of the world-wide web.

WORLD-WIDE WEB

In the beginning . . .

The world-wide web . . . the killer application for the Internet. Like catching lightning in a bottle. Such things just don't emerge, full-blown, from the head of some programmer, overnight. Like the Internet, the world-wide web crystalized a number of things "in the air," at the time: Vannevar Bush's Memex machine, 1945; Ted Nelson's coining of the terms "hypertext" and "hypermedia," 1963; and Douglas Engelbart's *ON*line *S*ystem (NLS), 1968.

Tim Berners-Lee is credited as being the web's primary architect. In the early 1980s (before the invention of gopher), he conceptualized *linking* in a new way. He began by envisioning a way for computers to enable a new way of tracking and linking both related and unrelated subjects . . . like calendar dates and address book information about people and their particular areas of expertise . . . much as the mind often works, freely associating to make an idea index, or mental road map. Up until then, the hierarchical or tree model had been the standard organizational model, but with his way you wouldn't have to " 'climb up a tree' all the way again before going down to a different but related subject," as he put it.

In the late 1980s, he had a chance to make his thoughts a reality when he was working at CERN (European Center for Nuclear Research), an organization of high-energy particle physicists based in a region at the border of Switzerland and France, but scattered over the world. He found a useful way of applying his idea for the high-energy physics community.

We'll use an analogy for what he invented, based on the kind of situation that high-energy particle physicists face. Scientists may theorize on and on, but must ultimately render empirical evidence in support of their theories. They run tests, write up their tests, and read write-ups of others', and evolve theories requiring new tests to prove. And everything's all footnoted. (Footnotes may refer to other theories, test results, articles in scholarly journals, books, or unpublished doctoral dissertations, etc.) But what if a scientist wants to read the cited material while in the primary document? Even if they could get all the cited material to CERN, at the border of Switzerland and France (which now you could, with ftp)— could they keep, say, three books open at once, at the pages which referred to each other, and follow along?

▶ *Hypertext*

Everything is deeply intertwingled.

—TED NELSON

This process of linking is now commonly called hypertext. One way of grasping it, at first, is as if it were a huge school—in which every room has doors leading directly to every other room.

HYPERTEXT

Footnoted texts and footnotes within footnoted texts, all laid out for immediate reference from within the primary text.

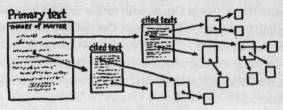

MULTIMEDIA

Text is merged with graphics, video, sound, etc..

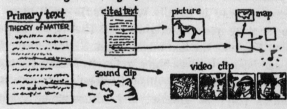

To get the hang of it, suppose we're reading *The Hypertext Shakespeare*. We've come to Hamlet's most famous soliloquy, "To be, or not to be . . ." This is where the melancholy prince contemplates suicide. When we come to the part, ". . . when man might himself his own quietus make with a bare **bodkin** . . ."—we see bodkin is a link, because the text is in bold, or another color, or underlined. We wonder, "What *is* a bodkin?" and so we move our cursor to it and click on it.

And here we see it's not a dagger at all. There's a little

picture and it's really a kind of pin. Invisible **fairies** used one to prick the mortals in **Shakespeare's Midsummer Night's Dream**. In **Elizabethan** times, men carried a bodkin in a sheath around their **belt** . . . etc., etc.

So let's say we want to know more about Elizabethan times. It's marked as a link, so we click on it. And we get a picture of Bette Davis, with ruffles around her neck, wearing a crown. And we read that Elizabeth was the Queen of **England** . . . and, being American and maybe not knowing the difference between England and Nicaragua, we click on England. And we get a map of the British Isles, with text.

Okay. Enough. Let's take a few steps back.

In this made-up example, we see an instance of how hypertext can work. And if the links are well-done (the operative word is usually well-*edited*)—we'll never be too far away from our original text. That is, on the page about England, the text might begin, "England: the European island that was home to Queen **Elizabeth**, under whose reign the bard William **Shakespeare** wrote such famous plays as **Hamlet** and **Midsummer Night's Dream**, wherein a **bodkin** was mentioned . . ."

This way, if we'd originally been reading about **costumes**, and fell into either *Hamlet* or *Midsummer Night's Dream*, we could always easily get back to **costumes** via the **bodkin**.

Of course Shakespeare wasn't originally written this way . . . but now it's possible. And, to give a related example, all major encyclopedias now have hypertext versions—including one, *Encarta*, which doesn't even have any linear, paper corollary.

▶ *Interface: interactive multimedia*

So the first kind of interface we see that the web has, hypertext, is *interactive*. (Purists argue that real interactivity would be where we might be reading about costumes and click on links for Shakespeare and Elizabeth, and the software would remember our choices, and, in the future, offer us options based on our personal tastes.)

And in our hypertext Shakespeare example, text merged with other media. We not only read—about bodkins, Queen Elizabeth, and England—but saw pictures, maps, and movie stills, too. This is what's called *multimedia*. Click on the map, and the map might turn into an animated, aerial guided tour. Click on the picture of the actress as Queen Elizabeth, and we might see a short clip from the movie. Click on a button for sound and we might hear "To be or not to be . . ." as recited by Sir Laurence Olivier, Mel Gibson, or Kevin Kline.

To digress for just an instant, many people aren't clear on what's interactive multimedia—is it like buying a mug at McDonald's with characters on it from the latest Disney cartoon? But now we know. We've seen an example of interactive multimedia on the Internet, called the web—and so has the cd-rom industry. Indeed, many in that industry have been noticing certain advantages of networked telecommunications technology over fixed discs and players. For example, online material can be updated and revised, in real-time, on demand, rather than an entire new edition having to be pressed. Plus, the web can be collaborative—enabling users to interact with other users across its interface. (Berners-Lee originally intended the web to be collaborative, not just an information system).

▶ *Linking*

Much as any one gopher links to all other gophers, a world-wide web site can form links to any other site. But, though gopher can link to other sites, it doesn't *interlink*. That is, gopher is basically hierarchical, not hypertext (the way the web is).

To take our example of the Local Global Information, Inc. site, if we displayed it on the web, it would be like spreading everything out in one environment, like a big, boardroom table. People could then open whatever speeches, articles, and quarterly reports they wished, and hop from an open page in one to any other page on the table.

Just as all gophers form a common gopherspace, so do all web sites make a common webspace totality.

Plus—and this is awesome—links can be made to anything else in the whole Internet.

That is, from any web site, links can be made to gophers, to ftp sites, to telnet sites, to Usenet conferences, and so on. A listserv can even be subscribed to from within a web site.

To repeat, the web's potential reach extends throughout the whole Internet.

Any given web main menu (aka home page) can potentially teleport us to anywhere and anything on the Net, and back.

To put this point in perspective, we recognize it's a

common phenomenon for a new technology to subsume previous models within it, just as TV added pictures to radio. Faxes often still have a separate telephone speaker/receiver. Portable sound systems, such as the boom box, include not only a radio, but also a tape deck and cd player. Someday the web may be but a node in a bigger web.

Ole Jacobsen, a twenty-year Internet veteran, uses an excellent analogy to sum it all up. We resume with a book or a paper (no matter which), fairly scholarly in nature. At the end of the document is a numbered list of references. Taped to each of those entries is a string of red yarn, which runs down the aisles of the library to that particular item—and attaches to the item it refers to. If the reference was to a quotation on page 54 of a Mark Twain book, the red yarn would take us to page 54.

Books and papers to which red yarn leads likewise have references to other papers or books. These, in turn, have strings of blue yarn running from them, to the items to which they refer. And those texts have strings of green yarn running from them.

Meanwhile, new books and papers are always being added, and new strings of yarn go out from them to the other books and papers. Thus, the path from one reference to another may never be the same twice (though, eventually, the environment would be hard to move around in).

Plus, the links can be not only to things on the shelves, like actual books, but also the *latest* version: today's weather report, for example.

And these items can be anywhere in the world. The library door leads directly to all the doors in the world.

Thus he shows the web's features of hypertext (the yarn), interactivity (the paths may never be the same), multimedia (a weather satellite image), and erasure of boundaries of time and space (the latest version of something, anywhere in the world).

Like gopher, the web supports a search engine—many of them, in fact—which can browse all of webspace and yield a hot list. Plus, its search engines can search within text, as in an index. (However, a web search will only rarely point to gopher sites. This is another reason for keeping your list of personal gopher bookmarks separate from your list of personal web bookmarks.)

The difference between surfing through gopherspace and the web, however, can be like that between taking a shopping list to a general store and a multiplex mall.

Just as there are gopher sites consisting solely of links to other sites in gopherspace, according to subjects (subject trees), so, too, can web sites be equivalent directories, atlases, and almanacs of the Internet, by subject.

And as with gopher, we can form our own links. But the web goes beyond gopher by including the whole Internet in its range—any site, or any node within any site, anywhere on the Net.

Having sensed how a menu of personalized gopher links can custom-tailor the Internet for you, we can see how a personalized directory of web links can extend that possibility—to the max.

Web bookmarks can bring what's in the background right up front, and vice versa, as you wish. They cut through any extraneous stuff along the way (extraneous to you). It's your personal map of the Internet. Now your primary Internet stops can be sitting on top of your very own customized dashboard, next to your customized steering wheel, in your customized vehicle.

This is truly awesome.

▶ *Gear*

You need two primary things besides the usual Internet gear to be able to surf the web:

1) As we've mentioned, you must have what's called a full Internet connection, such as SLIP (Serial Line Internet Protocol) or PPP (Point-to-Point Protocol).

2) You need software on your own computer to be able to browse the web. Mosaic, Netscape, and Spyglass are three common names. By 1999, there may be many others.

GOPHER	WWW
Menu (text) interface	Graphical interface (point-and-click)
Hierarchical (tree)	Interlinked (crystal)
Forms a totality with other gopher sites	Forms a totality with other web sites
Links within other gopher sites and other Internet sites	Links within other web sites, most Internet sites, plus within files
Veronica searches in subject lines	Can use wais to search in text as well
Bookmarks	Bookmarks
Subject trees	Directory/almanac home pages
Like a general store	Like a megamall
Only technicians can create a site	Anyone can create a site

Plus, as we've said, you need high-speed access if you want to access pictures and other multimedia features. Otherwise, you'll spend time waiting for them to transmit, like being in a taxi caught in rush-hour traffic.

Note: The Information Resources in the Appendix tells you about the Lynx web browser for accessing the web without using Slip or Ppp, and without using multimedia. This is ideal for low-tech users.

▶ *Web culture*

Since its popularization in 1992, people have started setting up their own web servers, besides the one in CERN, at breakneck speed. It's like the Gold Rush, or an oil cat. Everyone scrambling to stake their claim in cyberspace out along the new, web frontiers—even if they don't know what it is yet.

The latest craze is to have your own web site, your own home page on the web, even if it's only one page. As of this writing, four hundred new ones pop up per day. Printing your e-mail address on your business card is now passé for some; the latest fashion is to print the url to your web home page. Where people at parties in the 1960s commonly asked "What's your sign?", in the 1990s it's "What's your url?"

A web url (universal resource locator) is prefaced http:// (http standing for hypertext transmission protocol). Then it may add www to the domain name, or not. Plus, if it's not specifying the home page itself, it commonly includes a path. A previous example would now be this:

http://www.logloinfo.com/speeches/Net for Bankers

That will take you directly to a copy of the speech—even if it's sitting on another machine than Local Global Information's (thanks to the client-server relationship).

One of the emergent web trends (often called Cool Links) is to put a small teleportation pad at the bottom of the page or on a separate button, linking to other web sites of related or just possible interest. This adds value to a site, giving the visitor an added bonus. Some people have web sites solely devoted to cool links. Besides Netscape's, check out http://www.pointcom.com/ which links its Top Ten web sites, ranked in terms of content, presentation, experience, and popularity. There's also Best of the Web (the Net's Oscars), http://gnn.com; Cool Site of the Day, http://www.infi.net/cool.html; and Frontier Inn's Golden Nuggets, http://www.walcoff.com/frontier/pick.html. And Chris Babbs reviews new web pages in her column in *Boardwatch*—and makes these websites available at her own home page: http://www.aquila.com/babbs.bookmarks.

In the beginning of the next section, our Almanac, we'll visit a site on the web called Yahoo!, consisting solely of a subject directory of other web sites—one of several such "lists of lists." And since the web is growing exponentially, there's always a reason to visit Yahoo! from time to time.

For those already on the web: One of the charms of the web is that if I send you the url of a site I want you to check out and you read the url while in a web browser, then all you have to do is click on it. If, that is, it's an url written in the html (hypertext mark-up language) code of the web.

Just as people have been creating unique home pages, so they have been sending each other their bookmarks. It's like sending someone a scrapbook of personal snapshots. A person's bookmarks reflect where they've been—and allow others to see those same sights.

▶ *Perspective*

What's made the web such a success? The creation of ubiquitous software has certainly been one of the driving forces. To appreciate this, we flash back to the early 1990s, when the web was still incubating. The CERN visionaries had teamed up with Internauts around the world and engaged in online discussion and experimentation—setting up a demonstration site people could telnet to, making files available through ftp, and holding discussions via e-mail and forums.

About two years after the web's official unveiling, a 20-something student at the University of Illinois named Marc Andreessen, who'd been following the developments online, suddenly announced, out of the blue, that he'd invented an interface software (browser) to utilize the web, which he called Mosaic. While Berners-Lee's original browser was for an uncommon computer called NExT, Andreessen's could work on *both* PCs and Macs. And its programming was based on a language (source code) which anyone could learn to use in an hour (html, hypertext mark-up language). Distributed for free (over the Internet, of course), its popularity quickly spread.

Within the first year and a half of Mosaic's availability, web sites on the Net multiplied literally a hundred-fold. The Internet community took to the web like a duck to water.

Meanwhile, enter Jim Clark.

Clark founded Silicon Graphics in 1982, and helped make them a leader in 3-D graphics computers. But he quit as chairman twelve years later because the company wouldn't get involved fast enough for his taste with the growing networked, online world. He stewed around for a year, shopping for options, then "discovered" Andreessen. He introduced himself to the whiz kid—by e-mail of course—inviting him to form a company with him. (Andreessen recalls, "In Illinois, starting a company seemed like a sort of an unnatural act.")

A company called Netscape was formed, to make a commercial product out of Mosaic—reborn as Navigator. For the first time, Net software was made a commodity! Within their first year, their staff of two grew to 220. On the morning of August 9, 1995, their stock was made available for the first time and caused a stampede unprecedented in the history of Wall Street for any comparable initial public offering. Meanwhile, they made each new version of their web browser available over the Internet (a commercial version of the software is expected in 1996).

Among Navigator's many features, one of the most crucial was the inclusion of an icon—a key—in the lower left-hand corner.

Normally, the key was broken. But if it was joined together, that icon was intended to indicate a secure commercial transaction was being performed—online.

The doors of the Net were about to open for business.

We'll explore the impact of the web on several areas of life in the second half of the book. However, it's the web's commercial potential that drives its image as the Killer App, the software that will make the Net irresistible to the masses. So a few preliminary points relating to that commercial potential are appropriate.

The web can transform much of the Internet into a mall, making serious window-shopping out of netsurfing. How? Well, a picture's worth a thousand words, and a video's worth a thousand pictures. Because it's multimedia, the web can *show* items in online catalogs: big widgets, little ones, yellow, red, and aluminum ones. With all its storefronts able to lead immediately to all the other storefronts, it makes window displays in rectilinear malls look as prehistoric as a painting of a bison on a cave wall. Moreover, just as Internet culture often offers free samples of things, so has the web become a premier site for demonstration models and free test drives.

If you see something of interest . . . sample it . . . find you like it . . . click on it, and enter your credit card, cybercard, or virtual banking account number—you've ordered it. *Bing, bang, boom.*

And a good web site is, in and of itself, a great ad—and with such enormous foot traffic at some sites, a mere decal can be like a big billboard at a busy intersection.

Advertisement and point-of-purchase have merged —as have possibly, too, warehouse and distributor.

An additional virtue of the web is that it can record the "clicks" users make at a site. This is possible with other kinds of Net sites, too, but in the web, the "clickstream" has become very important. Demographic statistics are very useful in selling a client an ad (equivalent to billboard space), amid all that foot traffic.

The use of the word "hits" can be deceptive, however. It doesn't indicate the number of different users, just the total number of clicks registered overall. And web-site clickstream statistics will become even more problematic as more people use robot software to go out onto the web and bring stuff back for them automatically. Nevertheless, in 1994, the web did a brisk business in attracting hundreds of millions of dollars' worth of advertising revenue (billboards and sponsorships).

You don't have to be, as they say, a rocket scientist to begin to imagine why the web is being touted as the Internet's killer application—enabling each user to transform it into unique, interactive, multimedia interrelationships. The implications are of such an order of magnitude that the statistics alone are absolutely incredible.

Where the web accounted for about 17 percent of Internet activity in 1994–1995, by the end of 1996 it may comprise at least half of the Net. In 1993, there were one hundred computers (servers) dedicated to the web; by 1994–1995, there were thirty thousand. Web traffic grew 341,000 percent in 1993, and 1,151 percent in 1994. While the size of the Internet doubles every year, the number of web sites doubles every two months.

Suddenly, the web has become a kind of glue that seems to be turning the Net into a workable, global medium for the exchange of ideas and commerce, overnight.

Corporations can use it as an internal corporate network (rather like Lotus Notes).

Anyone can be an entrepreneur on the web. Any individual can now be a publisher, or an arcade, gallery, storefront, or whatever other kind of public presence they wish.

Whether for shopping, work, or fun, it has the ability to turn a couch potato into a mouse potato. That is, you know you're a webaholic when you see any word that's underlined, like this, and you want to click on it.

Last, but hardly least, the web is of incalculably great use for corporate communication, for commercial Internet service providers, and for average users—as a universal graphic user interface to the Internet. The Internet is no longer an ordeal. Instead: point and click! The web puts e-mail, forums, ftp, telnet, and information resources all at your fingertips, and in a way so that they can be intertwingled.

And so, having taken a complete tour of those very elements, at the end we've returned to where we started from.

The Internet.

PUTTING IT IN PERSPECTIVE

We now have an overview of the whole Internet—what it is and its key components. Next, we'll put it into some perspective.

Let's begin where we just left off, with the web. Newcomers often confuse the Net with the web. Some people think the Internet is Netscape or Mosaic. Even if we're web-savvy, we can easily get lost in its floating, point-and-click hyperspace.

We now know, however, that the web is an application *within* the Net that can include the whole Net within *it*. Our understanding of the vocabulary of the Internet as an entire system will help us realize the web's potential to the fullest.

To wind up our tutorial, we'll see how you can put all this together and create with it, to make new things which never existed before. We'll also outline two simple exercises, one to refine your Internet awareness, the other for budgeting your time.

Then, in Part 2, we'll detail examples of the Net in action: putting it in perspective, as it continues affecting our world.

THE INTERNET IS A MEDIUM WITH WHICH TO CREATE

> A ship in port is safe, but that is not what ships are for. Sail out to sea and do new things.
>
> —ADMIRAL GRACE HOPPER, Computer Pioneer
> (http://www.hopper.com/hopper.)

Now that we've learned our ABC's, we can apply our grammar. To follow the analogy, now that we've gained a new vocabulary, let's look at syntax, which literally means order or arrangement, as in the orderly array of troops. So let's march our vocabulary through some paces.

But let's not tramp over well-worn territory. Rather, let's strike out for new terrain. To do so, let me give you two examples of how this might be done, to fertilize your own native creativity and inspire your natural curiosity.

▶ *Finding a syntax for your vocabulary*

The first example is theoretical. Just around the corner, we're going to look at ten areas which each have a rich, robust Internet population: education, journalism and publishing, business, fun and games, computers, etc. But, consider this first:

Not only does the Internet link every major library in the world together into one big megalibrary. No— moreover, the Internet itself is one gigantic library. Its resources extend beyond magazines and books, written and digital, going off further into things like conferences of people, about whom books and magazines are written. And——

Not only is the Internet networking educational institutions together at all levels—K–12, middle school, and academic. No—moreover, the Internet itself is one big school. It's an open campus for basic education, upgrading and retraining, advanced research, and lifelong learning. And——

Not only is the Internet becoming a new major vehicle for businesses large and small, but—

The whole Internet is a business.

In five short years, three major, new Internet professions have sprung up. First, there were the providers, who leased their Internet connections. Then came the solutions industry, applying Internet applications to business situations, to give clients a public presence on the Net. And now we're just beginning to see the commercial software applications being invented and marketed. Each of these fields employs a number of different jobs. In the future, there will be many more similar, new Internet careers.

▶ *Leveraging new opportunities*

Our second example is a down-to-earth, literal occurrence which reveals another kind of pattern.

Sometimes, I extend my services as a consultant. In San Francisco, we have a fine, new, multimillion-dollar, multicultural arts museum, called Center for the Arts, in Yerba Buena Gardens. They've curated the largest exhibit of Philippine art in the world, for example, plus hosted such traveling shows as the largest retrospective of post-war Japanese art, plus another of Brazilian art, and so forth. So their director of communications asked me if there was any such thing as an Internet translation service.

I didn't know of any but said I'd find out. Ideally, I like to put twenty-four hours between a question to me and my answer—to allow for things like serendipity, the subconscious, and scouting the Net. So I went home, turned on my computer, and checked my e-mail. Because I'm an information scout, I subscribe to a few mailing lists that make me a target for receiving such stuff. Well, there was a message, out of the blue:

> Hi! My name is Vladimir Melankov. I translate 7 languages, and I'd like to make my services available to everyone on the Internet . . .

(He was in Moscow.) Hmmm, very interesting. I talked with some of my ex-Soviet friends. They told me that they'd learned many languages at school. The Swiss learn many languages because they border on many countries. Communism, on the other hand, was considered to be an international revolution, to sweep the globe, so they were being prepared in advance.

My mind started to unroll a scenario. So here were all these people who speak several languages . . . who need hard currency . . . many of whom are connected to the Internet. But that's not all.

Practically every country has at least one university, and many are on the Internet. Every university always has a bevy of skilled translators.

Imagine: if I were to call up Mr. Berlitz tomorrow and say, "Sir, I'd like to franchise a dealership for a new Berlitz school" (assuming, hypothetically, that they even franchise Berlitz schools). He'd say, "Where? I've been established since 1878 and I have one in every major city of the world. Paris, London, New York, Beijing . . ." And I'd say, "Cyberspace, sir."

But, no! I've landed onto something here far beyond any Berlitz. My Rolodex of translators could be almost unlimited. If I had a client, say, trying to resolve a costly fishing dispute between two parties speaking two very different dialects, I could probably find a skilled interpreter online at one of their local universities. Plus, I might find my clients online, if I liked. I needn't confine myself to local clientele. I could send text or a spoken recording over the Internet (for no toll)—and get back a translation I could give my client as a digital textstream, for direct editing or typesetting, as well as print out in hard copy.

Okay. Let's step back from the example and see how it works, in order to appreciate and apply its underlying structure. What essentially I'd be doing with an online Berlitz would be to take a situation in the real world (translation) and some situations in the Internet (availability of translators) and leverage them off each other to create new opportunities.

Think of it this way: you might see two situations in the real world and one in the Internet, then consider a constellation that they might form. Or it might be one situation in the real world and two occurring in the Internet. One of the messages here is that each of us is a unique individual, each of whom will see a different set of patterns given the same whole. If we were in the Grand Canyon, you and I would both be in awe, but our eye would each pick out different details.

Or to return to a previous analogy, each of us can see the same data, but a different formation.

No one knows everything there is to know about the Internet. So in your own voyages hence, you may spy two different factual things out there—associated together in a combination that nobody else might have put together. Another part of the puzzle (a second message, here) is realizing that much of the Information Revolution is not necessarily coming up with new information but merely making it in formation.

Put another way, much of the Information Age involves moving information around, rather than inventing it. This is a digital version of the way the service industries move papers and files from one skyscraper to another. Internet Berlitz is one example: mediating preexisting customers with preexisting suppliers in a preexisting profession—in new ways. Another example is when I sold the magazine article about Chinese Internet presences, in one day. I'd taken information I'd seen on the Net about which people not on the Net might be interested to know. Even people already on the Net might not know about it, because people tend to aggregate around their own interest areas.

The Internet is wide-open virgin territory. There isn't one way to use it. Learn what others have done. Benefit from their history. But customize it for yourself. Be on the lookout, too, for new opportunities.

The Internet is a new medium—to not only customize

but also with which to create—for sheer fun and maybe even some profit, too.

▶ An exercise: *mapping your own orientation*

Before we wind up, let me suggest two things you might do to help map your Internet journeying.

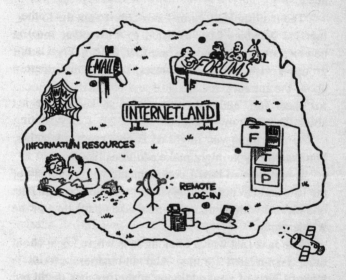

First, let's take another look at our map of Internetland. This is a rendition of our tour of the Internet's five prime sites. What I'd like you to try to do is redraw it yourself on a larger piece of paper. On it, draw each of the five sites on the perimeter, out at the margins. And, in the center, on the sign that now says Internetland, instead, write in your own name.

Now, in between your name and each application, write what you're currently doing with it. For example, you might write:

"E-mail is how I get my assignments from work, when I telecommute, and how I turn them in. It's how I send mail to family members. It's also how I keep in touch with an old high-school friend of mine who now lives far away.

"The mailing list forums I subscribe to are the following: the Newbies List, to listen to what other Internet newbies are saying, and the Jazz List, for fun. The Usenet groups I visit are news.newuser, to swap information about the Internet, rec.arts.golf and alt.binaries.cartoons for sheer fun, and soc.culture.china to keep informed about China for my sideline."

The next thing you might do is note cross-references. For example, you might make additions like this:

"E-mail is also how I communicate with members of the lists and Usenet groups, when I want to communicate one-on-one with them, rather than take up the time of the whole group.

"The Jazz List which I belong to is where I hear about other jazz-related forums. And alt.binaries.cartoons is where I hear of new additions at the ftp sites dedicated to cartoons."

Plus, you might even note, off in the waters surrounding the Internet island, the relations between online and offline worlds are like this:

"E-mail is also how I communicate with my editor, but we've found it isn't good to discuss text in any detail by e-mail: we find the phone is still generally the best for that. Through a site on the web is how I send a fax to an old schoolmate who isn't on the Internet, without my accruing a toll.'' Etc.

This will help you refine your understanding of each application and their interrelation, in order to use them to the fullest in an ecology of communications, both Net and non. Then, when somebody asks *you* to tell them everything you can find about widgets in seven hours, you'll know where in the Internet you'll go first, what you'll do after you go there, and so forth.

▶ *Budgeting your time*

There's no set measure of how long it takes to become adept at navigating the Internet. Being Net literate, you can now pretty well teach yourself, through trial and error and sheer practice. (In the bibliography there are urls for online guides, tutorials, and even hands-on exercises.)

If you're a total Net novice, you may want to try all the things we've mentioned at least once, then concentrate on getting good at each, one at a time. The order we've laid out is a recommended one to try.

But building skills takes time. How much time? Compare it to typing: whether you learn to touch type or do two-finger typing, you might spend more time learning than you'll actually spend using the skill. Once you've learned the skill, it can save you time.

Once you've become comfortable that you're Internet literate, the next thing I'd suggest is to budget your time.

EXERCISE:

Get pencil and paper and ask yourself this:

"How much time do I think I'd like to spend online? An hour a week? An hour every other day? Two hours a day?"

Draw a circle, representing that amount of time, and immediately shade off 15 percent. Label this slice *S* for SEARCHING/SCOUTING/STAYING ABREAST. With the Internet, this is an automatic given. It comes with the terrain. It's not a broadcast, there's no central dial, and it's a moving target (*see art, opposite*).

This leaves just one line to draw, from the center to the circumference, dividing WORK and PLAY. Whether you thought you were going to use the Internet just for fun, or just for work—believe me, you're sure to find a bit of both. Somewhere, someday, you're going to fall upon a gopher site or find yourself in a forum that you'll want to visit again and again. And eventually you'll see ways of putting the power of the Net to work for you, to put you on the leading edge.

After you've read Part 2, you might refine the pie by adding additional slices: medical research, virtual volunteering, etc.

And you'll want to ask yourself this:

"How much time do I think I'd like to spend online? An hour a week? An hour every other day? Two hours a day? Five hours a day?"

How much time do *I* spend online? Some work assignments, such as research, can take me anywhere from an hour to a day or two. I'd say I'm very comfortable and happy averaging a half hour to an hour (max) a day. That might not be a bad measure to consider for yourself.

Remember, time online doesn't include dealing offline with files you'll save and send.

Now you have a manual and a steering wheel. The keys are in your hands. An almanac of ideas and compass points—atlases and travel guides—follows immediately.

Happy trails!

ALMANAC

This half of the guide is an almanac.

You now know A) what the Internet is, B) what the Internet can do (its tools), and C) how to frame the Internet in perspective for yourself. Now we'll flesh out its possibilities in greater detail.

First we'll concentrate on the Internet as a whole, again, but in a different light. We'll see how the Next-Generation Internet will be a convergence of different usages. Then, before we explore ten of those usages, we'll focus on the Internet in terms of subjects, rather than tools.

Finally, our Almanac will wind us through the ''Top Ten'' Internet subject areas. Rather than dwell overlong in commentary, we'll point out the culture and point to specific sites—for you to put into perspective as you wish. The order of the subjects is not as logical as in the Tour (more, rather, like Harper's Index), but, in the end, the key issues and themes will gel in your own mind.

In each of these ten subjects, we'll not only pick up pointers we can use today, but we'll also glean different clues in each that will help us understand Internet . . . the Next Generation.

INTRODUCTION

DOTTING THE I & CROSSING THE T'S IN *INTERNET*

Let's start by defining three terms that are often used when the Internet is discussed: *online*, *cyberspace*, and *information superhighway*.

▶ Online

Online merely refers to the state of being connected with another device. If you're at your ATM, you're online with your bank. If you're using the phone, you're online with whomever you're calling. Using the Internet, you're part of that online world. That's all there is to being online.

▶ Cyberspace

By now, most people hear of cyberspace and don't really know what it means. This is a much more general term than "the Internet." The Internet is a subset of this bigger phenomenon called cyberspace.

Cyberspace refers to the realm of all the telecommunications activities—all the ATMs, faxes, satellite transmissions, fiber-optic long-distance phone calls, the whole schmear. The word was coined by a science-fiction writer—William Gibson—who pioneered a new genre called "cyberpunk." In his novel *Neuromancer* (1984), he described it like this:

> Lines of light ranged in the nonspace of the mind, clusters and constellations of data . . . All the data in the world stacked up like one big neon city, so you could cruise around and have a kind of grip on it, visually anyway, because if you didn't it was too complicated, trying to find your way to the particular place of data you needed.

Suddenly, it seemed, here was a word that expressed this insanely great *mesh* that some network pioneers had been living with and using and working on for twenty years, without sounding too insane, and just as the Net was entering its risky Phase Two, internetworking networks together!

It's a useful concept—for having that kind of grip he mentions. Taking the word apart, we might be surprised to find that "cyber" doesn't mean "computer," but "control," having a grip. But it's the "spatial" part that's really useful.

Because *thought* is spatial.

We think in terms of spatial metaphors.

We speak of thought as being *deep* or *lofty*.

Consider: "con" = with; "sidere" = stars. When we consider, we're part of a constellation.

We look *within,* to "*mansions* of the soul"—or shake a finger *at* idle, ineffectual intellectuals out there in their "ivory *towers.*" Within or without, spatial metaphors help us conceptualize ideas. Imagination needs a place, its space to unfold.

We already looked a bit at spatial metaphors when we first talked about interfaces and gui's. Macintosh presented computing to us as a desktop: a visual, spatial metaphor—filled with icons.

The Internet can seemingly erase boundaries of space. Metaphors of location, space, are useful for us to keep our mental bearings. First-time users of the Internet often need a map and a literal reorientation in space. A similar example is found in everyday life. When you've put your card into the ATM at any bank branch, your body may be at the corner of, say, Maple Street and Corkscrew Avenue, but where are you punching the ATM keys *to?* And where is your money when it's in a bank?

Cyberspace.

I once worked at the Federal Home Loan Bank, where on my orientation day, I was shown an aluminum petty cash box, downstairs, with only fifty dollars cash in it, exactly, in case of emergencies—the only real money in the building. Meanwhile, millions and billions of dollars came and went through the building all day in the form of thousands of little points of light on computer screens. Indeed, just one transaction today may access three different banks via two separate satellites in the space of a mere sixteen seconds.

Just as there's no Central Bank anywhere, there's no central Internet, either. So, when we're online with the Internet, it helps to have a metaphor to help locate ourselves: our actions are taking place in cyberspace.

Some people extend the word to locate where their consciousness is when they're online. This is esoteric. Frankly, you're on your own with that one.

There's a slew of spatial metaphors: surfing, navigating, cruising, farming, mining the Internet. Fishing with nets. Exploring the wilds with a butterfly net. See if you prefer any for your own feel for it. You might make up spatial metaphors of your own and coin a useful new word or two that way.

▶ *The information superhighway*

Right now, the Internet is information's biggest highway. So, for present purposes, you could say the Internet is the information superhighway. Fine.

However, there's a bunch of lane mergings ahead, off on the horizon. It's called convergence. New lanes are expected to crop up and merge, making one big super-highway of information: five hundred TV channels . . . every movie that ever existed, available on demand from a kind of video jukebox . . . home shopping . . . distance learning . . . video conferencing . . . telemedicine . . .

So the Internet might be today's harbinger, the bell-wether, if you will, of a convergent Information Super-highway of the future, linking medicine, business, education, entertainment, etc.

Assuming, that is, the phrase still sticks. Some have nominated PLANETARY MIND UNDER CONSTRUCTION, while others are more keen on local use, as in Free-Nets. Some Star Trek fans prefer the concept of an Information Transporter Room.

Historically, the phrase ''Information Superhighway'' was coined by Vice President Al Gore, a big Internet booster (whose father was a senator who pioneered America's interstate highway infrastructure). It makes a

TOWARD A NATIONAL INFORMATION INFRASTRUCTURE

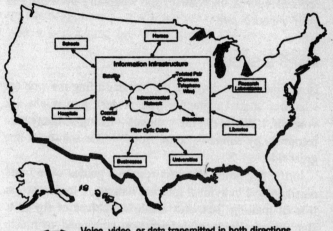

← Voice, video, or data transmitted in both directions

good buzzword, a spatial metaphor, easy to think about. But the Clinton Administration replaced it with National Information Infrastructure and Global Information Infrastructure when it became apparent that the metaphor wouldn't hold up under rigorous scrutiny. (It also became politicized. For example, a highway is centralized; space is decentralized.)

Though we will see multimedia applications by the dawn of the 21st century, it may take until our grandchildren's generation for accounting streams and textstreams to merge.

It is prudent to say that no one knows the final outcome. But we can pick up clues along the way as we tour the Net next by subject. (If it helps you get a handle on it, consider your ability to cruise the Net through specific *tools* as your X-coordinate, and searching by *subject* as your Y-coordinate.)

MAPS & SCOUTS

Next time you're cruising the Net or surfing the web (or whatever spatial metaphor you prefer), you might ask yourself, "Where did these menus—listing so many neat resources by subject—come from?" The answer is one great ride.

In the beginning, Internet resource guides were organized around individual Internet formats or tools, such as lists of mailing lists, and archie's archives of ftp sites. But the amplitude of information continued to mushroom—as did the kinds of tools, such as gopher, wais, and the world-wide web.

And so some people began creating *subject*-oriented information resources such as the gopher subject trees. And similar trailblazers became Internet scouts, taking up outposts on the frontiers, seeing what's new to come over the mountains and sharing the word with all the Netizens back at the campsites.

▶ *John December's Tools for Computer-Mediated Communication (CMC)*

Our first information pioneer is John December. In 1992, he undertook an independent research project as part of his academic work as a student of online communications. He searched for information about the Internet scattered across the Internet itself, found twenty-two unrelated sources, compiled them into a master list, and posted it to the only Usenet conference at that time with the word "Internet" in it. Quite quickly, his list grew to well over two thousand entries.

Today, he monitors and draws on information from mailing lists and from using archie, ftp, gopher/veronica, wais, and the web, updating his list frequently—the best list of its kind I know of. (To give due credit, completely independently of December, Scott Yanoff publishes a smaller list online, also of interest, the first and fifteenth of every month at alt.internet-services. For more information e-mail inetlist@aug3.augsberg.edu or point your web browser to http://www.uwm.edu/Mirror/inet.services.html.)

December's CMC list is also available in a hypertext format on his own web site, as a launch pad for exploring the Net, a recent development that came about in an interesting fashion. Kevin Hughes, a student at Honolulu Community College, scanned the list into hypertext and sent December a version, to return the favor. And, yes, all of this is free to all fellow Internauts. (Recently, he put a price tag on some of his work: he co-authored a big book about the web, in the encyclopedic *Unleashed* series of computer books, but put a big portion of that online, too.)

His atlas, or list, makes an excellent example of how most everything you could want to know *about* the Net (and most anything else) is *on* the Net. Sometimes, though, it's more helpful to download and print out indepth resources like this in hard copy. Then, for example, you can mark the places you like and cross off the ones you don't; later, you can check an updated version of the list against your old one to easily see what's new. For all the Internet Yellow Pages books on the market, this is still my personal favorite top-level subject guide to have at my desk.

Where to find it:

1. CMC Information Sources guide:
   http://www.rpi.edu/Internet/Guides/decemj/internet-cmc.html
2. Internet Tools Summary guide (tools for networked information dissemination and retrieval):
   http://www.rpi.edu/Internet/Guides/decemj/internet-tools.html
3. Internet Web Text:
   http://www.rpi.edu/Internet/Guides/decemj/text.html
4. Computer-Mediated Communication Magazine:
   http://www.rpi.edu/~decemj/cmc/mag/current/toc.html

▶ *The Clearinghouse*

Another example of Net cartography originated in 1993 when Lou Rosenfeld, then a librarian at the University of Michigan, wanted to create a central site for subject guides which scholars in particular areas were organizing. Lou's library students interned as volunteer archivists, then later as part of an accredited course. They supplemented their archie, veronica, and wais searches by asking people in mailing lists. Plus, they'd personally check to make sure each resource would be still active as of the date of their posting.

So, today, in the midst of the Internet, stands this mighty Clearinghouse, whose subject-guides list primary, relevant resources for exploring a given subject. The most popular topic has been (need we say?) the Internet, visited four times more than the other guides—which now total over three hundred!

The project has migrated over to the web, where the majority of guides now have direct links to the resources themselves. Many mailing lists and Usenet conferences are listed here, by subject—including, but hardly limited to:

adult distance education; Africa; aging; alternative medicine; animals; anthropology; artificial intelligence; biodiversity; book discussions; Buddhism; business; Christian resources; citizens' rights; computers; cross-cultural studies; cyberpreneurship; disability resources; diversity; emotional support; employment opportunities; futurology; law-related guides; library-related guides; magick; midwifery; mysticism; networks; non-profit organizations; personal finance; philosophy; post-Soviet and Eastern European resources; psychology; public policy; religious topics; social aspects of computing; television; Tibetan studies; travel; women's topics; writers

Where to find it:
 By ftp or gopher:
  una.hh.lib.umich.edu   path: /inetdirs
 By web: http://www.lib.umich.edu/chhome.html
 ("chhome" stands for "clearinghouse home page.")

▶ *Gopher Jewels*

Then, with the popularity of gopher, hot-linked subject-oriented lists of gopher resources became even more widespread. Building subject trees on a gopher site—mapping gopherspace by topic—became quite a respectable pastime. Probably the ultimate of such activities was the Gopher Jewels project—a compendium of subject trees and other top-level resources. If you're familiar with the new *Encyclopaedia Britannica*, you could think of it as a Propedia: a "top-level guide" to resources, by general category. It terminated in 1994, but not before branching out into a mailing list and a site on the web.

While it was a collaborative project, credit largely goes to yet another pioneer, David Riggins, as creator, researcher, and author. In its heyday, it had the largest collection of pointers to such topics as AIDS information, grants, and Free-Nets, while keeping track, too, of electronic journals, sources for environment, law, computers, new countries coming online, etc.

Today, its entire menu links to over 2,300 pointers to gopher compass points. Because this is gopher, the links are all active. You can cruise everything with the standard menu interface. Plus, Gopher Jewels not only allows you the option of jumping up one menu level, common to gopher, but also directly back to the main menu, from any directory. And it allows key-word searching of all its menus as well as offering help features and archives. It makes a beautiful pipeline for surfing the Net.

Its main menu categories are a baker's dozen, many of which themselves cover a range of options:

community, global, and environmental; economics, business, and storefronts; education, social sciences, arts, and humanities; engineering and industrial applications; government; health, medical, and disability; Internet and computer-related resources; law; library, reference, and news; miscellaneous; natural sciences, including mathematics; personal development and recreation; and research, technology transfer, and grants opportunities

That's the main menu. If we went one level deeper, from any of those, we might find some actual files plus some more menus, directories, and subdirectories. We've been learning about the Internet, so if we pick that, we'd get a menu offering us this:

1. **A List of Gophers With Subject Trees/**
2. **Computer Related/**
3. **Internet Cyberspace Related/**
4. **Internet Resources By Type (Gopher, Phone, Usenet, Wais, Other)/**
5. **Internet Service Providers/**

The first item holds a menu of about thirty other subject trees, besides Gopher Jewels, each of which includes Internet in an alphabetically arranged menu of gopher links. The second, Computer Related, focuses on IBM vs. Mac, etc.

What does number three, Cyberspace Related, mean? Here you'll find seventy links to various special interest groups—such as the Alliance for Public Technology, the Civic Network, the Clearinghouse, CNIDR, Commercial Internet Exchange (CIX), etc.

Or, besides the Net—if we'd picked, say number

twelve from the main menu, Personal Development and Recreation, we'd get something like this:

1. **Employment Opportunities and Resume Postings/**
2. **Fun Stuff & Multimedia/**
3. **Museums, Exhibits, and Special Collections/**
4. **Travel Information/**

Employment? Employment links to dozens of places where jobs are posted (academic and otherwise), and where you can post your resume.

What about number two? Fun stuff. What *kinds* of fun stuff? Oh, like—

aviation, bicycling, fantasy, games, gardening, humor, magazines, music, pets, pictures, recipes, restaurants, sports, tv/film. Plus—my favorite: our old friend, good-old Miscellaneous—which contains (hold onto your hats!), as of the last time I checked, aikido, amateur radio, an Arabian horse breeders' marketing network, astrology, beverages (a wine-drinkers' forum and beer homebrewing information), birds, boating, bread, ceramics, coffee, comics, crafts, Dr. Fun (a daily cartoon), dreams, jewelry, kites, metalworking, mime, model railroads, Monty Python, multimedia, photography, quilts, radio, Star Trek, robotics, rowing, science fiction, scuba, skating, skydiving (don't try it at home), sounds, spoonerisms/malapropisms, Survival Research Laboratories, UFOs, video laserdiscs, virtual reality, and wolves. (Don't ask why skydiving isn't under aviation. Just take it under advisement: this is how the Internet works.)

Under those miscellaneous headings are mostly files, but also a few menus of yet further subsubdirectories . . . such as an archive of magazines, asking which issue do you want to look up. And, meanwhile, back at menu number twelve, we still haven't browsed museums, exhibits, and special collections yet, nor checked out the travel information. But, again, one of the nice things about gopher is you can always return to its main menu, then launch off to another site in gopher space, and then return to your main menu again, teleporting all around cyberspace with the menu as your guide, using it as your surfboard.

Needless to say, I've linked Gopher Jewels to my own personalized home page of gopher bookmarks. A menu of 100% pure manna.

Gopher: cwis.usc.edu. Www: http://galaxy.einet.net/gopher/gopher.html

▶ *Net.Happenings & Info Scout*

My own favorite topic on the Internet is the Internet. Since the Net is still in its infancy, watching it grow before your eyes can be fascinating, in and of itself. (Sometimes, I imagine this might be what cinema was like a century ago, when audiences shared the excitement of a new discovery every week: the close-up, cross-cutting, recorded soundtracks, a new star, new genres, etc.)

It's one thing to read about new Net developments—and another to actually be *on* the Net regularly and *discover* them for yourself, in the Net itself. (This harkens back to what we were saying about how part of the charm of forums is being *in* them, as they unfold.)

The best way to monitor the Internet's daily news, as it were, may be through a project called net.happenings. It was started by Gleason Sackman, a former high-school science teacher, in North Dakota. First, computer literacy and word processing crept into the curricula he taught. But as to the online world, "My learning curve," he confessed, "was not a curve but a straight line up from ground zero." Soon he was operating an educational BBS. Way back in 1991, he found himself working for an online educational group, Sendit, scouting resources on the Internet of possible interest to North Dakota's online K–12 community.

Nobody else was doing this, so he cross-posted his findings to some of the educational mailing lists, until someone suggested he start a list of his own. Now he monitors one hundred forums and receives six hundred to seven hundred e-mail messages/day. Out of that, he produces five to fifty messages a day, reaching about six to seven thousand readers, with news of the Net itself. Sort of like an Internet town crier. Each message has a topical tag in the subject line, for easy reference (or filtering); in addition to Net sites (telnet, gopher, web, etc.), topics include faqs, books about the Internet, online netzines (e-journals, magazines, and newsletters), and new software—plus teleconferences, workshops, meetings, seminars, and symposiums. (If the existence of regular expositions and seminars confers legitimacy to any topic, then the Internet has more than come into its own, judging by the number of gatherings now being organized in its name every month, across the land.)

How to find it:

To subscribe, e-mail listserv@lists.internic.net and leave the subject line blank. In the message body, put "subscribe net-happenings."

Usenet: comp.internet.net-happenings
Gopher: gopher.mid.net 7000
Web: http://www.mid.net/net, gopher://ds0.internic.
net:70/11/pub/list_archives/net-happenings.archive

InterNIC (Internet Network Information Center), which lent disk space, listserv, and technical support for net.happenings, began as a project of the National Science Foundation (NSF). Having established NSFNet in 1988 (an infrastructure that generated millions of new Internauts), NSF took the next step to bridge the gap and set up InterNIC to help educators and researchers use the Net more effectively. Susan Calcari, with a background in data communications at such companies as BofA and Sprint, wrote a proposal for a full-time position of just staying in touch with the warp-speed current of Net resources and events. In so doing, she pioneered a new official title: Internet Scout.

In addition to monitoring the Net's rambunctious cornucopia and attending such major meetings and expos as Educom, Interop, Comnet, and IETF (Internet Engineering Task Force), plus working with a couple of other projects, she finds time to publish an Internet newsletter, Info Scout, aimed primarily at educators and researchers.

If net.happenings could be compared to a daily newspaper, Info Scout is more like a weekly magazine, taking the time to spotlight key, representative resources and emergent trends as well as curious tidbits—plus posting events and news. Each issue begins by mentioning the highlights, then proceeds by application—web, gopher, lists.

How to find it:

To subscribe, e-mail listserv@lists.internic.net, leaving the subject line blank. In the message body, put "subscribe scout-report <your name>."

The web: http://rs.internic.net/scout_report-index.html

▶ *Yahoo!*

The web has also become the latest medium for Internet mapping. Danny Reagan, Managing Editor of the *Abilene Reporter-News,* for example, has included a web help page in the local directory at the paper's site with links to several magnum, top-level, atlas-type web sites, such as The Yellow Pages, MegaLinks, The Awesome List, Guide to Cyberspace, the Internet Index, etc. As such, it's a Square-One web home page of web atlases and web directories; http://www.abilene.com/arn/webhelp.html

But the most famous web-based Net atlas is . . . Yahoo! (Yet Another Hierarchical Officious Oracle). Like many other aspects of the computer age, Yahoo began as an idea, grew into a hobby, and lately has turned into a funded, full-time passion. In April 1994, David Filo and Jerry Yang, two engineering students at Stanford, started making web bookmarks to keep track of their personal interests on the Internet. By the end of the year, their home-brewed list was becoming a rainbow of topics, a whole subject web. They made it available to everyone else on the Internet, via the web, over Yang's student workstation. To keep it up-to-date, they developed their own software to help them locate, identify, and edit material stored on the Internet, which they set up on Filo's student workstation.

Soon, the traffic on Jerry's workstation was handling three hundred thousand visitors to Yahoo . . . a day! They recall, "It became pretty apparent by the end of 1994 that we couldn't carry on as we were. The Net was growing much too fast for two guys in a small computer lab to handle it all. We were faced with one of three choices: never sleeping, doing a poor job, or seeking help. We were much too fond of sleeping and much too proud of Yahoo to let it slip into ill-repute."

Marc Andreessen (Mr. Mosaic/Navigator) invited Filo and Yang to move their files to one of his computers. Filo and Yang started a company, found financing, and now have over a dozen sleep-deprived employees, instead of two. Hundreds of sites are added per day. Rather than charge subscription fees, they kept access free to users (and people listing sites). Instead, like an online magazine, they have advertisers (aka sponsors). Their *What's New* section separately lists daily additions to their guide: last time I checked, it averaged 500–700/weekday, 150/weekend, plus Reuters has been giving them hourly newsfeeds to keep the site *ultra*-timely.

The San Jose Mercury News recently summed up much of the whole phenomenon—subject-guides, top-level directories, atlases of the Internet—quite neatly when they noted that "Yahoo is closest in spirit to the work of Linnaeus, the 18th-century classification system [genus/species] organized the natural world."

How to find it: http://www.yahoo.com

So where did all the subject-menu almanacs, atlases, and compass points come from?

The machines didn't make them. Rather, they reflect

synergy at work. Synergy between machines that can easily track and store information, then make it available to any number of seekers simultaneously, and people, who are able to make connections between things and classify them into more and more complex systems.

These almanacs, atlases, and compass points are available for further synergistic applications. Adapt them to the ecology of your own Internet usage. And be grateful to the people that make them possible. They come in very handy.

Now let's take a tour of our own almanac of the Net, and amplify our awareness of the Net's possibilities. In the words of information scout Susan Calcari: ''Hold onto your keyboards, 'cos this is just the beginning. And all of us using the Net now are on the ground floor.''

PLACES TO GO &
THINGS TO DO

Digitizing human communication and making it real-
time and on demand . . . networked . . . interactive multimedia—nobody knows the ultimate form it will take.
Meanwhile, for us to maximize its advantages and mini-
mize its problems, it helps to have a good, working metaphor for its uses. Or metaphors. (Parts of one interactive
intermetaphor?)

The best metaphors often come from inside personal,
first-hand experience. So naturally, librarians will compare the Internet to one big library; educators, one big
school; business people, a business; the entertainment industry, one big entertainment outlet; religious people,
one big church basement or Sunday picnic. Etc.

In the rest of this book, we'll look at ten such primary
areas, where the Internet's importance is being keenly
felt.

Each has practical resources you can try for yourself.

Each gives you models for how you might use the Net
to shape your future—

—and even how *you* might shape the future of the Net.

Note: Web sites are given for most resources in Part 2,
as the most common url. Readers without web access
(without even lynx—*see Appendix*) and those who prefer
gopher, please bear in mind: many web sites have corresponding gopher and ftp sites. Use the basic domain

name from a web url and try hacking around. For example: http://www.example.org/amazingstuff/info. html might also have a link to gopher.example.org and ftp.example.org; or maybe just example.org. And, if you only have e-mail, you can try seeing if anyone responds to messages sent to info@example.org or admin@ example.org. In a few instances, post addresses are even given for people who don't have computers yet. All urls in this book were current as of press time. Please check your favorite search engine in case an address is no longer active.

LIBRARIES

> Information literacy requires that the learner recognize the need for information, be able to identify and locate it, gain access to it, and then evaluate the quality of the information received before organizing it and using it effectively.
>
> —V. E. HANCOCK, *Information Literacy for Lifelong Learning*

Historian and California State Librarian Kevin Starr observes: "Libraries provide the capital necessary for us to understand the past and plan for the future. And when the tectonic plates of civilization shift, libraries are often the first to feel the tremors." Libraries and librarians are on the front lines of tomorrow's information revolution—whole new dimensions are opening up in the degree Master of *Information* and Library Science. So what better place to begin our subject-driven exploration of the Information Age than at a library Information Desk?

Indeed, libraries and the Internet each require the special skills of managing large collections of information: no wonder the Internet is often compared to a gigantic library.

In the future, many will naturally come to their local library to familiarize themselves with new information systems, as they have in the past for other things. A library is a familiar, common point of access. Moreover, libraries are trustworthy because they aren't really competing with anyone else in the community over turf.

And, as information specialists, librarians can help orient people, help them navigate, and help them evaluate the information and the kind of information they are seeking. (People will ask all kinds of things: "Are the lyrics to 'Wooly Booly' on the Internet?" "How do I start a business on the Internet?" And "What's R. L. Stine's e-mail address?") People come to libraries too not only for answers, but also to help find out what their question is and refine it through successive askings. And the Net is providing a forum for librarians to share difficult reference questions (stumpers), to discuss questions of administrative policy, and to keep abreast of the new technology.

Library-related forums can be very good ways of keeping tabs on the Information Revolution. The monthly electronic journal, *Current Cites,* for example, is an indispensable monthly bibliography of magazine articles, by subject, with brief abstracts. To subscribe, e-mail: list serv@library.berkeley.edu with the message sub cites <your name>. On the web, http://sunsite.berkeley.edu/CurrentCites.

A major Internet issue being discussed in libraries is

the Virtual Library. This is the recognition we discussed when we put the Internet in perspective: librarians are keenly aware that not only can they use each other's databases but that they also have at their disposal the whole Internet itself to use as a library.

We've seen an example of how one academic library department added the human component to the Internet search tools and came up with the Clearinghouse. Similarly, in studying the important question of providing mass Internet access as a Virtual Library—librarians have recently arrived at some interesting decisions as to applying Net tools to mirror ordinary library patronage. Librarians are skilled at handling different *types* of questions—that is, people usually have simple questions requiring a quick answer, while a fewer number are engaged in research requiring more time. Thus, access to e-mail might be the first thing to offer a patron, as the equivalent of the answer to a simple quick question. More intermediate-level answers could be gained by asking members of a pertinent Usenet group. Advanced-level answers would be using veronica and a web search. Note, these levels refer both to the depth of the answer but also to the level of Internet skill required. Thus the libraries show how real-world questions can be answered on the Internet, in unique ways.

We'll return to the Information Desk, and the public libraries' model of free information resources, at the end of our subject almanac, when we address the question of access: will the Internet be made available to all? Or will there be redlining; Information Haves and Have-Nots?

Meanwhile, here are a few virtual libraries and library resources worth a visit.

InfoPeople is a one-step Internet library reference desk, based in California. Along with California libraries, it includes comprehensive links to library-related resources; information about the Internet and the web; and web, gopher, and telnet sites at academic and public libraries around the world (such as LibWeb), as well as federal, state, and local governmental links.

How to find it:
Gopher: library.berkeley.edu:7000.
Web: http://www.lib.berkeley.edu:8000.

The Library of Congress, founded by John Adams and Thomas Jefferson, calls its information system Marvel (Machine-Assisted Realization of the Virtual Electronic Library). Theirs are probably the best home pages for federal information sources—gophers, library catalogs, and databases at such places as the National Institutes of Health, the national Library of Medicine, NASA, and so forth.

The ftp and web sites contain the catalogs to a number of exhibits: "Revelations from the Russian Archive"; "Rome Reborn: The Vatican Library & Renaissance Culture"; "1492: An Ongoing Voyage"; "Scrolls from the Dead Sea"; and "The African-American Mosaic."

As the nation's central library, it provides other librarians an electronic information exchange, ALIX (Automated Library and Information eXchange).

The library, too, has mapped an excellent Internet subject tree—using the Internet itself as a library—including BBS's, e-journals, and databases, entitled the Global Electronic Library.

How to find it:

Gopher or telnet: marvel.loc.gov. (If telnetting, log in as "marvel.")

Ftp: ftp.loc.gov.

Web: http://lcweb.loc.gov/

The Library of Congress also maintains Locis (the Library of Congress Information System), which accesses over 27 million records, including federal legislation (since 1973), copyright records as of 1978, braille and audio, descriptions of over thirteen thousand research organizations (primarily in science, technology, and social sciences) that answer questions and supply information to the public—and the Library of Congress, which contains bibliographic records for materials in the library, including serials, microforms, maps, music, visual materials (films, filmstrips, posters, prints, photographs), computer files, and manuscripts, as well as their unequaled collection of books.

How to find it: Telnet locis.loc.gov.

[*Note:* The Library of Congress is one of the few Internet resources that is not available twenty-four hours a day. Rather, it is only accessible during its normal business hours.]

The National Digital Library Federation was created in May 1995, following the Library of Congress's leadership role in raising as a national issue the need for a digital library. Founding participants include Yale University, The Library of Congress, Pennsylvania State University, Harvard University, Emory University, University of Tennessee, Stanford University, Princeton University,

The New York Public Library, University of California Berkeley, Commission on Preservation and Access, National Archives and Records Administration, University of Michigan, Cornell University, University of Southern California, Columbia University. Together, they intend to establish a National Digital Library, making materials accessible which document the building and dynamics of America's heritage and culture to all citizens as well as students and scholars. Putting theory into practice, the creation of such a network is expected to raise significant issues of policy, funding, organization, scholarship, technology, and law. Furthermore, to be successful it demands participation of many institutions of government, business, and education. Thus, this collaborative effort not only stands to be a valuable national resource, but, from the standpoint of process, can also provide an opportunity to evaluate and resolve many theoretical problems and issues facing the Net through practical action.

For more information: http://palimpse.stanford.edu/cpa/ and http://lcweb.loc.gov/NDL/per.html.

The Internet Public Library, of and for the Internet community, is the result of a graduate seminar in the School of Information and Library Studies at the University of Michigan in winter 1995. Laid out like an ordinary library, its youth section has created some marvelous online books for kids. The reading room links to online literature from around the Net. Plus there's a classroom, an exhibit hall, a MOO, and librarian services. And its reference desk has been able to answer 70 percent of the questions it's asked. All in all, it's no mean feat, given that the entire budget has been $18/month for an allocated 200Mb of computer storage space. Http://ipl.sils.umich.edu.

Libraries for the Future acts as a network to keep libraries in the loop of the evolution of the National Information Infrastructure, on one hand, and to see that the NII operates in the public interest, on the other. Laura Powers, Field Director, states:

> Everybody has a memory of using their public library as a child or an adult, so we start where people are and talk about access to information, which everybody can understand. . . . We talk about information as a right, and the idea that democracy is founded on equal access to information. Ironically, as technology goes forward, public libraries are in trouble in many places. On one hand, there's talk about giving you video on demand, but possibly in your town library hours have been reduced by 30 percent.

How to find it:
Libraries for the Future
521 Fifth Avenue, Suite 1612
New York, NY 10175-1699
(800) 542-1918
E-mail lff@inch.com

EDUCATION

Knowing how to ask the right questions may be the single most important step in learning. The process that is conducted in order to find answers to the right questions leads to the point at which information becomes knowledge. It is at this point where facts are

internalized into personal meaning by
the learner. Information literacy—the
ability to access, evaluate, and use information from a variety of sources—is
central to all successful learning and by
extension to all successful living.

—CHRISTINA DOYLE, *Information Literacy*
in an Information Society

▶ *Lifelong learning*

I've been teaching the Internet at the Extension Division
of the University of California, where for a half century,
the catalog was called *Lifelong Learning*. Similarly, I
teach at the Learning Annex, California's largest adult
education/seminar organization. At both, people come
for various reasons, of course, but often for lifelong
learning—attracted to the Internet because they sense,
rightly, that the Internet is itself a campus for lifelong
learning. A global university without walls. It not only
offers courses for credit, and free faqs on every imagin-
able topic: it offers new ways to learn.

▶ *Distance learning*

The Internet invites innovation. At Worcester Polytechnic
Institute, for example, Professor Dave Cyganski, in collaboration with some students, created a world-wide web
textbook for his graduate course in Telecommunications
Transmission Technologies. This field's changing so rapidly, ordinary textbooks are often out-of-date by the time
they hit the stores. Professor Cyganski's students use lec-
tures and the online textbook, and also have access to
each other's work. Since advanced students tend to turn
their work in early, a high standard is set for the others.

The Internet is just beginning to be used in distance learning—where one teacher can teach one course remote, sometimes to a number of different locations. It's already possible to take courses over the Internet for credit at a number of institutions, such as The New School, in New York City. This can be very practical for the training industry, as well as traditional education. Combining this kind of Internet usage with videoteleconferencing for distance learning can create a synergy that's like a match made in cyberspace.

A hybrid form of distance learning is global tutoring. International Tutors, a pioneer in this new concept, offers nonprofit tutoring for preschool, primary, secondary, postsecondary, and continuing education students worldwide. It was created as an alternative approach to learning, using information technology. (Http://www.info.ramp.net/~it1.)

In sum, distance learning takes the schoolchildren's rhyme at semester's end:

> *No more pencils. No more books.*
> *No more teacher's dirty looks.*

and stands it on its ear.

For more information on distance learning, contact:

The Distance Learning Laboratory, http://www.coned.howard.edu/webpages/dll;

The Distance Learning Network, http://www.fwl.org/edtech/dlrn.html; and

The National Distance Learning Center, telnet ndlc.occ.uky.edu login ndlc.

▶ *K–12*

> Critical thinking, data analysis, problem solving, and
> independent thinking develop when students use a tech-
> nology that supports research, communication, and
> analysis.
>
> —MARGARET HONEY

Now that K–12 (kindergarten–12th grade) teachers, administrators, and students are able to use network resources developed by the most advanced researchers and
top academicians, the Internet is becoming a proving
ground for some dynamic, even sizzling examples. Imagine every student having access to the kinds of education
formerly reserved for "gifted" children—and rocket scientists. Indeed, students formerly considered slow learn-
ers have blossomed when given self-paced, online
instructional tools.

Wherever it is present, the Internet rejuvenates K–12.
It does more than jazz up otherwise dull subjects. For one
thing, it relieves some of the strain on America's
stretched educational infrastructure. An average K–12
course might require forty textbooks, and, if the course
is Physiology, forty frogs preserved in formaldehyde.
Thanks to networked communication, instructional materials (or the lack thereof) are no longer a factor. There's
a hypertext illustrated frog dissection available on the
web at http://george.lbl.gov/#froggy.

But this is, perhaps, only a superficial example of the
Internet's effect on K–12. It can transform not only the
infrastructure, but the very nature of education itself. For
example, there's the Kids Network (sponsored by the National Geographic Society, National Science Foundation,
and Apple)—an upper elementary curriculum of science

experiments which has introduced cooperative effort and interaction with professional scientists into their curriculum, using real and engaging situations with important social context and global awareness. Currently, the Kids Network is one of the largest network-based educational programs, with a quarter-million students participating a year.

One year alone, study topics were acid rain, weather, then lead content of water in public schools—with students in various locations studying the local phenomena, sharing the results of their investigation, analyzing trends and patterns, and then comparing their findings against national data and discussing them with the appropriate professionals. They thus learn about science by living the role as well as by learning the facts and concepts. And Kids Network projects have been interdisciplinary: international in scope, letters to research teams have been written in Language Arts, findings charted and graphed during Math, and follow-up measures discussed during Social Studies.

The role of the teacher can also be transformed thereby. The common refrain among educators using telecommunications is: the teacher is no longer the sage on the stage but becomes now the guide on the side.

And when it comes to the new media, the kids are often higher on the learning curve than their teachers. For younger generations, multimedia, the Internet, and interactive satellite-TV hookups are like wallpaper—part of the landscape. K–12 students are putting up their own, often very sophisticated, web home pages, and visiting each other's. Usenet hosts over a dozen K–12 forums, only a couple of them for the educators, the rest being for kids themselves. Here are a few instances of K–12 online, beginning with some excellent mail lists.

KidsTalk: In 1990, Norwegian educator Odd de Presno organized the beginnings of *KidLink,* a global dialogue of youth using e-mail. The idea was for kids between ten and fifteen to have a place where they could talk freely to each other without adult guidance or interference. The age range reflects the optimal period for learning a second language and for developing self-concept (in this case, to think of themselves as part of a global network of interdependencies). To join the group, a newcomer usually answers four questions:

1) Who am I?
2) What do I want to be when I grow up?
3) How do I want the world to be better when I grow up?
4) What can I do to make this happen?

Initially, participants would read all the mail, not only that of their personal keypals. But the two thousand messages a year at the beginning grew to nine thousand the next year. So four student participants became moderators, and mail was divided into three categories. And separate lists are also springing up.

In the new KidForum, a single topic is discussed for a month or two, often around a timely subject, such as the Olympics. KidProj is where kids discuss many projects at once. One recent project has been the creation of a multicultural calendar database, collating all the holidays and festivals celebrated around the world—to be made available for all KidLink participants.

During the Gulf War, a list formed called KidPeace, which included eyewitness reports from the missile attacks on Israel and deep expressions of concern from students who knew family members involved in the conflict. More recently, special forums have been created to promote dialog in foreign languages—Portuguese, Japanese, Spanish, etc.

And a separate list was formed to coordinate all these activities. At first, there were eight volunteer coordinators; now there are twenty-two. The Board consists of seven members, representing each continent.

And all of this is done through e-mail. Gopher global. kidlink.org.

Kidsphere brings K–12 students and teachers together to discuss general technological development. A particular focus here is international standards of communication. Currently, its community includes 2,500 subscribers, plus tens of thousands more readers over various local BBS's.

How to find it: E-mail listserv@pittvms.bitnet with "sub Kidsphere <your name>" in the message body.

The HotList. Gleason Sackman maintains a web site linked to K–12 Internet school sites by state, plus school districts, state/regional networks, and state departments of education. Http://www.send.it.nodak.edu/k12.

Schools on the Net. The Co-NECT School Exchange is a place where teachers, administrators, students, parents, and other members of the Co-NECT community can exchange information, materials, advice, products, projects, and ideas. The home page has desks for information and support on special topics, such as assessment, technology, professional development, and critical friends; each is managed by someone with whom to communicate directly by e-mail or phone. There is also an area online with detailed information for planning and organizing whole-school change.

Member schools maintain web home pages for sharing their current online projects, which can be re-created at other schools and/or joined in collaboration with those already involved. In the World Band project, each school has an electronic music studio with midi synthesizers and computer sequencing software. Using the Internet, students collaborate on studying music composition, sequencing and creating their own sounds.

The Exchange is a program of Bolt Beranek & Newman, pioneering inventor of Internet technology. Http://co-nect.bbn.com/

NetTeach News is a newsletter for K–12 networking education. It provides a forum for the exchange of information for and by the K–12 community about digital networks and networking resources, applications to education, significant events, and major international, national, regional, and state programs and policies relevant to K–12 networking. It is intended as a platform for many varied personal and collective travels to new "net-worlds" for educators around the globe and a pathway to many global living learning villages. Reach it at:

> 13102 Weather Van Way
> Herndon, VA 22071
> E-mail: info@netteach.chaos.com.

LM Net's focus is library media, but, as noted, librarians tend to be at the cutting edge of the Information Revolution. This mailing list is primarily for school librarians but also is a good place to "lurk" (along with hundreds of other nonlibrarian subscribers) just to hear daily news about Internet resources. With members in every state of the U.S. and elsewhere, LM_Net is a K–12 must.

How to find it: E-mail Listserv@suvm.syr.edu, leaving the subject blank. In the message, put "subscribe LM-Net <your name>."

Education Net is a community of interest spanning K–12 to academic. It's intended to assist educators in exploring the educational potential of the Internet. To subscribe, e-mail: listserv@nic.umass.edu. Leave the subject line blank. In the message, type "subscribe Ednet <your name>."

Education Net also maintains an ftp site at the Nic.u-mass.edu domain, listing mailing lists and Usenet conferences for educators.

AskERIC Virtual Library is an archive of at least eighteen education-based mailing lists maintained by ERIC (Educational Resources Information Center), as but one of the many educational resources it makes available to the educational community. It also offers a toolbox, faqs, Info-Guides, lesson plans, bibliographies, e-journals, news, and announcements. With over eight hundred thousand such holdings, it is the world's largest educational database. Not only can teachers, librarians, and administrators browse the digital library, but also it has a question-answering service, called AskERIC. Within forty-eight hours, a specialist will answer your question about K–12 education. Perhaps as important as the actual holdings is the fact that these questions are evaluated constantly, as the basis of ongoing adjustments to make the library and its services best meet user demands.

How to find it: Gopher: ericir.syr.edu. (If you telnet, log in as "gopher.")

AskERIC, e-mail: Askeric@ericir.syr.edu

▶ *Training*

As we shall see in more detail in our look at business applications, training is a very important use of the Internet. Training teachers in the Internet is a new critical issue. California's Telemation project trained over 450 teachers in 1994, providing a performance-based, discovery-oriented, student-centered Internet curriculum for a variety of situations.

In a paper entitled "The Information Highway and Our Children," Sally Bowman and Alex Curyea of the Computer Learning Foundation state:

> The Information Highway and the opportunities it provides teachers and children will radically change schools and education from what we experienced as children. . . . When most of us grew up, the accumulation of factual knowledge was important, or at least emphasized. In the information society we live in today, however, the volume of information is staggering and no one can master it all. The skills our children need include the ability to ask the right questions, a facility in locating information, and, most importantly, the ability to evaluate and apply information they find. . . .
> . . . Teachers cannot be merely tour guides showing

students all there is to see along the Information Highway. They must help students learn to narrow their search for information and evaluate the information they find, while still providing students with the opportunity to explore and discover new areas of learning along the way. This is perhaps the hardest kind of teaching.

▶ *The next step*

Commercial educational companies have offered schools network services, but the altruistic Internet community is still the center of the online K–12 community. Gleason Sackman has located 191 K–12 schools in the U.S. with Internet sites (seventy-two elementary, thirty-eight middle, and eighty-one high school). Quite interestingly, here, too, we find the Net's typical bottom-up model being proven out: this census outnumbers that of the state departments of education that are on the Internet (twenty).

Yet many K–12 schools don't have computers, and most schools don't have a separate phone line to the classrooms. (When was the phone ever considered an educational tool, until now?) If schools *are* wired, it is usually only to one place of access, such as the library or a computer lab. Buildings with asbestos walls cannot be wired at all.

As of this writing, less than a third of our public schools have any Internet access at all. Yet the next big step may not be merely bringing wire or wireless access into the schools. A number of teachers have said that superimposing new technology upon the existing school system is an uphill battle that will be won only when we rethink what school is and how it works. An overhaul of the educational system itself and its infrastructure is also needed. Otherwise, integrating technology into the system is only, as it were, putting a Band-Aid on deeper systemic problems. As educator David Thornburg states, "Our challenge is not to do old things differently, rather it is to do different things. . . . Our challenge, quite simply, is to use our tools to prepare people for their future, not our past."

This model—of networking as being but the harbinger of an even deeper paradigm shift—may hold in some of the other topics in our Almanac, as well. We've seen it, to a degree, in libraries. American medicine looks like a prime candidate to integrate the new information technology into the system while that very system undergoes major reform at the local level. We won't dwell on this theme in each topic, leaving it up to the reader to consider.

In education, to conclude, the Internet is opening the door toward a reexamination of the whole educational model. The Internet, for example, is inherently less authoritarian than the standard model. In this regard, an interesting online forum between K–12 students and college students about to graduate and become teachers has been set up—to bridge the traditional gap. Online, the future teachers and their future students better understand each other's generation, and come to see each other as human beings.

In addition to using peer learning, "just-in-time" learning, self-directed learning, etc., younger generations may become educators themselves, learning themselves to teach and train older people as well as their peers in new technology (if the older people are willing to change their mindsets and accept a curious role reversal). Information haves and have-nots are not only divided along lines of income, but of generation. Many teachers are Information Have-Nots, while kids are Information Haves for whom the new technology is commonplace. Thus, a new curriculum might include teachers and other students learning about information technology through multimedia, distance learning, and hands-on tutorials created by kids. The Visionary Stampede project (415-256-8929), in California, is working along these lines already.

This idea may prove viable for generations to come. Whereas today's older generation is struggling to grasp basic concepts like computers, modems, and multimedia, today's younger generation is already defined by changes in the generations of new technology—such as the Nintendo Generation vs. the Atari Generation. In any event, the Internet's potential is most crucially felt by our children, who are our future. We do well, as we teach them, to heed the lessons our children teach us.

BUSINESS

To survive, it is essential to adapt to change.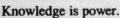

To adapt to change, it is essential to be informed.

Knowledge is power.

The Internet is the Information (Knowledge) "Superhighway."

And the times, they are a-changin'. An Information Economy is dawning.

Is it any wonder that businesses are coming online more and more?

This is such a huge topic that we'll just touch on the major areas of importance. We'll look at how the Internet can serve as an office network, able to take your business from local to global . . . how it can act as an early warning system . . . how information is itself a product . . . how corporations are becoming "virtual" . . . how it is important to coordinate the Internet into the ecology of other communications . . . how the Internet is training-intensive, and how to approach Internet training itself . . . how the Net presents new ways to work, including headhunting, re-engineering, and telecommuting . . . how the Internet is used for online commerce, both retail and business to business . . . and how the Internet is itself a business. Plus you'll find some top-level pointers in the sidebars to these topics, as well as cyberpreneurialism and finance.

▶ Networking

First came PCs and then laptops, putting computers into the hands of ordinary businesses.

Then came networking, LANs and WANs linking computers within an office and within branches. Networking puts facts into a more fluid pool, so they can be used in various formations. If you fill out a form and give it to a company, once it's digital, several departments can work on it at the same time, instead of one at a time, separately.

This also restructures management—putting initiative in more hands and creating more opportunities for collaboration. Workers' knowledge and insight can be incorporated at all levels of operations. And costs can be cut as various departments coordinate and streamline their

---

CYBERPRENEURS

Business Connection
   http://www.intbc.com
Commercial Sites Index
   http://www.directory.net
Cyberpreneurs Guide to the Internet
   http://www.lib.umich.edu/chdocs/cyberpreneur/Cyber.html
E-Net
   http://www.cyberzine.org/html/Entrepreneur/
   enetpage2.html
Entrepreneur Resource Center
   http://www20.mindlink.net/interweb/index.html
Entrepreneurial Edge Online
   http://edgeonline.com
Entrepreneurs on the Web
   http://sashimi.wwa.com/~notime/eotw/EOTW.html
The Information Center
   http://www.greatinfo.com
Internet Business Directory
   http://ibid.ar.com
The Internet Group
   http://www.tig.com/IBC/index.html
Small Business Administration
   htpp://www.sbaonline.sba.gov
Successful Marketing Strategies
   http://webhead.com/success

---

efforts, from research and development, design, and manufacturing through marketing and distribution.

Today, the Net makes an ideal solution to corporate networking situations. It matters not if some employees or subcontractors have Macs and others use IBM PCs. Resources on one machine can be distributed to the others. True to its name, the Internet can also internetwork one office network with such other networks as distribution and sales.

Every department within a large corporation can theoretically benefit from the Internet. For example, Security can use the Internet to monitor the read-out of video cameras. Human Resources can post job openings online and headhunt within employment databases. Fulfillment/Shipping can track merchandise from warehouse to delivery via computer—over the Internet. (For example, parcels sent UPS are tracked by computer through all phases of the delivery process. Users can now personally track their shipment orders over the Internet. Http://www.ups.com.)

Networked communication between labor, management, research, etc., by having them all on the same network makes terrific business sense. Initiating the changeover often boils down to which aspect has enough ''sizzle'' to sell the idea to a board which can't envision a bitstream.

The bottom line: using the Internet as a business network not only affords maximal interoperability but also brings to every office desk and workplace station all the additional resources of the Internet.

▶ *Local = global*

Setting foot in the Internet, we go from local to international in an instant. And this is of interest as today's economy grows ever more international, transnational, and globally interdependent.

LOCAL-TO-GLOBAL

Global Entrepreneurs Network
   http://www.entrepreneurs.net
International Import Export Business Exchange
   http://www.imex.com
Market Link
   http://nwlink.com/marketlink
One World Plaza
   http://www.owplaza.com
Trade Compass
   http://www.tradecompass.com
United Nations International Computing Center
   http://www.unicc.org

Our overseas clients, customers, and counterparts are now just down the hall. And companies can be not only international but global (transnational). That is, a global company can use its network to centralize its coordination and streamlining of research and development, design, manufacturing, and sales—while affording such decentralization as customization of the end-product at various localities according to regional taste.

▶ *An early warning system*

The Internet can also serve as an "early warning system" by networking a company with news of its clients, the competition, and new developments in the field. The Internet can draw potential clients closer to a business by providing an access site—a public virtual server—in the form of an ftp, telnet, gopher, or web site.

And it can bring a business closer to its customers and clients—using a forum as a focus group, and keeping track of the "hits" at a web site as a demographic survey—as quick, direct feedback as to what people like and what they don't. For instance, listen for a moment to Peter Drucker talking about the American department store.

> Nobody knew more about their customers than did these stores. Until the 1980s they held on to their customers. But they had no information about noncustomers. They had 28 percent of the retail market, the largest single share. However, this meant that 72 percent didn't shop at the department stores. And the department stores had no information on these people. And they couldn't have cared less. Thus, they were unaware that new customers—especially the affluent—do not shop in department stores. Nobody knows why. They just don't. By the end of the 1980s, though, these noncustomers had become the dominant influence group. They began to determine how all of us shop. But nobody in the department store world knew this because they had been looking at their own customers. After a time, they knew more and more about less and less.

The Internet can help business keep an eye on their competition through *their* public virtual servers, and through data such as SEC filings and quarterly earnings reports.

(Now that the Cold War is over, corporate espionage might become the next battlefield.)

For staying abreast of new developments in the field, the Internet provides tools on areas like scholarly research, new patents, trademarks, and product announcements—to be able to pinpoint emergent trends before they've become trends.

Information about clients/customers, competition, and new developments can all be thought of as an early warning system—designed to keep a business working on the leading edge of important news, trends, and information in the field as soon as they manifest.

A company with the Internet can do this for itself. Or it can hire a specialist to do it for them. And what would the specialist be selling?

Information.

▶ *Information as product*

As a Researcher for Local Global Information, Inc., I didn't invent widgets, only documented their existence and use. My report was a matter of moving and shaping facts from various information sources. As we've also noted when we talked about interfaces, information is putting facts in formation. A postindustrial economy sells services rather than goods—such as information.

This brings up a key question: who *owns* information? The slogan of many a Netizen is INFORMATION WANTS TO BE FREE. Many cite visionary tracts, such as this:

> If nature has made any one thing less susceptible than all others of exclusive property, it is the action of the think-

ing power called an idea, which an individual may exclusively possess as long as he keeps it to himself; but the moment it is divulged, it forces itself into the possession of everyone, and the receiver cannot dispossess himself of it. Its peculiar character, too, is that no one possesses the less, because every other possesses the whole of it. He who receives an idea from me, receives instruction himself without lessening mine; as he who lights his taper at mine, receives light without darkening mine. That ideas should freely spread from one to another over the globe, for the moral and mutual instruction of man, and improvement of his condition, seems to have been peculiarly and benevolently designed by nature, when she made them, like fire, expansible over all space, without lessening their density at any point, and like the air in which we breathe, move, and have our physical being, incapable of confinement or exclusive appropriation. Inventions then cannot, in nature, be a subject of property.

(The visionary author is obviously not Alvin Toffler, nor Peter Drucker. It's a visionary named Thomas Jefferson.)

Whether producing goods, services, or information—networking enables information. Incorporating information enables a business to add value to whatever it does, for their client and for themselves.

▶ *Virtual corporations*

Local Global Information, Inc. may have seemed futuristic. But not half as futuristic as it might have. Imagine a virtual corporation. A virtual corporation might not have a receptionist or even voice-mail. Instead, of twenty-one phone lines, one might be dedicated to connecting to five different e-mail infobots for frequently asked questions, and a direct-order catalog on a world-wide web home page.

A virtual storefront need not use an offline distributor. A virtual distributor need not own or lease a warehouse. But every time someone clicks on an item in an online catalog, their message might send a signal to a machine to dupe a tape, press a cd, print a book (much as a significant number of college textbooks now are being printed, on-demand), or have a Cad-Cam create an object.

A virtual corporation might have a CEO, a Board, management, and a workforce. But they might be working at other offices at the moment, in various parts of the globe. Futuristic, even utopian, as it may sound, these directions are being carved out already. For example, further on in this chapter, we'll look at CommerceNet. And in our next chapter we'll see how the Internet is reshaping the publishing industry model.

▶ *A new ecology*

The web has the potential to merge advertisement, distribution, warehouse, circulation, publicity, and point-of-purchase in one interactive multimedia tamale. It also has a unique culture:

- affinity-based (narrowcast),
- real-time (on-demand), and
- user-directed (interactive)

With the web, people visit a site out of some *affinity*. It isn't being broadcast at them. If they like what's there, they'll come again.

In the mass-production (broadcast) model, if a company wanted to capture more market share, traditionally it might print more catalogs. From ten thousand to fifty thousand, or five hundred thousand. A web home page now can make a catalog available to as many people with access as need it, ten or ten thousand, ten thousand or a quarter million. It's *on-demand:* if word catches on about your product and suddenly the demand for your catalogs doubles overnight, there are as many catalogs as need be. Increased demand doesn't decrease supply. There's as many as need be, all the time.

And it's *user-directed,* a matter of ''pull, rather than push.'' The reader isn't pushed down a straight path to get to the catalog, but pulls the material in, in bits and pieces, putting the links in a formation meaningful, comfortable, and appealing to them. (Everybody hops and skips through a catalog, for example, even though the pages are numbered 1–199.) Similarly, a buyer might help choose what product to make, or how to customize it—pulling a personalized product through an assembly line of options, as it were, rather than buying something pushed straight through production like a railroad. And this is real-time on demand, meaning that if an important change suddenly had to be made, such as a price change, all catalogs wouldn't have to be recalled; the change is effective the instant it's made to the file.

QUESTION: *How can people actually make money using the Net?*

To give the most simple example, consider the guy who decided he wanted to use the Net as his personal publishing company. He started a mailing list called Joke-A-

Day. He'd e-mail you and other subscribers a new joke every day. Subscription: $1 a year. In his first year, he estimated he had over 350,000 subscribers.

Supply and demand.

QUESTION: *If I go to someone's corporate home page, how can I tell how big or small a company they are?*

You couldn't. Nor would it matter, if they provide you with what you want.

Terribly simple. Yet there will be hundreds of thousands of dollars wasted, by companies big and small— failing to understand what the Internet can supply; its culture, its ecology.

It can level the playing field.

The web has already proven commercially successful at helping newer, smaller, and/or minority-owned businesses catch up with more established competitors in gaining exposure and distribution.

It requires understanding the medium as well as the audience.

Let's consider two hypothetical companies. Each has a home page on the web.

In one, the corporate logo fills the entire screen. At the bottom are four buttons: *Team, Reports, Products, Guest Book.* The only remotely interactive thing about it is that if we sign the guest book, we get on a list for junk mail. No thanks. And there's nothing here we haven't already seen from this company elsewhere, now just recycled. Been here; done that.

It's not so much a site as something that says, "We have a web site. This is it." (But a web site isn't just something you have, it's something you do.)

The other starts with a few small, cool graphics (small and not sucking up a lot of bandwidth). Five buttons are integrated into the design: *What's New, Blasts from the Past, Windowshopping, Our Favorite Links on the Web,* and a big *"?."*

It doesn't look like a print ad that has been shoveled into a computer screen.

Options are interlinked. So we can always pull the information as we wish.

It adds value by giving us some launch pads for more web surfing. If we like the choices, we'll come back here, for sure. It shows affinity—common special interests.

It's updated to feature new additions. Like the Net, it's evolving. We'll want to watch it change shape and grow, over time.

Maybe, instead of a guest book, there's a mailing list we can join—either via e-mail or direct from the home page—that lets us chat with other people interested in this site, at our mutual convenience.

Maybe the mailing list was started first, as a kind of focus group for the company to forge closer links to its market. Maybe the web site is so cool and customized in the first place because they'd actually spent some time online themselves, getting to know us, their audience, through the lists and newsgroups and conferences—as well as Net surfing to check out the competition and keep up with new developments.

And maybe the interactive multimedia works because it reflects the way the people who put it together worked together to put it up, reflecting a healthy corporate ecology. People interacting with each other. Across multiple duties and skill sets. Information intensive. Rather than as a segmented, bureaucratic office, channels of corporate communication cut off from the web department, not yet a truly networked working environment.

And rather than by a CEO hiring a pricy webmaster or webmistress. But whether in-house or outsourced, the webmeisters aren't to blame. The webmaster is, to paraphrase Peter Drucker, a toolmaker; the CEO is the tool user. CEOs must accept that if the computer is a tool, it is the tool user's job to decide how to use it. They must learn to assume information responsibility—along with everyone else on the team. Information responsibility is asking, "What information do I need to do my job? In what form? When do I need it? From whom? And what information do I owe?"

This isn't a question of David vs. Goliath, although this certainly can level the playing field. That is, it doesn't matter how big or small either of the two companies are. It does matter that they understand the new media to use it to advantage. It's not the old broadcast mode, one-to-many, we-talk/you-listen. It's one-on-one. (Sounds simple? It's a whole new ball game.) Companies that don't get that up front might be better served continuing to invest in print and broadcast. Waste is a terrible thing. Otherwise, somewhere down the line, CEOs, throwing money at the Internet without understanding the ecology, are going to be calling in their lieutenant, the Webmaster, and their flack, and asking, "Can anyone tell me what I'm paying six figures a year to have a home page for?!"

The web is proving profitable—seven-figures' worth this year—for its advertising merchants, selling billboard space on the Information Superhighway. It's easy to see why. Twenty-five seconds on SuperBowl Sunday are gone—<snap of the fingers>—like that! And maybe someone clicked to another channel. The Internet, on the other hand, is there twenty-four hours a day, on-demand. Real-time. One-on-one.

This is the Information Revolution. To paraphrase Dickens's opener to his novel about the French Revolution, it is the best of times, it is the worst of times.

Moral: Know your ecology.

▶ *Training-intensive skills*

Corporate training is a $50 billion a year industry. Once a company is Internet literate, they can use the Net as an orientation and training network, in such information-intensive fields as new product features, new procedures, technical maintenance, and sales techniques.

Networked distance learning saves expense on travel, duplication of materials, and productivity time away from work. A web site can make the training material available as needed—on the job. It can also present material in ways that are easier to learn, use, and remember—in byte-sized bits, for self-paced study.

How shall the company be trained in the Internet in the first place?

Here's a word to anyone about to train a working group—office, company, or organization—in Internet literacy. The buzz word about such training you'll hear in the corridors of Fortune-500 companies these days is *cas-*

cading—the way a waterfall spills over into a number of pools, which each, in turn, overflow into more bodies of water. To begin, someone is selected to train trainers. Then representative "team leaders" from each department are picked to be trainers, who will be trained and then go back to their department and train their department.

▶ *New ways to work*

Re-engineering
Re-engineering, and the requisite training for it, is one corporate rationale for the Internet; it can provide the managerial glue.

Big companies that had a dozen or two dozen departments now have eight middle-level managers who are no longer responsible for analyzing information and making decisions for particular groups: staying informed and making decisions can more readily be everyone's responsibility. This decentralization may also lead to a greater centralization of management—coordinating activities in a number of sites in a number of time zones—leading to a looser but also a tighter system. Local to global, for example. A corporation no longer has to choose between decentralization and centralization: it can do both.

Re-engineering, outsourcing, downsizing—for managers and others, these words can be synonyms for job loss rather than redeployment. Jobs and job descriptions become fluid. Positions become temporary contract assignments (raising questions of security for employees with families and kids). Learning becomes continual, Internet literacy becomes career-critical—as we'll see next.

The online job market

The Internet has been a barn-burner to human resources, both job-searching and head-hunting. A word-processed resumé is Standard Operating Procedure. An online resumé might be the next S.O.P. A digital resumé can be uploaded to an employer, headhunter, or online job agency—local, regional, or international. Most agencies have been for career-specific, mostly high-tech jobs, but many successful ones cover the full spectrum of job descriptions. A unique feature of a computerized employment database is that an employer and employee can search resumés for key words. A prospective employee, for example, could search based on job location, industry, company, job title, etc.

One of the most venerable online job centers is the Online Career Center. Begun in 1992, it is run as a nonprofit collaboration between Alcoa, Lilly, Procter & Gamble, IBM, Monsanto, and Aetna. Today, over two hundred subscriber employers pay a membership fee and annual dues, allowing them to advertise job vacancies. Other employers can pay agencies to post openings there. There's no charge for prospective employees to upload their resumés, or for potential employers to sift through them. The system currently posts about fifteen thousand job openings, with twenty-five thousand active resumés on file. Telnet occ.org, http://www.occ.org.

Sometimes, an electronic job bank comes about through sheer serendipity. At its inception, a European company, Trademarch, began linking potential importers and exporters, helping such countries as Sweden, on the periphery of Europe, find new trading opportunities. A spinoff has been its job bank, so companies seeking people fluent in English and Swedish, and potential recruits looking for openings in such companies, can find each other on the Internet.

More recent career centers include:

America's Job Bank, http://www.ajb.dni.us/

The Monster Board, http://www.monster.com

Employment Opportunities and Job Resources on the Internet, http://www.wpi.edu/~mfriley/jobguide.html

Career Path, http://www.careerpath.com

CareerMosaic, http://www.careermosaic.com

JobWeb, http://www.jobweb.org

Some recent books are Pam Dixon and Sylvia Tiersten's *Be Your Own Headhunter Online*, Alred and Emily Glossbrenner's *Finding A Job on the Internet*, and Joyce Lain Kennedy's *Hook Up, Get Hired!*

Telecommuting

As yet, the promise of telecommuting has not panned out on the broad scale. The majority of telecommuting has been by people who normally take work home after hours. It's still perceived by employers as involving an expensive investment, with the added possibility that a telecommuter won't actually do the work away from the workplace. When more offices are wired and more accustomed to networking, telecommuting may well become more common. Offices that have downsized, however, encourage it, and it's a viable alternative during maternity leave. For selected articles on telecommuting, http://www.cba.ziga.edu/tc96/resources/articles, and visit the Telecommuting Advisory Council, http://www.telecommute.org.

▶ *Online commerce*

> We believe we are all entering an era of more modern
> merchandising, better values, fewer losses, greater
> economies, a larger equivalent for the dollar and there-
> fore have a right to look for greater and grander suc-
> cesses than have heretofore been attained. With the
> almost phenomenal growth of wealth and buying power
> of our country, many new and more modern methods
> in the selling of merchandise will surely develop.
>
> —R. W. SEARS, 1909

In 1886, Richard Warren Sears sold watches to supple-
ment his income as a railroad clerk. The need for customer service led him to find a watch repairman. He met
a young watch tinkerer named Alvah Roebuck, joined
into a fruitful partnership, and soon they realized they
could sell more than just watches. In 1891, he came up
with a novel concept. Sears realized: "We've cheap
printing. We've got a postal service that goes everywhere. We've got a national railroad system to ship goods
anywhere. Why not make a beautiful book, put all the
stuff we have to sell in it, and give it away so that it
ends up in everyone's home." A century later, the Sears
company employs over four hundred thousand people
and still publishes a free catalog.

Thus began mail-order: aka home shopping.

People have been using specific Net forums for years
as classified ads for buying and selling stuff. With the
web, ordering pizza online started something new. Mail
order turned into e-mail order. Virtual shopping is now
poised for blast-off. Meanwhile, people are staking their
claim to cyberspace. As of this writing, there are over a
hundred thousand commercial domains; although it is not

certain how many are merchants, compare this number to the nine thousand nonprofit domains, five thousand network service provider domains, and the two thousand educational domains, and you'll see that the business of the Internet now means business. New web pages appear every other second—urls being given out on sides of buses and in TV commercials.

OPEN 24-HOURS-A-DAY

'60s Trading Post for the '90s
  http://www.artitude.com
All-Internet Shopping Directory
  http://www.webcom.com/~tbrown
American Shopping Mall
  http://www.greenearth.com
CatalogSite
  http://www.catalogsite.com
Deamer's Emporium
  http://www.wolfe.net/~cherokee/store.html
Internet Mall
  http://www.internet-mall.com
Internet Shopping Network
  http://www.internet.net
Mall of the Cyberspace
  http://www.zmall.com
Shopping2000
  http://www.shopping2000.com
Shops.Net
  http://www.ip.net/shops.html
Stuff.Com
  http://www.stuff.com
The Webfoot's Used Car Lot
  http://www.webfoot.com/lots/international.car.lot.html

Yet the culture is still one where most merchants balance the karma, giving something back to the Net in addition to taking the opportunity to post a catalog. Smart cybermerchants offer content, add value, rather than just set up shop.

A quick trip to Yahoo will point out some major kiosks, pointing to the future of online malls. For example, NetPlaza is very similar to a retail mall. There are different methods for browsing the stores and merchandise: alphabetical listings of stores, by categories of merchandise, searching for specific items or vendors, and random strolling. Inside a store, customers can view merchandise in groups or individually. Http://www.netplaza.com.

The critical factor seems to be payment transaction. New forms of currencies are springing up. Digicash. Cybercredit. First Virtual, for example, is a secure site acting as a bank account for online transactions, in lieu of using a credit card. (How the Federal Reserve will look on all this is yet another question.) For more information, readers might wish to read Dan Lynch and Leslie Lundquist's stimulating, thorough, and important book, *Digital Money*.

Meanwhile, the big, early, Internet business success stories may come not from selling direct to consumers, but, rather, business to business. Two pilot programs in this area in incubation are the Agile Net, based in Philadelphia, and CommerceNet, in California.

▶ *Business-to-business*

Professor Rolf T. Wigand, Professor of Information Studies at Syracuse University, reminds us that commerce is more than a transaction of supply and demand. "Commerce denotes a larger process, including aspects of information seeking and distribution, negotiation, trust, risk-taking, customer relationships, buyers finding sellers, sellers finding customers, after-sale service and support."

In a similar, larger process, CommerceNet is a gathering of small- to middle-sized businesses coming together to network among themselves about commerce. Besides learning about technological advancements and their applications, the network enables them to lower operating costs in a number of ways. Members with commercial products can sell them in a mall, The Internet Shopping Network, offering next-day delivery on more than 22,000 items. (Http://shop.internet.net.)

Buyers can browse multimedia catalogs, solicit bids, and place orders. Sellers can respond to bids, schedule production, and coordinate deliveries. A wide array of third-party value-added information services are springing up to bring buyers and sellers together. These services include specialized directories, broker and referral services, vendor certification and credit reporting, network notaries and repositories, and financial and transportation services.

Although many of these transactions and services already occur electronically, they require dedicated lines or prior arrangements. The use of an Internet-based infrastructure reduces the cost and lead-time for participating in electronic commerce, and makes it practical for both small and large businesses. For example, it enables pilots to transfer a printed circuit assembly design from a design group to subcontract manufacturing groups using the Internet.

Here's a CommerceNet scenario for the future:

Bill owns a small company that designs printed circuit boards. His four-engineer design group is located ten miles outside of Boulder Creek in the Santa Cruz, California, mountains. This morning, he checked his electronic mailbox on the Internet and found a message from Irene, a design engineering manager at a large computer company in San Jose. She asked him to look at a sensitive request for quotation (RFQ) she had just posted. The RFQ was open to only three firms, and the message was encrypted in such a way that only those three firms could read it.

After analyzing the RFQ, Bill again used the Internet to check for current prices for the integrated circuits needed to build Irene's board. He accessed several online catalogs for IC manufacturers and made rough estimates of the cost of materials. There was one thing left to deal with: a sticky design issue he didn't quite understand. He queried several engineers he knew at Irene's company via the Internet as well as an engineer in Amsterdam he had met at COMDEX [computer trade show]. The Amsterdam engineer referred him to an article in a back issue of an electronics association journal, which he promptly downloaded from the journal's Internet forum.

After lunch, Bill prepared a quotation and sent it, encrypted, to Irene. The bid was not only secret—it also was a legally binding offer. He mused about how his access to the Internet enabled his company to get jobs that used to go only to the ''big boys'' on the other side of the hill. His quotations were extremely accurate; he could always look up the most up-to-date prices and inventories via online catalogs. His designers were highly efficient; they accessed the latest applications and utilities from colleagues all over the world. And his cash flow was improved because he could send invoices and receive remittances via the Internet.

Irene, at the other end of the "electronics food chain," often remarked about how using the Internet had helped her company's profitability. The publications group cut printing costs by putting its data sheets, catalogs, and data books online. Her engineering group could take advantage of independent board designers; the other two firms bidding on her boards were in Oregon and Taiwan.

The bottom line: for Bill and Irene, the Internet is easy to use and secure. It provides access to services and information sources around the globe. It is a commercial tool, as fundamental as a spreadsheet or telephone, that they both need to stay competitive.

And, as we said at the outset, the bottom line for an agora-like CommerceNet is not only deals and net trade—but, too, the information exchange between industry leaders about issues, collaboration on pilot applications, and definition of standards and best business practices for using the Internet for electronic commerce, to help define the necessary theories and put them into practice. Http://ibs.commerce.net.

▶ *Internet as a business*

A thickish layer of hype pervades the Net. For example, one Internaut, reporting the statistic of the Net's 10 percent a month growth rate, concluded that, at this rate, everyone on the planet will be connected by the year 2003 (by which time, one out of three users might also be Elvis impersonators, too). Only a decade ago, five countries accounted for more than half the world's phone lines; right now, 90 percent of the world's computers are found in fifteen countries. However, whether or not everyone on the planet gets a phone and a computer, it looks like the Net is here to stay and continuing to grow. A survey by Veronis, Suhler & Associates found that a third of America's homes have computers, and a third of them had modems. By 1999, the percentage of computer households is expected to reach 44 percent—56 percent of them equipped with modems.

The same survey predicted, too, a long-term trend of the Internet surpassing online services in interest. In 1994, consumers spent $1.4 billion on online services and $48 million on Internet providers; by 1999, the total consumer spending for Internet access is expected to reach $3.5 billion, surpassing a predicted $2.6 billion spent for online services. Robert Broadwater, of Veronis, Suhler & Associates, said, "The image I have of online services is that you've got a bunch of isolated lakes. If you're in a rowboat, you can row out and see everyone on that lake. Over the horizon is a big ocean called the Internet. Now all of the rivers are beginning to enter the ocean."

Let's review a bit of history. The Net was fostered by the U.S. government through its high-risk Phase One. Thus 50 percent of the domains today are in the U.S., as are the majority of manufacturers of Net-related products, now showing robust profits. As PCs and laptops became more common and companies became networked in the 1980s, commercial domains and providers came to the fore. In the 1990s, a Solutions Industry sprang up, putting the power of the Internet to work for businesses, applying it to their various situations. In the shadow of Netscape, the development of commercial Internet software has just begun. Plus, there are new job titles springing up where none existed a year ago, thanks to the world-wide web, the latest being webmaster (or webmistress).

So, in addition to being an application for business, the Net is itself a business.

COMPANIES ON THE NET

1-800 Flowers
   http://www.800flowers.com
AT&T
   http://www.att.com
Blockbuster Video
   http://pwr.com/blockbuster
Buise Cascade
   http://www.bc.com
Chiat/Day
   http://www.chiatday.com/web
Chi Pants
   http://www.aonet.com/chipants
Crayola
   http://www.crayola.com/crayola
Eastman Kodak Co.
   http://www.kodak.com
Ford Motor Co.
   http://www.ford.com

Frito-Lay
   http://www.fritolay.com
General Electric Co.
   http://www.ge.com
Hershey's
   http://www.hersheys.com/~hershey
J. Crow Company
   http://www.ronin/com/jcrow
Jones Education Networks
   http://www.meu.edu
Kaplan Educational Careers
   http://www.kaplan.com
MCI
   http://www.internetMCI.com
Pacific Bell
   http://www.pacbell.com
Ragu—Mama's Cucina
   http://www.eat.com
Toys R Us
   http://www.tru.com
Virtual Vineyards
   http://www.virtualvin.com
Zima
   http://www.zima.com

As we've seen from the previous examples, we still don't know what final shape all this will take. From business, however, are sure to come major elements of any overarching *inter*-metaphor, for a national (and global) information infrastructure.

Only time will tell. For example, the digital word-processing revolution and the digital banking revolution have yet to merge data with accounting. Maybe our grandchildren's generation will have a better picture of what's . . . still to come.

ONLINE FINANCE

American Stock Exchange
  http://www.amex.com
Charles Schwab & Co.
  http://www.schwab.com
Commodity Traders Advice
  http://infomatch.com/~adas/adv.html
Dun & Bradstreet
  http://www.dbisna.com
Finance Net
  http://www.financenet.gov
Financial Economics
  http://www.finweb.com/
Financial Resource Guide
  http://libertynet.org/~beausang/aaafrg.html
First Chicago Capital Markets
  http://www.fccm.com/
Investment Resources
  http://infomanage.com/investment
Investor In-Touch
  http://www.money.com/ssnhome.html
JP Morgan
  http://www.jpmorgan.com/
Merrill Lynch
  http://www.ml.com/
Mutual Funds
  http://www.ai.mit.edu/stocks/mf.html
PC-Quote
  http://www.pcquote.com
Portfolio Accounting World-Wide
  http://pawws.secapl.com
QuoteCom
  http://www.quote.com

Salomon Brothers International
  http://www.sbil.co.uk
Security APL
  http://qs.secapl.com/cgi-bin/qs
Stock Market Data
  http://www.ai.mit.edu/stocks/prices.html
StreetLink
  http://www.streetlink.com

PUBLISHING

In the beginning . . . was the Word.

Four hundred years ago, Gutenberg made the Word available to all.

Now we are at the very beginning . . . of the electric word.

If desktop publishing made everybody their own Gutenberg, the Internet adds publicity . . . warehousing . . . and distribution.

Desktop has gone webtop.

The Net has not only spawned totally new words, as we've seen. It is opening up totally new worlds.

It won't replace paper. But it is transfiguring our use of words and pictures.

Here we might make the distinction that Marshall McLuhan pointed out about new media—they subsume the old media, within themselves. There are fax machines that still have a separate telephone within them. There are portable music systems that include tape decks and radio as well as cd-players. The web includes the features of the Net.

The Internet still uses words, but the old forms change within the new media. Classical poetry, for example, shed metrics and rhyme with the widespread use of the typewriter—giving birth to free verse.

Time will tell how the electric word will differ. Already, we're starting to feel the winds of change. E-mail and forums have caused a tremendous revitalization of the written word to a postFilm, TV era. We're only just starting to see how literature might be transformed by such concepts as faqs, hypertext, and multimedia.

The publishing model holds a powerful place in the future metaphor for the Internet. Think of the Joke-A-Day mailing list, for example.

Here follow a few essential angles to consider and compass points to check out.

▶ *Journalism*

Twenty-five years ago, it was news to a journalist or publisher that text could be manipulated from keyboard to draft—and then to editorial revision to design and layout and to print—all without rekeying, thanks to a word-processed "textstream." Photos, too, are now digital—shot, retouched, and printed without film—and thus merged into the digital stream. Today, information streams have become big rivers. San Francisco State University journalism professor J. T. "Tom" Johnson recalls this:

> When I broke into the business 25+ years ago, knowing how to type with at least two fingers was sufficient. If the paper, magazine, or station were small enough, we might have had to know how to load film into a camera or splice

tape. But that, and a good sense of the language and a smattering of libel law, got us by.

Today, dramatic shifts in the Information Environment have not replaced any of those techniques or specific bits of knowledge, but whole new layers of "must-have-to-survive-professionally" skills have been piled on. Those additional layers have serious consequences for training in the newsroom and classroom.

I'm trying to assemble a list of all the individual skills or pieces of knowledge that journalists need to know today that simply didn't exist in the profession 10–15 years ago.

For example:

—Formatting a disc
—Setting telecommunications parameters
—The difference between a serial and a parallel port
—Saving a file in a binary or ASCII form
—Knowing what "*" means or what a wild card is
—What is SQL, and how does it work?
—What are rows, columns, and cells?
—How to start a formula in a spreadsheet

Indeed, it used to be that the entry-level position at a newspaper was Copy Boy, messengering text around the building. As the Fourth Estate gets "totally wired," messengering is done today by computer networking. As of 1989, color photos as well as text could be phoned in, from remote locations. Far-flung correspondents and page production can all be coordinated via the Internet.

And the Internet can refine various processes, offering an extra edge. Reporters have been known to use the Net to get past the secretarial lions guarding the gates of VIPs, by finding where they hang out in forums and by sending them direct e-mail to get interviews. Here's the significance of Usenet calling its conferences news groups and Net news: they carry news of affinity groups who can provide firsthand background, testimony, and reactions; and it's people's reactions to events that often create new events.

There are specialized news services instantly available on the Net, such as Interpress, HandsNet, Pacific News Service, and New York Transfer. Hundreds of journalists at papers large and small, across America and in eighteen countries, talk shop, swap gossip, and share information daily—about hot news, new Internet resources, interviewing techniques, women in journalism, one-newspaper towns, etc., in such forums as CARR (Computer-Assisted Reporting & Research) and SPJ (Society for Professional Journalism).

During a major event or disaster, the Internet becomes a twenty-four-hour information command post. For example, within one hour of the initial tremors of the 1993 Los Angeles earthquake, Texas Tech journalism professor Randy Reddick began remote news gathering over the Net. First, he telneted to a seismic data computer in Oklahoma. From there he teleported to another in Berkeley's Office of Emergency Services (OES), right on the faultline.

He was surprised to find the OES computer rife with preliminary information which was updated throughout the day—proclamations from the governor, California Transportation Department breakdowns on highway status, overview and specifics on utilities (gas, electricity, water), aftershock times and magnitudes, Red Cross relief centers, press briefings, media advisories, FEMA involvement (Federal Emergency Management Association), damages, deaths, etc. Later that day, visiting the

Well, where many journalists hang out, and at a few "live" chats, he bumped into reporters from a few news agencies "trawling for color," who were, simultaneously, relaying to each other what they'd heard—leads which he was able to pick up on.

Still "charged" from surfing the Net through a disaster of such magnitude, he reflected afterward to other journalists, in one of the forums, this:

> Using only the Net (and understanding the danger of such), I could have produced at least a page (168″ SAU) of fresh, relevant news articles on a breaking story: main story, sidebars, human interest, etc. Aside from the art, these stories would have been just as good as about anything that went out over the wire, and probably as good as 90 percent of what on-the-scene media produced.
>
> My point is, the information was there in a timely manner, sources were available for "interviewing," and I never left my desk or lifted the phone. It would not have taken much effort to get some "friends" to snap some pictures, digitize, and post the images. No AP. No UPI. No AFP. No Reuters. No NYTNS. No LATNS.

In other words, the electronic audience at large has the same options (Associated Press/AP, United Press International/UPI, AFP, Reuters, The New York Times News Service/NYTNS, Los Angeles Times News Service/LATNS) as the reporters—and even the wire services. Of course, while the electronic journalist has any of the above Net options, so does the electronic audience at large.

As a rule, people who follow news over the Net tend to know about news items—and have discussed them with others—at least a day ahead of everyone else. And they can be informed in more depth, through forums which act as affinity-group newspapers and newsletters.

A slightly more recent current event reveals another angle of the power of Internet journalism. In July of 1995, *Time* published a cover article about pornography on the Internet, upon which certain members of Congress then tried to base legislation to constrain what people say and post over the Net. Within weeks, Internet reporters had discredited the study upon which the article was based. Not only did serious examination reveal the statistics to be seriously flawed. (The grossly inaccurate citation that 83.5 percent of all images on Usenet are pornographic was contradicted with the statement much later on that they comprise half of one percent [00.5 percent] of all Internet traffic.) Not only did people who were Internet literate understand that the report mixed up the BBS's and online services where the majority of porn exists with Usenet, but the credibility of the person who wrote the study was extremely suspect. The study had been written by an electrical engineering student, on a grant from his university. During time, it was also discovered, he wrote a paperback entitled *Pornographer's Handbook: How to Exploit Women, Dupe Men, & Make Lots of Money*—a copy of which was found and portions of which were posted on the Internet. This news was published by Brock Meeks in *Cyberwire Dispatch. Time* later did the right thing, ate crow, and publicly admitted the article's fatal flaws—a media giant rebuffed by Internet users with the power of their own press (computers and modems).

▶ *Information brokers, intelligent agents, & neural nets*

CyberpornGate was something of a nonstarter to begin with. The Internet is not a broadcasting system, like TV. Any parents with genuine concerns about their children's access of things on the Net can obtain any number of inexpensive, efficient softwares for blocking access to preselected subjects, such as CyberSitter and Net Nanny. (For information on how you can obtain a copy of a faq about this, e-mail us at our domain listed on the inside cover.) This brings us to the topic of narrowing—or widening—our access to certain areas on the Internet.

Now that everyone on the Net has the same sources as journalists, we can appreciate their abilities all the more: namely, how to not only search through vast fields of information but also winnow the chaff from the grain. Information brokers and researchers are not new, but now they can make their services available online. There are many Personalized News Agencies online (such as InfoSeek, First/HeadsUp, FarCast, and Newscast).

To stem the rising tide of information glut, software developers are coming out with filters (often called agents). "Bozo filters" will automatically block messages from specified individuals or those containing specified words. "Smart bookmarks" will keep tabs on specified web sites and report back changes. Intelligent agents will automatically look for and bring back information, like an electronic butler or good hunting dog. The next step is neural netware—the purist's true interactivity. A neural net evolves—evaluating your choices, and based on them, making decisions for you and offering you new choices.

It will be a longer wait, however, before these things can replace the journalist's ability to separate fact from misinformation, folklore, and hype—and, besides mere reportage, to create a story out of it.

▶ *Synergies*

Paper is a fixed and finite medium, as anyone can understand who went to buy a book or newspaper and found it was sold out—or if you tried to use a Xerox when somebody else was making many copies. It would be tempting to give as examples also the rising price of paper, and the sight of clear-cut forests—except that electric words may be creating even more demand for paper.

Models of traditional publishing and the Internet overlap but also differ—which can make for powerful synergies, just beginning to be explored. For instance, *The San Jose Mercury News* (aka *SJMerc*), in Silicon Valley, made a bold experiment in May 1993, launching an online newspaper called *Mercury Online*. On the one hand, *Mercury Online* overlapped with the *SJMerc*, taking stories published in the paper version and expanding them, online—making available all the wire-service articles, plus, perhaps, the reporters' complete interviews and notes, etc. But, too, it published its own exclusive material, not mirrored in the paper version. The logical assumption might have been that *Mercury Online* would steal away readers of the *SJMerc*. But the electronic *Mercury Online* increased the sales of the paper *SJMerc*. (An Internet version went up in early 1995: http://www.sjmercury.com.) Now there were more reasons to read the paper and different ways to use it.

Merc Executive Editor Bob Ingle says, "One of the tremendous advantages that a computer-based system has over physical product is that it's basically limitless. It's the never-ending newspaper, if you will."

In 1989, forty-two newspapers had online counterparts; in 1993, over a hundred; in 1995, thirty-two hundred. A very good compass point to them is Steve Outings' Commercial Online Newspaper Services, http:// www.mediainfo.com/edpub/e-papers.home.page.html.

Magazines are also setting up shop on the online world. *Time, Newsweek, U.S. News & World Report, The Economist, The National Review,* and *Consumer Reports* were among the first to have online counterparts.

Paper < = > Electronic. Not mutually exclusive, they both feed into each other.

And there are electric words that appear *only* online—as online newspapers, magazines, and books, which see paper and ink only if they're saved to disk and printed out. A seminal moment came in October 1994 when *Wired* announced that it was starting an online magazine, *HotWired*—with its own advertisers and a separate editorial department. Many of *HotWired*'s departments are the same, but they're called channels instead; the table of contents is called the front door. One of its best features is its NetSurf critical guide to other web sites, as well as a searchable archive of its own past pages. Http://www.hotwired.com.

Time Inc. has a mega–web site bursting with online counterparts to its paper magazines (visit, for example, *Vibe* and the *Virtual Gardener*), but in August 1995 the site itself became an online magazine by adding daily news feeds, stock quotes, weather updates, and sports statistics, plus much original content. Http://www.path finder.com.

On the other end of the spectrum is the zine scene—alternative, often radical, often cyber-savvy, self-published by and for a younger audience—an incubation site for some future potentials of online publishing. A selection can be found at gopher.well.com, and gopher.cic.net.

Two exemplary, very different magazines designed exclusively for the web are *Word* and *Feed*. *Word* is literary, mixing hypertext, image, and even sound—more like the experience of things hurtling by a traveling car window than large, enveloping texts to be absorbed while commuting. *Feed* is a very stimulating forum on current affairs, from affirmative action to virtual communities, and has a very innovative approach to dialogue. Http://www. word.com, and http://www.feedmag.com.

One of the first strictly online newspapers is *The American Reporter,* staffed by professional reporters and editors. Begun April 1995, its coverage of the tragic bombing of the Alfred P. Murrah Building in Oklahoma City, that very month, included an interview with the head of the day-care center, and coverage of terrorism hearings in Washington. The *Reporter* also scooped the rest of the press by a full day on the sequence of the explosion and the substance of the bomb.

To subscribe, e-mail Joeshea@netcom.com. In the message body, put: Subscribe AR.

Http://www.newshare.com/Reporter/today.html.

Additional online newspapers and magazines can be found in the Appendix.

In the mid-1960s, Pete Hamill coined the phrase "the New Journalism." The catch-all included not only such novelists as James Baldwin, Norman Mailer, and Terry Southern, but also Gay Talese, Truman Capote, Gail Sheehy, Rex Reed, Michael Herr, Joe Eszterhas, Barbara Goldsmith, Garry Wills, John Gregory Dunne, Joe McGinniss, et al. Today's paperless presses are ushering in the virtual challenger: Internet Journalism.

▶ ©?

Where does copyright fit in to all this?

You own your words.

The Internet is a public space.

A case can be made for both points of view. Intellectual property has been one of the fastest growing fields in the legal profession. Lawyers are massing at both sides of the river, preparing for battle. Meanwhile, here are some helpful hints for the layperson.

Navigate with common courtesy. For instance, can you make a link to an item in somebody else's web page and put it in yours? Sure, unless you see a copyright notice. Would you ask the owner of the site? It wouldn't hurt and might gain some encouragement in your common interest.

If you hear something in a Usenet group, can you reproduce it in something you're writing? You'd want to ask the author's permission, out of sheer courtesy alone. If you ask and are told no, back off.

▶ *Publishing models*

We've seen how the Net can add synergy to paper. And, able to cover news-as-it-happens just like a newspaper, the Net lends itself to being a news medium. Plus, as a distribution mode, the Net mottoes "Try it before you buy it" and "Give something if you sell something" apply to publishers, as well. Paper magazines gone online generally offer at least one sample article or story, along with tables of contents of the paper version. Book publishers often offer excerpts, as well. Stephen King, for example, likes the Internet and has made four stories available online. William Gibson tried making a novella available online only, entitled *Agrippa (A Book of the Dead)*, designed to self-destruct after one reading; hackers outsmarted the software and made it available to all.

But then there's the model of Joke-A-Day: you might have some item on your web site that people will pay 2¢ for, say, twenty thousand people per day. Now that publishing is accessible to ordinary people, it will be interesting to see what they publish, and what sells and what doesn't.

As an example of the way the Internet can stand previous models on their ear, consider the weekly news column "This Is True" that Randy Cassingham, of Pasadena, California, has been writing, with bizarre-but-true news items plus his commentary. In its first three months of publication, circulation was 120,000 (in eighty-seven countries!). He gives it away, over the Internet, but syndicates first publication rights (to, thus far, two newspapers, two magazines, and one radio station), with Internet release delayed a week afterward. And (unlike many Internet models) there are no archives: he publishes his archives and sells them as paperback books. (For more information, e-mail: TrueInfo@freecom.com.)

To get you started, here are some primary magazine and book compass points in the online world.

The Electronic Newsstand first opened in July 1993 "to provide the Internet community with easy access to a wide range of interesting information furnished by the world's leading publishers." After starting with just eight magazines, the 'Stand now has over 275. Besides an alphabetical list, there's listing by subject: computers and technology, business, entertainment. As a research tool, the entire Electronic Newsstand (current and past issues) is searchable by key word.

How to find it:
WWW: http://www.enews.com
Gopher: enews.com
Telnet: enews.com (log-in as "enews")

BookWire is the web home page of *Publishers Weekly*, which has been taking a strong, active interest in online publishing and interactive multimedia since August 1994. Their page includes links to 225 publishers and 150 booksellers, as well as libraries, a reading room, and an index of indexes to other sites: http://www.bookwire.com/

BookWeb is the web site of the American Booksellers' Association (ABA). In addition to stuff for book dealers, it features interactive chats with authors, such as Harlan

Ellison, Studs Terkel, and Newt Gingrich, bookstore home pages, and speciality topics. Its "Book Ports" links to plenty of other web sites: http://www.ambook. org/bookweb/

Book Port is an online book fair with online booksellers, online books, bound books, topical reading lists, editors' discoveries, literary experiments, etc. Http://www. bookport.com

The Internet Roadmap to Books offers a guided tour of the terrain, http://www.bookinfo.com/welcome/roadmap/ pgi/. It's brought to you courtesy of Daniel Kehoe, pioneer builder of an online book marketplace, who maintains two other sites: *Internet Bookfair,* where you can search the stock of publishers and booksellers, http:// www.bookfair.com, and *Bookport,* for finding online editions of books (such as *Netiquette*), http://www. bookfair.com.

As with examples in our previous chapters, the Internet won't replace or preempt preexisting outlets. But it does challenge them. When understood and used effectively, it enhances them. And as it transfigures how we communicate our world, it can transform that world itself—and ourselves.

SCIENCE

The tool solves a problem, and then creates new and more thorny issues not dreamable before. Technology, unlike science, does not even claim to reveal larger truths about what exists, but hints at more ways for humanity to change the world. Born of simple need and want, it emerges as an agent of human evolution . . .

The more we learn about how to use an instrument, the less we think about it as we use it. It becomes like an extra limb, a new way to reach out and change the world. But what is it precisely that is extended? Not simply an internal human idea, but an idea to act, a thought that engages the world, making the possible actual. The more we understand of this the more ways we conceive of how it may be put into practice. Our desires and intentions to act upon the world are themselves altered through the tools that we create to realize them.

—DAVID ROTHENBERG, *Hand's End*

▶ Paradigm shift

Scientific research has been at the core of the Internet from its very inception. To explore that further, let's take a big step back.

Historian of science Thomas S. Kuhn pioneered the commonplace usage of *paradigm shift*. A paradigm is an example or model. Learning to go from riding a tricycle to a bicycle would be a paradigm shift. In 1962, in *The Structure of Scientific Revolution*, he described how science undergoes such great upheavals of outlook and worldview wherein the map of the known world and the universe is reenvisioned.

Consider the Copernican Revolution.

Up until then, knowledge was held in single-copy manuscripts. To even know what the paradigm was entailed making pilgrimages beyond the walls of libraries in distant cities.

But then, thanks to Gutenberg, scientists could access at their fingertips the data of past observers, as well as the latest in visual aids, plus something like bibliographies. Thus Copernicus would note inconsistencies in inherited data. Following his own publication, scientists would have the basis for an alternative theory, which, in turn, would have to be tested against the prevailing one.

Now, flash-forward to the present. Scientists map the chromosomes of genetic inheritance on a chart resembling a bar code (such as on the bottom of the back of this book). When a new DNA sequence is discovered, the scientist adds it to that map, hyperlinked with accompanying text. And thousands of gene scientists around the world all instantly have a common copy of that newly revised map.

How?

The Internet. Geneticists around the world all share a world-wide web site. Thus, for example, if one geneticist posts to the web the new DNA sequence he or she has discovered on a gene related to a genetically based kind of blindness, it can be searched in relation to all the others—and if it resembles a DNA sequence involved in protein switching in another gene, then the possibility of a cure for the abnormality may have begun. The Genome Mapping Project is the largest and arguably the most ambitious study in the history of science. Http://gdbwww. gdb.org.

There's no telling what the next big scientific break-through, like Copernicus's, will be. Only time will tell. Until then, a number of paradigms compete for attention. (Maybe it will turn out that we *are* an atom in a cat's hair in some parallel universe, after all.) We *can* see, however, the paradigm.

For example, interactivity is becoming a standard for the Internet. Case in point: Serendip. Jointly conceived by professionals in brain research, computers, and, in the broadest sense, education, Serendip creates a test bed for the exploration and expansion of the interactive potentials of the web. Interactive exhibits, forums, and links to other sites are designed to create experiences of how one makes sense out of life—given its ambiguities, blind spots, and double messages: Http://serendip.brynmawr.edu.

Similarly, BMEnet (Biomedical Engineering Network) is a one-stop for its field: http://fairway.ecn.purdue.edu/bme. It contains a directory of every biomedical engineering program in the U.S., links to government and private databases, a library of technical journals, funding sources, job opportunities, etc. Plus, just as the Internet served as the incubator for the collaborative, interactive invention, development, and implementation of such tools as remote log-ins, conferencing, the web, etc., so too does the Internet enable scientists with a common resource for sharing new tools. For example, within BMEnet is a project developing tools for distribution over the Internet that enable medical students to practice with such costly biomedical equipment as magnetic resonance imagers (MRI) and heart monitors, the way pilots train on flight simulators.

Thus, just as Gutenberg's invention of movable type enabled scientists to read and compare contrasting theories and research from remote parts of the world, so, too, is the Net providing a new medium of information. (As David Rothenberg's quote at the beginning of the section reflects, technology plays an important role in section to shape science, as well as vice versa.)

In the remainder of this chapter, we'll consider just three scientific areas where the Internet is already providing particularly potent benefits: 1) medicine/health/fitness; 2) disability; and 3) environmental studies.

▶ *Medicine/health/fitness*

Like education, medicine is a field that stands to reap huge benefits from the Internet. Telemedicine was one of the featured applications when Taiwan unveiled its National Information Infrastructure in July 1995. At that inaugural debut, doctors were seen at different hospitals using linked computers to simultaneously access a patient's images and medical history, and make an onscreen diagnosis of the patient's illness. American investment in telemedicine over the next five years is estimated at $90 billion, largely from the military. Now surgeons can remotely visit the front lines, where the mortality rate of wounded soldiers has been 90 percent.

Technology developed for other military purposes is now finding medical adaptations. Now doctors can use 3-D models rather than X-rays as templates, with information conveyed back from the patient's interior by microsensors. Smart-bomb targeting systems can be used to pinpoint areas for surgery. (Such research is further enabled, interestingly, by the fact that the military, unlike private hospitals, can't be held liable for malpractice suits.)

Medicine is the most rapidly consolidating industry and stands on the verge of major reform, certainly at local levels. But billing and fees and telesurgery are only a part of the field's transformation in the Information Age.

A patient's medical information is often stored at many locations and includes a variety of data, such as doctor's notes, lab results, insurance, billing—as well as multimedia (CAT-scans, ultrasound, magnetic resonance imaging, X-rays, etc.). Telecommunications enables them all to be merged, into one multimedia medical record, and called up on-demand and even real-time (as during a test or operation) from remote sites. Where time is critical, a radiologist still in robe and slippers at home can render a diagnosis from an accident victim's CAT scan, rather than rushing to the hospital. Collaborative research and diagnosis via networks can augment the role of the sole practitioner, as health sites are interlinked. As videoteleconferencing becomes more mature, doctors and patients can visit more frequently, eliminating needless trips to the hospital.

The Internet provides individuals a channel to become self-educated, as through medical databases and specialized information providers such as Medlars. These are useful for researching a diagnosis or just understanding the terminology. Internet forums dealing with a particular medical ailment act as twenty-four-hour support lines.

The Internet has played its role, too, in the tragic AIDS

saga. Anyone with Internet access has been able to tap into a vast pool of international information. In addition to linking to a dozen major databases (World Health Organization, National Institutes of Health, Johns Hopkins University, etc.), the Centers for Disease Control has hosted a daily mailing list which has been one of the Internet's most striking achievements. To correspond with the CDC's Clearinghouse, e-mail: aidsinfo@ cdcnac.aspensys.com. Their web site is http://cdcnac. aspensys.com:86. Gopher Jewels is also an excellent gateway to major databases. And the Usenet group sci.med.aids has an 80-page-plus faq. (Parts are starting to date, however.)

Here are some other representative medical resources of various kinds. *Note:* Readers inclined to hypochondria are warned against Med School Syndrome, developing the symptoms he or she reads about.

Preview the Heart is a tour wherein you can actually watch the exchange of oxygen and carbon dioxide between the capillaries and arteries, among other neat things. Http://sln.fi.edu/tfi/preview/heartpreview.html.

National Library of Medicine's History of Medicine has at least two projects well worth a visit:

1) HyperDOC: The History of Medicine is a searchable database of sixty thousand images from the world's richest treasury of medical prints and photographs. Exhibits include *Paracelsus—500 Years, The Art of Medicine in the 21st Century,* and *Caesarean Section.* Upcoming topics include health care for Native Ameri-

cans and medical arts in Islamic culture. Http://www.
nlm.nih.gov/hmd.dir/hmd.html.

And there's the Visible Human Project. Using CAT-
and MRI-scans and cryosection images, it is creating
complete, anatomically detailed, three-dimensional rep-
resentations of the male and female human body. Http://
www.nlm.nih.gov/extramural_research.dir/photos.html.

Virtual Hospital, for use by both physicians and patients,
is a continuously updated medical multimedia database.
It provides patient care support and distance learning to
practicing physicians and other health-care professionals.
Information for patients, for example, includes multimedia health books on cardiovascular, endocrine/metabolic,
gastrointestinal, and immunologic systems, and such
departments as anesthesia, dentistry, dermatology and
family practice. Http://indy.radiology.uiowa.edu/Virtual
Hospital.html.

U.S. Department of Health and Human Services provides
links to government agencies, such as the Indian Health
Service, Occupational Safety and Health Administration
(OSHA), the Centers for Disease Control (CDC), the National Institute of Diabetes and Digestive and Kidney
Disease, and the National Clearinghouse for Alcohol and
Drug Information, "the world's largest resource for current information and materials about alcohol and other
drugs"—plus links to other Internet sites. Http://www.
os.dhhs.gov.

Let's Talk Health links to forums that discuss topics like
allergies, cancer, CFS (chronic fatigue syndrome—an

unexplained phenomenon well represented on the Internet), and fitness (exercise, diet, etc.). Http://www.social. com/health/hypermail/mlists/index.html.

The Good Health Web is a page geared toward the consumer and includes many forums, Usenet groups, and faqs, as well as links to health-related mailing lists. Http://www.social.com/health/index.html.

The Karolinska Institute in Stockholm, Sweden, provides a collection of links to Internet resources about diseases, disorders, and a few related topics, loosely classified by means of the Medical Subject Headings (MeSH) indexing vocabulary. Http://www.mic.ki.se/Diseases/index.html.

Repetitive Strain Injury (RSI) is a growing hazard of frequent users of computers, affecting the hands and arms. The most common is Carpal Tunnel Syndrome.

The University of Nebraska has one of many web pages devoted to this phenomenon. Theirs is preventative, rather than curative: Http://engr-www.unl.edu/ee/eeshop/rsi.html.

Rural Medicine: At Marshall University, West Virginia, the School of Medicine has a home page dedicated to improving health care for those who live in rural areas. It's home to the RuralNet Rural Health Gopher Server and Rural Health WWW—subject-oriented access to health-care-related servers around the world, focusing on those resources most relevant to rural health care. Http://musom.marshall.edu/.

Natural Medicine, Complementary Health Care, & Alternative Therapies: This nonprofit organization is dedicated to reuniting the art of healing and the science of medicine, and furnishes a big atlas of alternative/holistic medical resources, as well as links to other web pages. Http://www.amrta.org/~amrta.

HEALTH RESOURCES

America's Lifeline Online for Health/Population Trends
    http://web.syr.edu/~cakincai/lifeline.html
B&B Health Watch Health Links
    http://rampages.onramp.net/~indebt/index.htm
Balance Fitness on the Net
    http://tito.hyperlink.com/balance/
Consumer Health Information
    http://www.hirs.com/constemp.html
Cyberspace Telemedical Office
    http://telemedical.com/~drcarr/
Health Center
    http://netcenter.com/netcentr/health/index.html
HealthNet
    http://hpbl.hwc.ca/healthnet/#medapp
Healthwise
    http://www.cc.columbia.edu:80/cu/healthwise
Interactive Medical Student Lounge
    http://falcon.cc.ukans.edu:80/~nsween
Medical Hot Links
    http://www.mcli.dist.maricopa.edu/links/med.html
MediCom
    http://www.medi.com/Lobby/
Wellness Web
    http://www.wellweb.com/wellness
Whole Internet Catalog's Health & Medicine Page
    http://near-net.gnn.com/wic/med.toc.html

The World Health Organization has excellent reference materials, both in its virtual library and its three search engines. Writers visit this site for biographies and statistics, and travelers check its international travel and health information on vaccination requirements and health advice. The site is updated to include recent data—past updates include the Ebola virus outbreak, the Global Polio Eradication Campaign, and the World No-Tobacco Day: http://www.who.ch/

▶ *Fitness*

The best medicine is preventive. Staying in shape is fun, but (like yoga) it's a science, too, as well as an art.

A good place to research what's online here are the faqs in such Usenet groups as Misc.fitness. And for those who pump iron, there's Misc.fitness.weights. The Yahoo directory is just starting to find fitness items on its radar screen; however, there are already thirty-nine subtopics under Running.

The HealthInfo gopher covers exercise and fitness resources, such as guidelines for developing your own programs—starting with knowing how much is too much, determining your target heart rate, stretching properly, and building up to progressions and recovering after hard exercise. Http://riceinfo.rice.edu/health&safety/Health Info/. Body builders will want to check out http://www2.your.body.com/yourbody.

▶ *Disability*

On the Internet, disability is no obstacle. Anyone able to access the Internet has access to just as many resources as anyone else. For the blind, this may mean using a voice-recognition and voice-emulation interface. For the severely handicapped, it may mean using a unicorn prong to type with, breathing Morse code into a small wire or tapping a knee against a desk in Morse code. In addition to all the resources anyone else might use, there are also special resources for people with disabilities. UCLA, for example, has a Disabilities and Computing Program (DCP) that is an excellent Square One. It centers on locally developed resources (which can provide a good model for other localities)—plus links to the vast Cornucopia of Disability Information (CODI) (valdor.cc. buffalo.edu), St. Johns' extensive resources, Equal Access to Software & Information (EASI), deaf education information, Recording for the Blind, and a dozen other major sites. Http://www.dcp.ucla.edu.

▶ *Environment*

Ecology is a science that filtered through to mass awareness in the late 1960s.

Seeds of that awareness are being planted every day on the Internet—such as the slogan THINK GLOBAL—ACT LOCAL. (Longer texts than those four words appear every July 4, when environmentalists post the latest Declaration of Interdependence.) April 22, Earth Day, is a busy time for eco-activists on the Net.

Here are compass points to some of the Internet's environmental resources.

The Environmental Issues Resource Center at EcoNet's home page is an atlas of forums, resources, and activists concerned about such issues as:

acid rain, agriculture, air, biodiversity, climate, endangered species, energy, environmental education and environmental law, forests, health, mushrooms and mycology, parks, population, recycling, seas and waters, sustainable development, toxic wastes and pesticides, trade, transportation, water (seas, oceans, and rivers), and wildlife.

It has hundreds of "ways you can live earthwise at home, at work, and in your community."

Since many K–12 educational organizations use IGC (EcoNet's umbrella) as their Internet provider, they easily link up with other IGC subscribers on other group projects with environmental components. So, for example, I*EARN (International Educational and Resource Network), which networks over one thousand K–12 schools in twenty-five countries, has prepared a project on monitoring watersheds with an associated EcoNet group, such as GREEN (Global Rivers Environmental Education Network). Http://www.econet.apc.org/econet/.

The National Resources Defense Council furnishes the latest news from Capitol Hill, plus information on the state of our air, water, land, and health: http://www.nrdc.org/nrdc.

Rainforest Action Network's home page is sterling as well as needful. It's at http://www.ran.org/ran/.

Earth Island Institute's home pages are worth a look, too, at http://www.earthisland.org/ei/.

Three Usenet groups to visit are talk.environment, sci.environment, and misc.activism.progressive.

And who says environmentalism, conservation, and the Internet are for the birds? There are plenty of local and national birding organizations on the Net.

To join a birdwatching mailing list, e-mail to:

listserv@arizvml.ccit.arizona.edu

In the message body, put:

```
SUB BIRDCNTR <your full name>   (Central US)
SUB BIRDEAST <your full name>   (Eastern US)
SUB BIRDWEST <your full name>   (Western US)
```

And the National Audubon Society has a home page: Http://www.audubon.org/audubon/.

▶ *Miscellaneous*

Orienting ourselves through the Internet strictly subject-by-subject has its limits. Topics overlap. (The Net itself compensates, however, by cross-posting and hyperlinking.) For example, to bring law into the picture, in 1995, Professor Stanton Glantz, at the University of California's medical school, a leading critic of the tobacco industry, obtained four thousand pages of often sensitive documents from inside Brown & Williamson, the cigarette company. Along with the American Medical Association and the curious, lawyers suing cigarette companies have found these papers of landmark significance. So UCSF librarians scanned them and made them available on the Internet, where they can now be viewed by the whole planet. Http://galen.library.ucsf.edu/tobacco.

The Medicine and Global Survival working group has a web site containing research, reviews, news, and informed opinion pieces of major worldwide threats to health and to our collective well-being and survival. They state the following:

Among these threats are the possession and use of weapons of mass destruction, including nuclear, chemical, and biological weapons; environmental and social destruction due to war, pollution, overpopulation, overdevelopment, and the inequitable distribution of the world's resources; natural and human-caused disasters; and large-scale abuses of human rights.

M&GS takes a special interest in the social and ethical responsibilities of physicians and other health professionals with respect to the issues of war, the environment, medical research, and humanitarian assistance.

Http://www.bmj.com./bmj/mgs/index.html.

The above two examples show that, in an ever interdependent world, people can freely cross categorical boundaries to collaborate on areas of mutual affinity—and their impulse to do so is empowered by the Net.

COMPUTERS

In the very beginning, before comput-
ers, the American Constitution had de-
creed a national census be taken every
decade. Near the turn of the last century, our country had grown so that it
became evident that it would take a decade just to tabulate the results, so an open competition was held for a new system. A young engineer named Herman Hollerith won, with a machine that automatically counted holes in punch cards—the basis of a company he later founded in 1911, International Business Machines (IBM).

The growth of computers since then has been exponential, to say the very least. George Gilder tells the following story to dramatize the impact:

> The Emperor of China was totally infatuated with this new game of chess that had been invented for him and said, "I'll give you anything you want in the kingdom as a tribute for this wonderful game you gave me."
>
> And the inventor said, "Well, I want one grain of rice. I want one grain of rice on the first square of the chess board, which has sixty-four squares, then I want two grains of rice on the second square. Four grains of rice on the third square, eight grains of rice on the fourth square, and so on."
>
> . . . And the Emperor happily granted this apparently modest request, and everything went fine for the first thirty-two squares. He could produce the several billion grains of rice fairly well on a quarter square mile of rice fields. But after the first thirty-two squares, things began to get interesting.
>
> There are two ways the story ends. One is, the Emperor went bankrupt because after sixty-four squares, this was several billion trillion grains of rice, which would take the entire surface of the earth, plus the oceans times two to produce. The other end of the story was that the inventor lost his head.
>
> But in any case, to get some perspective on how this applies, Raw Kurzell estimates that by 1993 there had been exactly thirty-two doublings of computer power since the first digital computers were invented in the early 1940s. So we've now completed the first half of the chess-board, where things really become interesting and where the Emperor began to take notice of this process.

One application for computers that Herman Hollerith probably never dreamed of is the Internet. Now a single computer can access millions of others.

There was a lag of about a decade before computer

manufacturers made the Internet an option. Now, as more and more people share information and do work across it, the Net is becoming a computer "platform" itself.

The Internet has become a "killer application" for computers. Indeed, many are buying their first computer just so they can access the Net.

Naturally, the Internet is a treasure chest of information about computers—traversing communities of programmers, computer science majors, and ordinary users. For example, when WordPerfect 6.0 debuted on the market, one user tried it out, created a software package that would fix all the bugs, and posted it on the Internet. On the Internet you can find computer information based on applications, platform (PC or Mac), protocol, society, software, programming, philosophy, or market. Beginners, intermediate, or advanced, the Internet is an oasis for people with computers.

The future of the Net and of computers seems ever more entwined. It may become commonplace for standard computing software, such as word-processing and spread-sheets, to program in an Internet interface, as, too, for cd-roms to interface with the Net. However, someday there may well be alternatives to computers as the only form of Internet terminal. Oracle, the second largest software company next to Microsoft, is already testing in Britain an "information appliance" which would plug into the telephone. The box would interface with not only the Internet but also interactive TV, video-on-demand, fax, and telephone. In this paradigm, any necessary software can be transmitted through the network. This reverses the traditional relation between hardware and software: here, the software (the application) is the primary attraction,

COMPUTING RESOURCES

C\net
   http://www.cnet.com
Computer Intelligence Infocorp (computer industry market research)
   http://www.compint.com
Computer Literature
   Gopher://chop.isca.uiowa.edu:70
   Path general/wbachman/netserv/comp/lit.mnu
Computer User Groups
   http://www.melbpc.org.au/others/index.htm
Dell Computer Corp.
   http://www.dell.com
Digital Equipment Corp.
   http://www.digital.com
IBM Personal Computers
   http://www.pc.ibm.com
IndustryNet
   http://www.industry.net
Microsoft
   http://www.microsoft.com
The Most Popular Computer Sites On The Web
   http://www.iol.ie/~kmagee/compco/popular.html
Novell Inc.
   http://www.novell.com
Oracle Corp.
   http://www.oracle.com
PC Catalog
   Gopher or telnet: pccatalog.peed.com
      (if using telnet, log-in as "gopher" and at the password
      press "enter")
   Http://www.peed.com.
PC Software Harvest Broker (freeware)
   http://www.town.hall.org/Harvest/brokers/pcindex/
   query.html

Shareware Search
  http://vsl.cnet.com/
Silicon Graphics
  http://www.sgi.com
Software Exchange
  http://www.hyperion.com/usox/
Software.Net
  http://software.net
Spry Inc
  http://www.spry.com
Spyglass Inc
  http://www.spyglass.com
Sun Microsystems (with links to the must-visit *SunSites*)
  http://www.sun.com (See also http://java.sun.com)
Tandem Computers
  http://www.tandem.com
Tandy Corp.
  http://www.tandy.com
Toshiba America Inc.
  http://www.tais.com
Ultimate Macintosh
  http://www.best.com/~myee/ultimate_mac.html
Windows Archives
  http://coyote.csusm.edu/cwis/winwworld/winworld.html

and the hardware is merely a tool to plug into a wall for data. It's as if we were buying software, with the equivalent of a computer being given away along with it, like getting a free razor with the purchase of razor blades, or a disposable camera with a roll of film.

In other words, the Information Revolution's paradigm shift is not only affected by the future of personal computing—it might affect it as well.

ENTERTAINMENT

> Play is older than culture . . . culture arises
> in the form of play. It is played from the
> very beginning.
>
> —JOHAN HUIZINGA, *Homo Ludens*

▶ Sports

In its community-building, the Internet can resemble sports. Sports have brought people together since time immemorial. On Usenet, for example, you can find people getting together to talk about their favorite sport, such as:

```
archery, badminton, basketball, billiards, bowl-
ing, boxing, bungee, caving, chess, climbing,
cricket, darts, fencing, fishing [saltwater and fly],
foosball, golf, hockey, horse-racing, jet-ski, jug-
gling, korfball, lacrosse, lasertag, maulball, of-
ficiating, Olympics, paintball, photon, pool, pro
wrestling, racquetball, rowing, rugby, running,
skating, skateboarding, skiing [Alpine, Nordic, and
snowboard], skydiving, squash, swimming, tennis,
triathlon, waterskiing, weightlifting, wind-
surfing.
```

Many have faq files too. ClariNet has daily newsfeeds on the major sports, by team. Teams and leagues have their web home pages. And the Internet has other resources for most of these sports, plus

```
air hockey, auto racing, body-building, canoeing,
cheerleading, coaching, croquet, danball, footbag
(hacky sack), gymnastics, handball, martial arts,
rodeo, shooting, sports schedules/scores/stand-
ings, sumo, surfing, table tennis, track and field,
volleyball, walking, water polo, and, the sport of
the 21st century, world whiffleball.
```

The Internet Baseball Archive, for instance, contains softball simulations software, major/minor league schedules/stats, and ticket information. Ftp: eucalyptus.cc. swarthmore.edu in /baseball.

ESPNet's popular SportsZone is the Internet counterpart of the TV station; http://espnet.sportszone.com. Of no less interest is SportsLine USA, started by some cyberpreneurs as a web site for sports fans, by sports fans, featuring a scorecard, newswire, exclusive columnists, photos, odds, chats, employment, and links to other sports web sites. In their stable are the NFL Players Association, plus Joe Montana, Arnold Palmer, Wayne Gretzky, Monica Seles, Andre Agassi, and dozens of other superstars. Http://www.sportsline.com. Another winning site is Nando, http://www.nando.net/sportserver. And for the Super Bowl, check out http://www.super bowl.com.

For more information on Internet sports resources, there are special directory editions in both the Internet *Pocket Tour* series and the *Net Guide* series.

▶ *Games*

Who would have imagined? Even with Arnold Schwarzenegger's box office receipts, movies have been outgrossed by software. Games have become the number-one attraction of the Infotainment Industry, generating over ten billion dollars in revenues in 1995. And the Internet is getting in on the action.

The Net enables a number of people (multiusers) to hook up from remote sites at once and interact. Depending on the software application the host site is running, they can play *go,* chess, checkers, or computer games unique to the Net. And if they add a multiuser dimension to a web site, then people can even play popular titles over the Net.

If you've grown tired of outsmarting your computerized chess game, you can play real people "live" online. You don't have to register, but if you do, your game will count toward a rating; if you like, you can play other people at defined levels. Telnet: coot.lcs.mit.edu 5000, iris4.metiu.ucsb.edu 5000, ics.onenet.net 5000, and chess. onenet.net 5000. For advanced players who can pay $25–50 per year, there's the sleek server at chess. lm.com 5000.

When people speak of Chinese chess, they usually mean the kind where you try to move your pieces to the other side first. To play this kind, telnet coolidge. harvard.edu 5555. On the other hand, if you're thinking of the Chinese game called *wei c'hi,* which the Japanese call *go,* telnet either hellspark.wharton.upenn.edu 6969, lacerta.unm.edu 6969, or bsdserver.ucsf.edu 6969. If you're a fanatic, you may be delighted to hear that international *go* competitions online have included players from over twenty countries.

Steven Spielberg and Robin Williams have been known to play backgammon with each other . . . over the Internet. Telnet fraggel65.mdstud.chalmers.se 4321 and log-in as "guest."

As with traditional board games, you can just watch most of them, and sometimes even kibbitz the players and discuss moves with other watchers.

Besides board games, there are puzzles, trivia, word games, mind games, and mazes online. There are even about sixty different "purity tests": gopher.ocf.berkeley. edu:/70/00/ftp/purity/.

For an awesome, hyperlinked, searchable site about games and gaming, http://www.gamesdomain.co.uk.

But the most popular game right now is Doom. When the makers of Doom wanted to publicize their new creation, they gave away the game's first level, fully functional, over the Internet, for anyone to download, free. Being customizable by its players, with new features you can plug in, many of Doom's add-ons are being shared on the Net. And people with the proper software are playing each other, live, over the web. For complete information, e-mail ap641@cleveland.freenet.edu, and in the subject line put "Doom Faq Request." To play Doom online: http://www.dwango.com. For links to Doom web sites, http://doom-gate.cs.buffalo.edu.

And ImagiNation is a huge multiuser game network, sponsored by AT&T. It has such casino-type games as blackjack, liar's poker, poker, roulette, slots, LeftyLibs, and Veracity; board games, such as backgammon, bridge, checkers, chess, cribbage, euchre, FlipFlop, *go*, hearts, and spades; plus MedievaLand and SierraLand, with such items as The Fates of Twinion, 3D Golf, Boogers, Paint-Ball, and Red Baron: http://www.imaginationnet.com/.

What if you only have e-mail? There are both traditional and Internet-based games you can play by mail. For example, to play Diplomacy online, send mail to judge @shrike.und.ac.za with "help" in the body of the message.

For more information, there are special editions on games in the *Net Guide* and *Pocket Tour* series.

▶ *Gambling*

According to one trade journal, Americans wagered $394 billion in 1994. Just as online sports sites will tell you the odds, so, too, will some Internet sites give you a chance to place your bets, offshore. The Internet's ability to erase spatial boundaries here is enabling bettors to lay their money down in regions where it's not illegal to do so, not unlike betting done by phone to Canada or the Caribbean. Were it ever to go to court, it could be a legal bombshell. As Prof. I. Nelson Rose, of Whittier Law School, put it to the *L.A. Times,* "Applying antibookie statutes to the Internet is like performing brain surgery with stone tools. It might work, but the result will be awful messy." If anyone has a problem gambling, they shouldn't even touch these sites. Ultimately, the biggest problem online gambling may pose is to kids; concerned parents who use "smart screen" software to block access to unwanted sites, or monitor usage, will want to include the word casinos.

Bettors who want to try a little gambling might want to visit WagerNet, in Belize, http://www.vegas.com/wagernet, or Casinos of the South Pacific, http://eagle. sangamon.edu:8081. At Caribbean Casino, based in the Turks and Caicos Islands, you need electronic DigiCash to play poker, blackjack, lotteries, and sports betting: http://www.casino.org/cc.•Sports International, based in Antigua in the West Indies, offers sports betting (mini-mum $50 wager), plus casino games while you're waiting: http://www.intersphere.com.bet. Check local and state restrictions on offshore sports betting before you register. Sites without monetary transaction include betting pools, http://www.hal.com/~markg, and Virtual Vegas, http://www.virtualvegas.com.

▶ *Entertainment*

Given the Net's exponential growth, the entertainment industry is eyeing it with great interest. And the Net holds great potential as a delivery system for the entertainment industry.

For example, a future Blockbuster Video site may let you browse and order online, and spool up your selection for playing on your computer screen at a specified time.

Moreover, the niche-targeting and community-building that the Net enables holds a wealth of possibility for the world of entertainment. Two representative online entertainment magazines are *Gigaplex!* (http://www.gigaplex.com) and *Mr. Showbiz* (http://web3.starwave.com/showbiz). The Emmys and the Oscars have their own web pages: http://www.emmys.org/tindex.html and http://ampas.org/ampas.

Usenet is full of fan clubs for TV, music, movies, and sports stars. Yahoo lists over one hundred sites for stars, and about seven hundred for individual programs. And web pages that include reader forums are ideal for the devoted followers of shows that command minute attention to the smallest detail such as "X-Files" (http://www.delphi.com/xfiles, http://www.cs.uml.edu/~ccashman/x-files/x-files.html, http://www.neosoft.com/sbanks/xfiles/xfiles.html, and http://www.rutgers.edu/x-files.html) and

"StarTrek" (character-specific pages, clubs and organizations, official Paramount pages, fans' pages, Asimov's pages, pictures and ascii art, sounds, games, simulations, articles and reviews, Federation history, faqs, checklists, warp velocities, subspace, transporters and replicators, other Treknology, Borg screensaver, Captain Kirk singing "Mr. Tambourine Man," etc. (http://voyager. paramount.com, http://www.tos.net/tosguide, http:// ccc-shop.wpi.edu/rogue/trek, ftp://coe.montana.edu).

And you never know who might turn up. Consider the following example: The Usenet "Northern Exposure" fan club (alt.tv.northern-exposure) created a faq surpassing any of the books on the series. People who live in and around Roslyn, Washington, kept the group updated as to gossip from the set. And, after lurking (silently reading the group for several weeks), one of the actors came forward—and admitted that participating in the conference was entertaining for him, too. He revealed such fascinating arcana to the group as how show members got things past TPTB (the powers that be).

▶ *Humor*

How many people on the Internet does it take to screw in a light bulb? I dunno, but the world's biggest collection of light-bulb jokes has appeared on the Internet. For instance, how many members of the Starship *U.S.S. Enterprise* does it take to change a light bulb? Answer: seven.

```
Scotty will report to Captain Kirk that the light
bulb in the Engineering Section is burnt out, to
which Kirk will send Bones to pronounce the bulb
dead. Scotty, after checking around, notices that
```

they have no more new light bulbs, and complains that he can't see in the dark to tend to his engines. Kirk must make an emergency stop at the next uncharted planet, Alpha Regula IV, to procure a light bulb from the natives. Kirk, Spock, Bones, Sulu, and three red shirt security officers beam down. The three security officers are promptly killed by the natives, and the rest of the landing party is captured. Meanwhile, back in orbit, Scotty notices a Klingon ship approaching and must warp out of orbit to escape detection. Bones cures the native king who is suffering from the flu, and as a reward the landing party is set free and given all the light bulbs they can carry. Scotty cripples the Klingon ship and warps back to the planet just in time to beam up Kirk, *et al*. The new bulb is inserted, and the Enterprise continues with its five-year mission.

Is the Internet having fun yet? One Usenet group—Rec.humor.funny—has over two hundred thousand jokesters. Now and then, people even summarize all the jokes in a certain category (like light-bulb jokes, or lawyer jokes) and post a big anthology of them. The Web's getting whimsical and witty, with such sites as:

The Dilbert Zone, http://www.Unitedmedia/comics/dilbert

Comedy Central, http://www.comcentral.com

Where the Buffalo Roam, http://plaza.xor.com/Wtbr and

The Wrecked Humor Page, http://www.cs.odu.edu/cashman/humor.html

From time to time, it's not uncommon for waves of jokes to wash over a group in a mailing list on any topic. Jay Leno's home page (http://www.nbctonightshow.

com) not only has his calendar of guests, but also has jokes updated daily. Dave Letterman updates his Top Ten list on the Internet, via a mailing list and the web (http://www.cbs.com/lateshow). And my boss at school and I often swap computer jokes with each other and a small circle of friends by e-mail. In short, the Internet is a great place to hang out if only to catch the latest joke before it starts making the rounds—plus the ones no one else ever hears.

▶ *Travel*

Not all Internauts are mouse potatoes, judging from the great amount of travel resources online. In travel forums, people trade gossip about places to go and things to see. City.Net will tell you about over six hundred and fifty cities in the world, http://www.city.net.com. Condé Nast's *Traveler* (http://www.cntraveler.com) and *Tripod's Travel Services* (http://www.tripod.com/travel/) include a number of informative features.

▶ *Miscellaneous*

In 1990, John Romkey hooked up his toaster to the Internet. Telnet in to his Net site and you could look through a video monitor at his toaster. Strange, but weird. It spawned a craze of its own. Someone else hooked up a Leggo Loader. A campus coffee percolator is monitored by a camera, and the camera is hooked up to a web page, so that the lazybones in the computer department can know when the coffee is ready—and everyone else on the web can, too. An upside to this is that now there are annual Christmas trees put online every year.

The latest twist in this trend is Tele-Garden, a virtual community plot, where you can operate a robot arm over a planter box to plant your own seeds, water them, and watch them grow, alongside other telegardeners. Http://www.usc.edu/dept/garden.

ARTS

> When businessmen gather together, they discuss art. When artists gather together, they discuss business.
>
> —OSCAR WILDE

▶ Pictures

When painters no longer painted exclusively on walls of cave or church but used canvas instead, art became mobile. This meant, too, an artist had greater choice of subject, but then had to get the word out.

Now, the Internet can get the word out, exhibit the work, and even sell it before the paint has dried. And the Internet opens access to media without paint, to collaboration, and to experiment.

The list ranges from @art, African art, Ansel Adams, apparitions, arboretums, Asian, and astronomical—to 3-D kinetic art, the Smithsonian Institution, Survival Research Laboratories, Andy Warhol, something called the Weird Workshop, world art treasures, and Yale University's Peabody Museum. In between, there are things like Bucky Fuller and Japanimation, pottery and electronic poetry.

Now that it's becoming not just text-based but multi-media, the Internet is becoming the world's biggest arts happening.

We've often spoken of Internet culture. Now we can glimpse how cyberculture can transform general culture.

For one thing, on the Internet, the boundary between High and Low Art is porous. The Louvre (http://www.louvre.fr) exists side-by-side with a museum of international graffiti (http://www.gatech.edu/desoto/graf/Index.Art_Crimes.html). Each has its url, but the boundary between them persists, insofar as neither adds the other to its Cool Links list.

If you're PostModernist, the Internet is PostModernist: there's no core, but what you make of it. Each facet of the crystal can be as important as any other. The Fluxus conceptual art page, for example, is laid out like a board game, a game of chance: http://www.panix.com/fluxus.

And the Internet is Classical if you're a Classicist. The hierarchies are still there. The Canon. For example, it took three hundred years for Dante's works to spread to all of Europe; today, all major commentaries on Dante in the world are being collated and merged together for the first time into one central repository, linked to his text, at the Dante Project. Telnet: Library.darmouth.edu, and log-in "connect dante."

High-, low-, or middlebrow. Take your pick.

Culture in the Internet can be free-associative, self-directed, and shared. For instance, the Australian National University's excellent online museum has many exhibits.

You can take one any time, using hypertext as your tour guide. Touring the palace of Diocletian at Split (http://rubens.anu.edu.au/), if the text refers to a word you wish to know more about and it's highlighted, click on it. The word arch, for example, will instantly produce for you an illustrated history of the arch.

As in real life, art online can be uplifting, vitalizing, ennobling, empowering—or entertaining—or escapist. That is, we can spend an hour visiting Diocletian's palace without ever realizing that a few clicks away people have been telling firsthand of a war raging unstopped for over three years there, in what was Yugoslavia. In the Internet, as in real life, the boundaries of art do not change. War is not art. And art has never stopped a war.

But art makes us aware, if not awake.

America is becoming more and more awake to the many possibilities of art. Our art museums are becoming more and more popular to broader numbers of citizens; New York museum attendance outranks that for all the city's professional sports teams combined. On the Internet, museums, too, are beginning to come into their own.

At last count, there were over two hundred and fifty museums and galleries online. Major, multimillion-dollar museums as well as uknown artists are opening up their galleries and studios to the public. Works in archives too rare for the public to handle are being digitized and made available on the Net, and artists unrepresented by galleries have a virtual venue. *OTIS (the Operative Term Is Stimulate)* is the granddaddy of purely virtual arts museums. Based (physically) in Omaha, Nebraska, it's "a gallery, an exhibition space, a database, a browseable sketchbook of the world's artists, artists of all disciplines and cultures."

Otis invites any art that can be somehow digitized into a binary file and displayed on a computer screen, and there's no charge for exhibition or to view or copy images. Its organizers state: "Beyond mere storage/exhibition of images, OTIS seeks to involve artists with one another via collaboration." Indeed, the Internet's ability to mediate collaboration should prove very fruitful to the art of the future—especially to those new interactive/ multimedia arts which, by definition, involve multiartist interaction to produce.

Works on Otis will remain there in perpetuity, in "digital immortality." Its organizers state the following:

> Otis seeks to make today's art available to future generations. Utilizing the pure information binary storage of images and the subsequent ease of replication and distribution, the plan is to so widely disseminate the gallery as to ensure its perpetual existence. The growing vastness of the Internet should itself guarantee that anything stored on Otis for any length of time will make its way to thousands of computer screens and onto thousands of digital storage devices. Images can then never be destroyed, and hopefully the structure of Otis will provide an easy and congenial method of browsing and appreciating the art of today's artists for the children-at-heart of 2113.

How to reach it: Ftp: sunsite.unc.edu. Path: pub/ multimedia/pictures/Otis

Web: http://www.otis.org.

FineArt Forum is one of the best specialized, top-level guides to art online, begun way back in 1987. It has three components: 1) it produces a monthly e-mail digest, 2) its online gopher contains a database of arts-related material, including a directory, 3) it hosts, since 1994, an interactive, multimedia site on the web. The web has more up-to-date directories than the gopher, such as Jane Patterson's list of art-related mailing lists, which includes: arts deadlines (competitions and contests), arts management, book arts, ceramics, comics, dance, digital video, fantasy costume, historic costumes, lighting, medieval performing arts, puppet theater, quilting, 3-D photography, and wearable art.

How to reach it:

To subscribe to FineArt Forum, e-mail: fineart_request@gu.edu.au with the message "sub fineart <first-name last-name>." To cancel your subscription, e-mail to listproc@gu.edu.au with the message "unsub fineart."

Gopher: gopher.msstate.edu/11/Online_services/fine art_online.

Web: http://www.msstate.edu/Fineart_Online/home.html.

Besides these, and the subject directories, Michael Clark has recently published his extensive survey of Internet art resources, called *Cultural Treasures on the Internet*.

And the Internet itself is becoming an art gallery, as people design more and more pictorially fascinating web pages. For example, some digital artists have discovered a glitch in Netscape that will produce a shimmering flash

FEAST YOUR EYES

Adobe
  http://www.adobe.com
Art Links
  http://www.fine-art.com/link.html
Art Online
  http://www.terra.net/artonline
Casbah
  http://www.dsiegel.com
Center for the Arts, Yerba Buena Gardens
  http://www.hia.com/hia/yerbabuena
Clement Mok Designs
  http://www.cmdesigns.com
Communication Arts
  http://www.commarts.com
DesignOnline
  http://www.dol.com
*George Eastman House International Museum of
Photography & Film*
  http://www.it.rit.edu/~gehouse
Golden Road
  http://www.goldweb.com
Internet Museum
  http://www.artnet.org/iamfree
Leonardo Museum
  http://www.leonardo.net/museum/main.html
Online Visual Literacy Project
  http://www.pomona.edu/visual-lit
Outpost
  http://www.users.interport.net/~outpost
World-Wide Arts Resources
  http://www.concourse.com/wwar
Ylem (artists using technology)
  http://www.ylem.org

of colors and they program that effect in to their web pages. Other artists are creating images that have pictorial links within—using images as navigational points rather than words. One has created a mystery told entirely through pictures, which the user interacts with.

Architecture, fashion, design, and typography departments at universities have richly designed pages, as do independent design companies. If your calling card speaks for who you are, these pages speak for themselves. However, you can appreciate good design wherever it occurs—such as at a site for mountain biking, called MudSluts (http://www.rubyslippers.com/funhouse/index.html) or flyfishing (http://www.flyshop.com).

And, speaking of artists painting on caves: important cave paintings were discovered in Combe D'Ardèche, France, December 1994. Only one month later, they were displayed worldwide: http://www.culture.fr/gvpda.htm. (How long did it take for the Dead Sea Scrolls to be published?)

▶ *Sounds*

Two compression softwares have made pictures widely available on the Net: gif (graphics interchange format) and JPEG (Joint Photographers Experts Group). Then along came MPEG (Motion Picture Expert Group) and people into sound discovered it could do compression from ten to one, while retaining cd-quality sound fidelity.

Music.

Another M word is *MIDI* (Musical Instrument Digital Interface), which, with the appropriate hardware, enables musical information such as note names, durations, etc., to be recorded into your computer and "played back" on any sound source. And *Mbone,* which enabled the Internet to broadcast the Rolling Stones live.

The computer has become a microphone, sound studio, and its very own MTV.

Four-dimensional (4-D) media (like video and film) still soak up a tremendous amount of bandwidth. But if you're looking for just sounds, however, there are ftp warehouses chock full of sounds, with everything from London's Big Ben tolling midnight to Jack Nicholson doing his chilling Joker laugh. (I've downloaded a little loop of Tibetan monks chanting Om, which I play while I'm working at the computer if I'm particularly stressed, and it helps me chill out. But sometimes the recording I also have of the theme to the "X-Files" also has the same effect.)

For some sounds warehouses, ftp to sunsite.unc.edu/pub/multimedia, sounds.sdsu.edu/sounds, and ftp.funet.fi/pub/sounds.

4-D arts are still in their Internet infancy. Yet some examples of music's presence today might be harbingers of directions toward which the Internet dial might be tuned in the future.

One example is a music directory. You say you want to find a known band? The Ultimate Band List can point you to six hundred bands on the Net. Http://www.american.recordings.com/wwwofmusic/ubl/ubl.shtml.

You say you're looking for unknown bands?
Our next example is the Internet Underground Music

Archive (IUMA, pronounced yewma)—one of the most illustrious cyberpreneurialism success stories so far. In late 1993, two twenty-something friends, Jeff Patterson and Rob Lord, based (physically) in Santa Cruz (down the vine from Silicon Valley), California, met when Patterson wanted to post a demo of his band on the Net and Lord helped him use mpeg to do so. Then they both looked at each other and said, "What if other bands could do this too?" So they set up a site where independent musicians could make their work available on the Internet for anyone to download and listen to. They're not a distributor—you can order direct from each artist—but they have created an alternative distribution model.

A visit to the site is practically mandatory just to gander at the design of their interface. The style effectively collages retro-1950s imagery—the excitement over technology, such as home appliances and space exploration—to capture the excitement of exploring today's Net technology. Music can be selected by genre—from classical and jazz, to all the many niches of contemporary modern music, with today's ultraspecific names like speed metal and hardcore industrial, which is where Iuma really holds its own. "The concept of teenagers with a cultural identity of their own," Lord points out, "was only invented in the 1950s. And then it was pretty simple. Now there's a tremendous differentiation of teenagers. Take rave music, for example: there's jungle, tribal, trance, and ambient. Do you know how much the fans of each of these subsubsubgenres want to know about the latest? Damn, do they want to know."

Using the open system of the Internet to create an open

music exchange quickly clicked. They soon had as many groups as the Ultimate Band List. Music mogul David Geffen visited the site one night—and *discovered* two groups and signed them up for juicy record contracts. And when they were gathering about 3,000 visitors a day, and 45,000 registered users, Iuma took the plunge and became a business. Downloads remain free, but with all that foot traffic, they began to sell ad space (sponsors) at this new kind of hi-fi lp party. "At first we found it difficult to shift from a group of inspired volunteers in a clubhouse into a professionally run business," Lord recalls of the transition. "But you can be a for-profit company and be really altruistic. I don't think that we're fundamentally different now from how we were at the start."

Boasting 350,000 "hits" per week, the site now plays host to over 700 bands, plus a half-dozen online music magazines—including *Addicted to Noise,* whose online counterpart has *daily* music news, soundclips, etc. (To dial direct, http://www.addict.com.) We say, Yo, check Iuma out. Awesome. Http://www.iuma.com.

You say you're looking for some music, but you don't know what?

HOMR, a product of MIT's Media Lab, recommends music to you based on your likes and dislikes. How? First, you rate a select number of musicians from its database—out of about 2,500 musicians, total. Then your profile is matched with profiles in the database, which are similar to yours. It can be very accurate.

One person who tried it out found the music it recommended included a song she'd been trying to identify for weeks after hearing it on the radio. The more who try it, the better it gets. This is the harbinger of true interactivity. Http://ringo.media.mit.edu/ringo.html.

You say there's a megaevent you can't go to, but you wish you could?

The 25th anniversary of Woodstock (1994) didn't try to repeat the incredible original. Lightning doesn't strike in the same place twice. Or does it? Woodstock was the first music megaevent with an Internet counterpart. If you visit the site today, not only can you get a good rundown on the events, but there's even a scrapbook. People had their picture taken, and a microphone recorded their impressions. (Comparing the first scrapbook entries with the last, it goes from kind of quick, excited exuberance—to mellow, laid-back drawl.) Http://www.well.com/woodstock.

Whatever happened to Adam Curry, the MTV dj?

Adam is testimonial proof that there is life after MTV. He's now a dj on the Internet, with his own online service—Metaverse—featuring music charts, video and sound clips, and juicy gossip. And of course he links to home pages devoted to particular artists—Frank Sinatra to Nine Inch Nails. Http://metaverse.com.

You say you want to visit a rock-and-roll fantasy theme park? Rocktropolis is the place for you: http://www.underground.net/rocktropolis.

You say you're into chants? (No, I don't mean men beating a drum on a vision quest. Remember way, way back in the summer of 1994—when high art hit the top-40 with medieval chants?) Scholars of chant have their very own cool web site, called Cantus. Cool? Like that master gene map, it's a central database for chantologists around the world—plus, it mingles art history, church history, and hagiography: Gopher://vms.gopher.cua.edu/gopher_root_music:[_Cantus]

And for all you Deadheads, the Grateful Dead's alive and well on the Internet. (When Jerry quit the gig a bit early and traded in his guitar for a celestial harp, his signature was reborn overnight worldwide as the Internet held a noisy, heartfelt, mass wake in forums and on the web. For days, people posted a line or two—to Jerry and to each other—about one or two a minute.) If you're a Deadhead, you won't want just one, so here's a bouquet of urls, for a hatful of virtual rain:

Http://www.dead.net
Http://www.sirius.com/~jmelloy/jerry.html (our favorite roadside shrine)
Http://www.icstrategies.com/garcia
Http://sedona.uaphys.alaska.edu/~price/ded.html
Http://www.primenet.com/~bobkirk/index.html
Http://www.uccs.edu/~ddodd/gdhome.html
Http://pathfinder.com/people/jerry/index.html
Http://www.jagunet.com/ideal/garcia
Http://www.cs.cmu.edu/~mleone/dead.html
Http://wl.iglou.com/hippie/hippie1.html
Http://rockweb.cybercom.net/cgi-bin/nph-jerry-chat
Http://www.human.com/jerrymail

If the thunder don't get you, the lightning will.

Artists are microcosms of the human condition. What do they strive after? What will they do next? And, meanwhile, how do they survive?

On the Internet, artists keep on truckin'.

GOVERNMENT

▶ *World affairs*

 . . . one big family hugging close to the ball of Earth for its life and being.
—CARL SANDBURG, *The Family of Man*

It's natural so many Internet books should have an image of the globe on them. The Net gives us literal opportunities to widen our horizon as to what we consider ours. When we're chatting in a conference, sometimes we stop and notice that a correspondent is in Moscow or Singapore. Sometimes we don't even notice it.

Let's think back to the Internet's origins. In the beginning, the Internet was, in part, a strategic military application in the face of global war. It wasn't as commonplace as it is now to think of our collective well-being. Now even our economies are globally intertwined. We realize more and more that we're part of a network, all bound together. Call it Spaceship Earth. When anyone on board goes down, the snarl-up could cost money, even lives.

This realization brought 282 international delegates, following the horror of World War II, to convene on April 25, 1945, and draft a charter for the United Nations; http://www.un.org. Things no longer happen in one part of the world anymore. Today, we're more aware of our global interdependence, in terms of health, security, economy, and ecology.

In his groundbreaking book *Global Communication & International Relations,* Howard Frederick states, "Today, communication among nations must be a two-way process in which partners—both individual and collective, carry on a democratic and balanced dialogue in which the mass media operate in the service of peace and global understanding." Certainly, the Internet can play a large role in facilitating such dialog.

Whether between nations—or within government agencies of the same nation and region, as well as within and between corporations—collaboration on projects using network telecommunications such as the Internet can not only eliminate wasteful duplication, but also help bridge issues of difference and mediate areas of common concern.

Now that the Cold War between capitalism and communism is over, we might consider nations in terms of how they allocate resources between the private and public sector—and their degree of openness with regard to information.

The dramatic roles that modern information technologies have played in closed societies are worth a brief recital. In 1969, after Soviet tanks crushed the Prague Spring, a Soviet journalist asked Brezhnev where could he write an article about it. Brezhnev replied: "Write it all down, but only in a single copy, and send it only to me." When the Xerox came along, it helped create a powerful underground press movement in Russia. (Now that the Iron Curtain is down, the world can read dozens of revelatory documents from the archives of the KGB, http://sunsite.unc.edu/pjones/Russian/outline.html.)

In 1979, the Ayatollah Khomeini smuggled tape cassettes he made from exile in France to his followers in Iran, which were duped into thousands of copies and played in rallies in huge mosques; following his revolution, he led his nation on a retreat from Modernism. Today the Internet is banned in Iran.

Fax and modem, camcorder and satellite played key roles in 1989 when three million Chinese people stood up and nonviolently challenged an unchallenged system (which, in turn, the government said was all made up by CNN). Tiananmen Archives, including the boy who stood up to the tanks, are available on the Internet for all to see and judge for themselves: http://www.cnd.org/June4th. All three instances, above, represent information societies in varying degrees of openness.

Free flow of information has always been essential for our own democratic way of life, as the former Iron Curtain countries are now learning for themselves. Each citizen is expected to be able to draw from a number of points of view as to the issues facing them, so as to cast informed votes thereon. Open access to information is thus essential to a democratic way of life.

In a closed information society, information media act as a running dog, obeying a master. In an open information society, information media can act as a watchdog as well as a lapdog—and, now, even as a retriever.

What next? People who live by reading the future in a crystal ball may come to eat ground glass. The best we might do could be to acknowledge, as Frederick points out, the growing global awareness of the freedom to communicate (including the right to associate and to privacy) as an essential freedom—a right more extensive even than freedom of information (the right to inform and be informed).

► *Access*

> I know no safe depository of the ultimate powers of the society but the people themselves, and if we think them not enlightened enough to exercise their control, with a wholesome discretion, the remedy is not to take it from them, but to inform their discretion.
>
> —THOMAS JEFFERSON

The largest producer of information in the world is the U.S. government, which is also the largest national consumer and distributor of information. America is literally a commonwealth of information. Yet, when President Clinton's administration took office, the White House communications system itself still had an antiquated telephone switchboard, with an operator wearing a headphone (much like Lily Tomlin's character, Ernestine), plugging cables into slots. President Clinton recalls, "I walked into the Oval Office—it's supposed to be the nerve center of the United States—and we found Jimmy Carter's telephone system. No speaker phone, no conference calls, but anybody in the office could punch the lighted button and listen to the President talk. So that I could have the conference call I didn't want, but not the one I did."

As of June 1, 1993, the White House went online: http://www.whitehouse.gov.

Also to go online during the Clinton administration have been the Library of Congress, the IRS, the National

Archive, NASA, the Department of State, the CIA, the Pentagon, the Department of Energy, the Commerce Department, the Consumer Information Center, and the Small Business Administration, to name but a few—as well as hundreds more state and local agencies. (For a beginning directory, telnet fedworld.gov or http:// www.fedworld.gov., furnishing over one hundred federal BBS's, courtesy of the Federal Technical Information Service. There are a couple of books devoted to indexing government resources online. *Washington Online,* for example, by Bruce Maxwell, author of a book on Washington BBS's, takes each access point and breaks it down, explaining what's available and how to get there.)

The following is a quick example of what can happen in the transition from print access to digital. When President Clinton announced the NAFTA agreement on a Wednesday, a publisher produced it as a "quick" book by Monday. Within a week of publication it shot up to the bestseller charts. Folks online, however, knew it had been posted on the Internet the day it was announced— for free, and in a more fluid format.

Thomas (after Thomas Jefferson) is one of the most recently touted federal web sites. Here, you'll find the Congressional Record of daily proceedings on the House and Senate floors searchable by key words, bill number, or sponsor, and full text of legislation and major "hot" bills currently receiving floor action in Congress. There are the gophers for the House and Senate; e-mail directories of representatives and committees; faqs, including "How Our Laws Are Made"; plus links to C-SPAN (Cable-Satellite Public Affairs Network) and other sites: http://thomas.loc.gov.

State and local governments are following suit. California—with proportionately the most Net access of the nation—has an equally exemplary home page on the Web—with a subject-driven almanac approach, plus timely updates (such as up-to-the-minute freeway traffic): http://www.ca.gov. The Golden State also has local sites online such as the Association of Bay Area Governments (ABAG), http://www.abag.ca.gov, in Northern California.

And, in Southern California, since 1989, Santa Monica has been building its marvelous, pioneering model of electronic democracy it calls Public Electric Network (PEN). PEN provides information about City Hall (from legislation agenda to environmental programs, from the Planning and Building Department to airport and bus information, from park schedules to bid deadlines) and civic organizations (neighborhood groups, disabled and senior citizens services, community services, schools, cultural arts). Numerous, convenient online forms enable citizens to conduct transactions online, such as getting a building permit, renewing a business license, applying for a library card, and checking out a book. It also enables citizens to send e-mail to city officials and departments (required by the city manager to respond within twenty-four hours), community organizations, and other PEN users, as well as to participate in online forums about such topics as city issues, education, science, California, and the nation, leisure, etc.: http://pen.ci.santa-monica.ca.us/.

The Clinton administration reversed a Reagan policy that had defined government information as a commodity, often available for sale to private industry. Instead, the new policy advises government agencies to maximize the amount of information available to the public and prohibits them from charging more than the cost of delivering the materials. Implementation of the new rule falls to each agency and department to comply with in its own way (but Congress may enact some of the policies into law). A recent case of interest is EDGAR (Electronic Data Gathering, Analysis, and Retrieval System).

From January 1994 to October 1995, a nonprofit Internet Multicasting Service maintained Edgar as a site on the Internet, making available the corporate filings at the Securities and Exchange Commission (SEC) and the Patent and Trademark Office, twenty-four hours after their filing, for free. During that time, it sent out some 3 million SEC filings and 1.5 million patent documents to individuals, Wall Street firms, and college students.

Then the grant ran out.

At that point, the project's director, Carl Malamud, put the project in the lap of the federal agencies themselves, saying that the recent Republican "Contract with America" mandated them to take over the project or start an equivalent one of their own. He was referring to the 1995 Paperwork Reduction Act, calling on agencies with public records stored electronically to provide "timely and equitable access" in an "efficient, effective, and economical manner."

The SEC took it over, saying it would entail no new employees and only a modest cost. SEC Chair Arthur Levitt, Jr., stated, "Taxpayers and shareholders have already paid to compile this information; they should not have to pay again." Referring to one private company's offer to take over the site, making files available for browsing for ten minutes, after which there would be a fee, he added, ''A library that charges people by the page or by the minute is no longer a library.'' In addition to the new site address, http://www.sec.gov, the information is mirrored with additional materials at http://www. disclosure.com.

Another aspect to the issue of access is the question of access to the Net for the broad base of citizenry—not as consumers to be targeted, but as citizens to be informed, for the public good. As of this writing, for example, there's a petition filed by Apple Computers before the FCC (Federal Communications Commission) to allocate 300 MHz of spectrum (dubbed the National Information Infrastructure Band) for high-capacity, unlicensed wireless data, to be allocated for free, public use. The petition states, ''To a very significant extent, networks will be built, and services provided, only when they can be justified by anticipated advertising revenues, service fees, access charges. . . . The NII Band would advance a host of public policy objectives, including assuring that all segments of society have access to the 'Information Superhighway.' '' For more information on the current status of the petition, http://www.warpspeed.com. (Another transmission medium that might easily support such service would be cable.)

▶ *Security*

The government has a stake in seeing that the Internet provides its constituency with better access to it. And the government can play a role in seeing that its constituency has better access to the Internet. Now we turn the frame around, to the question of the government's access to its constituency. To do so, we must first prepare the ground with a preliminary issue: security.

QUESTION: *How secure is the Internet?*

As of right now, not very. The phone, cellular networks, and computers are all vulnerable.

QUESTION: *Can someone put a virus in my computer through e-mail or reading a file online?*

No. It would have to be through software that you downloaded and used. That said, the occurrence of viruses is rare, and virus protection is always available online.

QUESTION: *Can someone crack into my computer while I'm online with my Internet provider?*

No. They might crack into your provider's server, but not *your* computer.

(Incidentally, cracking is the correct term, as opposed to hacking. In computerese, hacking is the general area of scouting around—which, as we've seen, becomes an essential part of the online world—rather than clandestine entry, or cracking.)

The classic book in this field is astronomer Clifford Stoll's *The Cuckoo's Egg,* which recounts the discovery in 1986 that ArpaNet had been cracked, and the subsequent stalking of its wily invader. It reads like a cross between a computer detective story and a science-fiction novel. A more recent title is Joshua Quittner and Michelle Slatalla's *Masters of Deception.*

In 1994, the Secret Service reported 2,600 attempted break-ins to Internet-linked computer facilities. And in 1995, a kid named Kevin Mitnick, having already served time in jail for cracking, violated his parole and went and did it again. Before he was caught a second time, he'd accessed billions of dollars' worth of information from remote computers, some of them Internet providers. Interestingly, he didn't use any of the stolen info: like a teenager hopping fences, he seemed more interested in cracking people's locks than doing any tangible harm.

Mitnick's capture was possible due to close collaboration between the government and the Internet community, and the nature of the Internet itself—that is, the immediacy of communication, the ability to copy files from machine to machine, and the availability of a pool of expertise and resources.

In the course of reporting the case for *Cyberspace Today,* I interviewed a number of people, including U.S. Attorney Kent Walker. When I asked him about users utilizing encryption software to prevent communication over the Net from being cracked, he said, "Encryption has many beneficial social uses, but unbreakable encryption poses a significant social threat where it makes it impossible for government to find out about criminal activity. The Department of Justice and the Administration strike a balance through Clipper Chip. [Clipper Chip is an encryption software with a kind of trapdoor that would allow the government access into a computer or computer network—with a warrant.] The goal is to encourage Americans to adopt strong encryption, as part of their privacy interests, but allows law enforcement, if need be, after government obtains a court order."

Critics argue that it would allow anyone else access, too. However, the government remains adamant. In fact, the government has for some time classified encryption as a munition, and thus bars it from export. (Netscape and Lotus cannot currently be exported as they have security technology in them.)

This has prevented any commercial software manufacturer from getting into the encryption field in any big way, because they'd have to invest in developing and marketing two programs, domestic and foreign. Yet, as we've seen, the Net inherently takes us local to global in the blink of an eye. Computer companies, specifically, sell more than half their products overseas, and weak security systems would open the door for foreign companies to gain that market. In short, along with the lack of a standard method for financial transaction, the lack of a strong standard of cryptography is a roadblock to the information economy.

Some critics of the government stance contend that the government is using outmoded criteria and is still low on the telecom learning curve, needing to be educated by its more technosavvy constituents. Stanford law teacher and activist Carey Heckman told us, ''Government representatives have security and law enforcement agencies whispering in their ears, 'If you loosen up and take away limitations on the export of encryption technology, bombs will go off in buildings,' and most representatives don't understand encryption technology. So they're made nervous.''

This also reflects an aftershock, as it were, to the Cold War, when advanced computer technology was classified as military technology. This is not to say the government's fears are unjustified now that the Cold War is declared over. Spies aren't about to all just fade away—when they can ply their skills at the new frontier of corporate espionage. And in 1995, the world witnessed a new kind of terrorism, one without a state, when a weird Japanese cult set off nerve-gas bombs in subway stations. The cult members were computer networked.

Federal "cyberswat" teams are beefing up their force. And Kevin Mitnick? He was sentenced quickly—to eight months, for but one of the twenty-one charges against him. The other twenty charges were dropped—it is believed, lest the facts about his techniques be publicly aired in trial.

Meanwhile, within a week of its going public, Netscape's watered-down foreign encryption was cracked by a graduate student in France. (Within about a month, the domestic version was also cracked.) And that same week, a ring of Russians were apprehended cracking into a Citibank electronic money transfer network, in the process of attempting to steal over a cool $10 million—yet a mere drop in the bucket. *Information Week* reports that online data theft in the U.S. amounts to over $10 billion a year.

▶ *Formulating policy*

> A country that works smarter; enjoys more efficient, less costly government, guided by a well-informed citizenry; that produces high-quality jobs and educated citizens to fill them; that paves a road away from poverty; that promotes lifelong learning, public health, and the cultural life of our communities: this is the promise of the National Information Infrastructure.
>
> —*National Strategy for Civic Networking: A Vision of Change,*
> CENTER FOR CIVIC NETWORKING

Thus far, the government has done the right thing in grubstaking the high-risk development of the Internet, funding it, sticking to it over the course of several decades, then getting out of the way. As a result, the U.S. today is the home of the majority of Internet users, hosts, networks, and hardware/software developers.

Today, the government is faced by such issues, as we've seen, of copyright, access, privacy, and security, as it tries to formulate the future of the national information infrastructure. As our accompanying diagram shows, the arena for formulating telecommunications policy is a web of many strands, posing many questions. For example, will the government apply new tax and accounting standards for new technology? Currently, the U.S. semiconductor industry faces five-year depreciation timetables for products with three-year life spans, for instance, versus Japan, where chip manufacturers write off their fabrication plants in one year. And what is the appreciable lifetime of software?

By way of another example, the Center for Community Economic Research (CCER) has noted that online commerce will have an effect on state and local taxes. With state and local governments already losing $3.3 billion each year to untaxed interstate sales, they stand to face devastating losses in local government revenue, which might call for government reorganization.

Of the eleven bodies in our diagram, we'll focus on citizen groups. Four such groups, actively working on legislative issues, provide excellent examples of how open the arena is in this formative phase. Then, in the chapter to follow, we'll continue the thread with a few

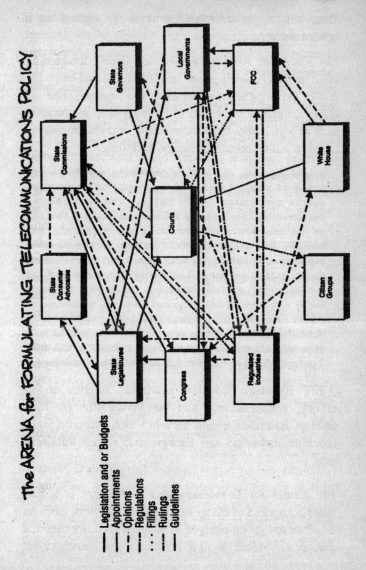

The ARENA for FORMULATING TELECOMMUNICATIONS POLICY

Legislation and or Budgets
Appointments
Opinions
Regulations
Filings
Rulings
Guidelines

more citizen groups whose activism is slanted more toward society.

The Electronic Frontier Foundation (EFF), founded in 1990, makes its voice heard in Washington and helps the rest of the population understand Washington. Their archives contain a great deal of issue-specific information such as legislation, legal information, and documents relating to online communications, including:

> a mailing list for online community activists and names of about two dozen relevant Usenet groups; alerts concerning legal, policy, and cultural developments affecting the online community; listings of online activist organizations—regional, national, and international; guides to the federal Freedom of Information Act; a tool kit of resources about online privacy, including anonymous posting and encryption; Congressional phone and fax numbers; a primer of lobbying and advocacy techniques; a list of newspaper and magazine e-mail addresses; a guide to Internet resources for nonprofit public service organizations; and Citizen's Guide to the Net, a primer on using the Net for activism and advocacy.

EFF maintains extensive electronic archives at ftp. eff.org, gopher.eff.org, and http://www.eff.org/. They have an automated e-mail address which will send you a brochure, calendar, and background: e-mail info@eff. org.

The Center for Democracy and Technology is a new voice composed of many key legal people from EFF. As an advocacy group pledged to advance civil liberties and democratic values in new computer and constitutional communications media, the Center pursues policy research, public education, and coalition building. Issues on their agenda are free speech, the free flow of information online, privacy, public access to electronic government information, and monitoring technology trends to identify developments which contribute to universal digital access and other democratic goals. E-mail: info@ cdt.org.

The Progress & Freedom Foundation (PPF) is a research and education organization, with a strong base in Newt Gingrich's camp, dedicated to "creating a positive vision of the future founded in the historical principles of the American idea." For the latest release of their provocative *Magna Carta for the Knowledge Age,* first drafted in 1994 by Esther Dyson, George Gilder, Jay Keyworth, and Alvin Toffler, http://aspen.pff.org.

The *GovAccess* mailing list is a sterling exemplar and very practical bulletin consisting of:

```
information, action-alerts, and often ardent advo-
cacy [about] effective citizen participation in the
process of our own governance; protections and im-
plications regarding constitutional civil liber-
ties; citizen-access to federal, state and/or local
government; government access to and records about
citizens—covert and overt; and federal, state, and
local legislation-in-process, statutes, regula-
tions, and court cases and decisions pertaining to
these issues.
```

For a brief description and subscription information, e-mail majordomo@well.com with the message: Info

GovAccess. As its editor says, "It's free—worth at least every penny you pay for it."

We note that GovAccess is maintained neither by a group nor by lawyers. In 1993, the editor, Jim Warren, single-handedly spearheaded a successful campaign to make California legislation and statutes available via the public nets without state fees.

As such, he's an example that the system works and that just one person can make a difference.

▶ *Toward an electronic republic*

Marshall McLuhan, patron saint of modern media studies, noted that as the speed of information increases, politics tends to move toward the immediate involvement of the entire community in the central acts of decision. Will the Internet replace government? Hardly. But it is very tempting to imagine, for example, how lawmakers would no longer be able to engage in filibustering if they held bill sessions over the Internet.

Along with the emergent importance of radio talk shows, the Net is becoming an important factor, too, in political discourse. Some public forums in Usenet with the prefix alt.politics have been logging one to three posts every minute, representing a very sizable chunk of population, possibly in the millions. And the web is proving a prime information outlet for legislators and political parties, conventions, and committees. Derek Baker, the Webmaster for the official Phil-Gramm-for-President page, told *Web Review:* "Our page lets the Senator go straight to voters with his message. And it's not just a 30-second sound-bite either. We offer up his entire welfare proposal, the entire text of every speech he makes, just reams and reams of stuff. This is unfiltered by the press or by pundits. It's straight from the candidate to the people.'' As of this writing there's a home page called Turn Left, whose slogan is YOU KNOW HEADING RIGHT IS A DEAD END: http://falcon.cc.ukans.edu/~cubsfan/. And there's a home page called The Right Side of the Web, which ''exists to counter all the socialism and moral anarchy you'll find on the web.'' It's at http://www.clark.net/pub/jeffd/index.html.

By autumn 1995, home pages for the 1996 presidential election were already up and running, even though it was far from certain which candidates would be on the ballot. (To receive an updated list of such sites, drop me a line at the address on the inside cover.) No less significant is the online presence of independent, relevant, factual resources for voters—for instance, Project Vote Smart (http://www.vote.smart.org), a self-described voters' self-defense system, and Votelink (http://votelink.com), an information-rich interactive polling station.

Now citizens can have much the same data as legislative advocates (lobbyists). At the same time as the Internet provides citizens with greater information about and closer access to the government, it also affords them greater influence *on* the government.

Legendary on the Internet is Dave Hughes, a highly decorated, retired army colonel, known as the Cursor Cowboy in Colorado Springs, where he's influenced legislation by posting local ordinances on his BBS there (telnet 192.160.122.1)—such as the bill to prevent the traffic to home businesses from disturbing neighbors, which also would have stilled modem- and phone-based home businesses. And his rallying cry over a matter of pending legislation regarding networks in education generated a significant flood of phone calls and faxes to Capitol Hill legislators—overnight.

More recently, *The Wall Street Journal* has reported the story of a thirty-two-year-old engineer, Richard Hartman, of Spokane, Washington, who'd never been active in politics. However, a new crime bill had provisions in it which incensed him—pork-barrel spending, in his view—and he said so in a forum on the Internet.

> [Hartman] received dozens of replies, some asking what *he* was doing to defeat [House] Speaker [Tom] Foley. So Mr. Hartman started a PAC called "Reform Congress: The De-Foley-Ate Project." He publicized it on the Internet and talk shows and raised $26,000 in small checks. The money paid for ads and an anti-Foley car parade . . . that had over 150 vehicles. Mr. Hartman's steering committee consist[ed] of 12 people from around the country, 10 of whom he . . . never met or even *spoke* with. They coordinated their activities on the Internet.

Speaker Foley lost at the polls (as did many other Democrats).

The same article, "We Are All Pundits Now," also quotes a progressive online activist, saying, "Voters . . . have come to believe they have just as much right to propose solutions as do Beltway policy wonks and experts."

While there aren't anywhere near over one hundred million voters using the Internet, as yet, it currently represents the reverse of an apathetic population, reflecting instead a very viable channel for informed citizen involvement in politics.

''The immediate involvement of the entire community in the central acts of decision'' via the Internet in a presidential election is still a revery. Yet we do see the Internet as itself an issue rallying a good deal of active political involvement. Even though shared modems doesn't necessarily mean shared ideas, there have been nonpartisan alliances over common causes, such as not drafting constricting limits to online freedom.

Currently, the politics of the Internet is open. Because the Internet is two-way, anyone can produce as well as consume information. You could even coin a symmetrical word for people both consuming and producing the same thing/at the same place—''prosuming.'' Radio, at its launch, was two-way; now, it's only two-way on the ham radio frequency. (On the other hand, an example of one-way asymmetry would be ''interactive'' video services currently in test phase, so-called ''interactive TV.'' There, the consumer has a range of choices, from a preset menu, but neither creates his or her own options nor interacts with other consumers.)

As Internet prosumers, we have an opportunity of determining for ourselves the outcome of this major new information system, while it's still in its formative stage. It may well be an education in democracy for an Information Age. As such, we can use the new technology, along with more traditional channels such as mouth-to-ear, in a democratic way to participate in its future—a future manifesting our deepest hopes and needs, as well as our greatest pleasures.

As we've seen, communication among numbers of people leads to shared experience, which forms a culture.

Here, Netiquette may be just another word for democracy. Netiquette and democracy make for good comparison. Like the Internet, democracy is not an entity or a thing. It's not something we have, but something we do. It's not broadcast—as over TV, or falling from the sky, on a silver platter, wrapped in a red ribbon, tied in a bow. Rather, it's do-it-yourself, and it involves taking power over your own life: tuning the dial—and taking part. Self-actualizing, autonomously. We've recently all seen that internationally. The extraordinary "ordinary people" of Russia, Lithuania, Poland, East Germany, Czechoslovakia, China, Tibet, Mongolia, and so forth, who stood up for democracy in 1989–1990, knew this, too—even though, for many of them, democracy was still something they had to believe in first before they could see it. On the other hand, America is the only nation in the world with the idea of democracy as its cornerstone, embodying it in action. Now the Internet demonstrates to us the process anew, perhaps because democracy's normative, always redefining itself.

Thus our Internet literacy can be an occasion for practicing and refining the arts of democracy. And perhaps the skills of democracy, in turn, will help us understand what kind of information infrastructure we should be building next.

Government does not come at the end of our road, here. Instead, to conclude our almanac, we'll look at the Internet in terms of society: that is, none other than we, ourselves. To paraphrase Lawrence Grossman, the former president of NBC News and of PBS, and author of the superb book *The Electronic Republic: Reshaping De-*

mocracy in the Information Age, democracy is a matter of citizenship as well as leadership.

SOCIETY

what is ——> is ——> up to us
—HOWARD RHEINGOLD

▶ *Civil society*

Civil society is independent of state and market sectors, composed of such things as church groups and parent-teacher associations, trade unions, cooperatives, service organizations, professional associations, chambers of commerce, hobbyists, and clubs. Civil society is becoming a global movement, as evidenced by the growing power of Nongovernmental Organizations (NGOs) in shaping the agendas and outcomes of the major United Nations world conferences in the 1990s.

An open society such as ours is composed of a dense mesh of these organizations. Because any one citizen is likely to be a member of more than one organization, he or she is likely to come into contact with differing opinions, a diversity of viewpoints. Such a pluralism can act as a healthy self-regulatory mechanism to our democratic process.

We often take this third sector, the public sector, for granted, yet it is one of the most dynamic sectors of our society today. And the Internet is an ideal resource for nonprofit organizations. Once it became clear that it was not a flash-in-the-pan fad, like citizen's band radio, nonprofits began using it as a way to not only disseminate their information but also organize for their causes. There are now enough nonprofits online to reach that critical mass enabling coalitions of grass-roots organizations to become viable and powerful. Lobbying, often requiring speed, can be done online at a greater pace as well as scope.

Electronic activism spans the political spectrum. The Institute for Global Communications is the venerable one-stop BBS/online service over substantive issues for progressive activists (http://www.igc.apc.org). Conservative activists can find affinity groups to work with through such web sites as Town Hall (http://www.town hall.com), and alt.politics.conservative, which has a very informative faq. And the Internet is a mainstream forum for such alternative movements as cooperatives, libertarians, objectivists, sovereigns, survivalists, etc.

In the previous chapter, we grasped how the Internet can enable the public to bypass professional lobbyists. (Actually, the Internet *is* a lobby: both a tool and object of lobbying.) Next, we'll look at Net resources for the public sector and for Internet issues in society. After that, we'll turn to women as an example of a social sector with various activist causes facilitated by the Net. And then we'll look at two electronic communities of place, to bring it all back home.

► *Nonprofit activists online*

The Contact Center Network links to thousands of non-profits, organized by topic and regional base. Http://www. contact.org. John December's online guide, discussed earlier, links to dozens of nonprofits involved in Internet communication.

Here are a few organizations exploring the possibilities of nonprofit activism online:

The Society for Electronic Access (SEA) is dedicated to making the world of computers and the communications links that bind their users together (cyberspace) open to everyone. They also believe that the same civil rights that protect our freedom in the physical world must prevail in cyberspace.

How to reach them:
The Society for Electronic Access
P.O. Box 7081
New York, NY 10116-7081
http://www.panix.com/sea

Computer Professionals for Social Responsibility is one of the most venerable online activist groups. Their mission is to provide the public and policymakers with realistic assessments of the power, promise, and problems of information technology. As concerned citizens, CPSR members work to direct public attention to critical choices concerning the applications of information technology and how those choices affect society.

E-mail to CPSR-Info@cpsr.org will automatically give you their brochure.

Center for Community Economic Research (CCER) is actively engaged in helping governments, community organizations, and educational institutions use Internet technology to enhance civic life. Its Economic Democracy Information Network (EDIN) supports and trains a whole range of community organizations in getting online. Http://garnet.berkeley.edu:3333/.

The Civic Network is a project of the Center for Civic Networking in collaboration with a growing number of individuals and organizations, including the Institute for the Study of Civic Values, Americans for Democratic Action, Sustainable Development Information Network, and the Millennium Report, and with links to other community-related subject trees. The site is an evolving collection of online resources dedicated to supporting civic life and civic participation. Http://www.civic.net:2401/.

The Internet NonProfit Center, begun in 1994, promotes information exchange among donors, volunteers, and nonprofit organizations, especially in ways that enhance an organization's accountability and strengthen its base of support. Its resources and links make it a perfect Square One for getting involved.
   How to reach them:
   The Internet NonProfit Center
   409 Third Street
   Brooklyn, NY 11215
   Http://www.nonprofits.org.

Impact Online is a new Internet nonprofit (launched April 1995), dedicated to helping people become more involved with other nonprofit organizations nationwide through donations, events, and virtual volunteering via e-mail. Their web site is building a community acting as a central point of communications and information on a

range of topical issues and organizations. Http://www.
iol.org.

▶ *Women*

> It is not the prerogative of men alone to bring light to
> this world.
> —AUNG SAN SUU KYI (pronounced Ong Sahn Sue Chee)

The Internet, as we've seen, fosters the formation of effective communities of interest. An excellent example of
that are women activists, using the Net in a number of
ways. It also represents a paradigm shift of its own.

A survey found that guys tend to see computers as a
toy, whereas gals see them as a tool. Thus might guys
have been more apt to use the Internet in its more difficult
infancy because, as a toy, they could tinker with it and
get it to work, whereas women would prefer to be able to
just turn it on, use it, and then turn it off without having
to fiddle around. However, with a graphical interface, any
possibilities of such difference are minimized.

"Traditional wisdom" has dictated that computer science—like science and math—is not a field for women
(*i.e.,* "Why don't you do something feminine?" "The
boys won't like you." "It's too hard for you."). Yet, in
the computer industry there is just as likely to be as many
if not more women CEOs than middle managers; Esther
Dyson, digital maven and current EFF chairwoman, spec-
ulates this is so because many women give up working
within a system with a glass ceiling and go create their
own companies.

Recent statistics from NSFNet and the Georgia Institute of Technology estimated the number of women on

the Net at more than 8.5 million, comprising over 17 percent of the estimated 50 million people on the Internet today. However, the demographic survey of every organization on the Internet conducted by John S. Quarterman and Smoot Carl-Mitchell found the ratio to be less than two to one—about sixty percent male, forty percent female.

There's nothing implicitly feminist about women being online, yet some women's subjects are more appropriately private: chats about sexuality, support groups about breast cancer, etc. Other areas, by being publicly available to all, help round out the dialogue, so guys can "get it," too. (It doesn't happen in a vacuum.) Some are concerned with such universal issues as poverty and human rights; others are focused on employment discrimination, sexual harassment, and domestic violence. Plus, women may well want to network with other women—whether about haute couture or health, fitness or finance—independent of feminism.

The Internet has permitted an increase of communication between people with common problems—as internal communication and as long-distance network, to exchange information and influence decision-making. Just as this has been true for individuals, corporations, and cities, so has it been true for people concerned with women's issues in civil society. Interestingly, women's issues have afforded the possibility of global problems (poverty, population explosion, etc.) being dealt with globally. This became evident during the United Nations Fourth World Conference on Women held in Beijing, August 1995—history's largest forum of NGOs (nongovernmental organizations). Many participants were aware that the new technology held a dual potential: for empowerment or greater disparity. Yet they found that being able to use it within their realities and needs made an effective addition to mail, fax, diskettes, radio, etc., as a means for women to access material created by other women and for dissemination of points of view. And they came away convinced of the self-sustainability of small computer network nodes. Despite differences in language, as well as access to technology and information, the success of their computer networking led participants to set up networks linking them together to track government action on the paper they ratified and to mobilize protest against any backsliding politicians trying to squirm out of the plan to improve women's lives. All in all, the use of the Net showed its efficacy for communication within individual groups, networking with other groups, receiving and transmitting information (even sending large amounts of information, such as position papers, back and forth within a short period of time), and influencing the decision-making process.

WomensNet and the Association of Progressive Communications formed a team of 40 women from 24 countries, speaking 18 languages collectively, to provide computer communications services (technical, support, training, and informational) for all participants free of charge for the duration of the conference. And, for anyone with Internet access unable to attend, they furnished background, the documents of the nongovernmental organizations (NGOs), and daily updates, via e-mail, conferences, and their web site—the next best thing to being

WOMEN'S VOICES

Cybergrrl (includes SafetyNet Domestic Violence Resources)
  http://www.cybergrrl.com
Digital Women
  http://www.women.org
Femina (a map of online resources for women and girls)
  http://www.femina.com
Feminist News & Events (includes resources for giving
feedback to news media)
  http://www.feminist.org/news/1_news.html
National Organization for Women
  http://now.org/now
Voices of Women
  http://www.voiceofwomen.com
Webgrrls (women on the Web)
  http://www.webgrrls.com
Women Artists Archive (WAA)
  http://www.sonoma.edu/waa/
Women Homepage
  http://www.mit.edu:8001/people/sorokin/women/
  index.html
Women's Information Resource Exchange (WIRE)
  http://www.women.com
Women's Resources on the Net
  http://www.bestcom/agoodloe/women.html
Women's Studies, University of Maryland, Subject Tree
  gopher.inform.umd.edu:70/11/EdRes/Topic/
  WomensStudies/Other Gophers
Women's Web InfoNet
  http://cyber-active.com/wwin
World's Women On-Line
  http://www.asu.edu/wwol/

there. WomensNet is an online community of individuals and organizations using computer technology to advance the interests of women worldwide. Similarly, one of WomensNet's goals is to get more women online. However, WomensNet leans more toward activism in community issues within a global context—issues such as poverty, violence, education, and equity.

Gopher: gopher.igc.apc.org

Web: http://www.womensnet.apc.org/womensnet/

At the outset of this book, we defined networking as interacting with a community of interest and exchanging information via computer. Now, at the close, we'll look at using computers to enhance the interaction of citizens regarding civil affairs—civic networking—essential to a healthy civil society.

▶ *Community networks*

East is east, west is west—but, in the end, home is best. Some of the best models for and uses of the Internet are right in our own backyards. While it creates communities of interest, how do we use it to talk about locale-specific issues, about where we live? We'll take a look at two American communities, Cleveland and Blacksburg, using the Net's power to create community networks (as well as networks of communities).

A Free-Net is both a community network and a network of such communities. It all began in Cleveland in 1984, almost by accident. Tom Grundner was working at Case Western Reserve University's Department of Family Medicine, where he started an informal BBS with his

Apple II Plus for the purpose of linking local medical clinics, to close the gap between Cleveland's far-flung residents and staff. Word, however, quickly went out through the community at large—and ordinary citizens were using the dial-up number to post medical questions to doctors. Within weeks of launching his BBS, in fact, it was flooded by so many of these calls that the system crashed.

If you have lemons, make lemonade. Tom, wisely, opened the door wider, rather than put a lock on it. He started a BBS, St. Silicon's Hospital & Information Dispensary. The most popular forum continued to be where people posted medical questions—and, now, doctors answered, within a day—which he dubbed Doc in a Box. When Doc in a Box was publicized, AT&T sent him some classy computer equipment for high-power networking. Legend has it, the card on the gift read, "Expand the concept, and report back." Grundner began networking other sectors of his community who moderated their own special-interest forums and helped spread the word around town. That network grew and now currently handles up to twelve thousand visits a day. Grundner now heads an organization called the National Public Telecomputing Network (NPTN), which is the hub to over 100 Free-Nets across America.

Big online services grab news headlines. But these low-bandwidth, by-your-bootstraps, grassroots-level civic Free-Nets deserve our attention just as much. They're like a complete virtual town within a real town. But the idea is not to replace the real communities, but to support them.

When you connect to Cleveland Free-Net, the civic metaphor is consistent through over a dozen options:

- The Administration Building.
- The Post Office—for sending and receiving e-mail.
- The Public Square—with such things as a cafe where you can chat with other users, a kiosk for adults only, a podium for electronic speeches, also adults only, a singles partyline, a speakeasy, a nonsexist special interest group, etc.
- The Courthouse and Government Center—with a courthouse (with legal information), the Freedom Shrine (with historic documents, more about which in a sec), contacts to local representatives, governmental (800) hotlines, the National Weather Service, county engineer's office, safety and environment, Institute for Democracy in Education, the year's federal budget, and I.R.S. information.
- The Arts Building offers culture high and low— literary, theatrical, musical, audio, visual, and culinary.
- The Science and Technology Center includes the local Museum of Natural History, IEEE (Institute of Electrical & Electronic Engineers), a computer corner, NASA, home, yard, and garden, environmental discussion, and special-interest groups for solid waste, functional MRI, and skeptics.
- The Medical Arts Building is a big complex, housing St. Silicon's Hospital, The Handicap Center, Alzheimer's Disease Support Center, Psychology and Mental Health, The Byte Animal Clinic, The Center for Inter-

national Health, Substance Abuse Education, The Pediatric Information Resource Center, Safety and the Environment, and the state bioethics and nursing networks.

- The Schoolhouse has a lounge for local students to hang out, and one for teachers and administrators, a library, plus a program called Academy One, the electronic schoolhouse, with information, curricula databases, and bulletin boards of interest to administrators, teachers, and students. Plus it hosts special multidisciplinary projects linking remote sites, along the lines we've seen in our chapter on education.

For example, a Cleveland school was a launch site and mission control for a full-scale space shuttle they'd made. An elementary school in California was designated as an "alternate landing site," and filed hourly weather reports. Another school in Ohio, acting as "Solar Tracking Station," monitored the National Bureau of Standards shortwave radio broadcasts for reports of solar activity and reported them to Mission Control. All schools correlated the "launch" with a week-long series of educational activities incorporating science, computers, and space.

- The Community Center and Recreation Area.
- The Business and Industrial Park features a personnel office for local employment information, a travel agent, a computer room, a tax advisor, an insurance office, legal information, a local newspaper syndicate, a place for car talk, the latest economic information from the U.S. Department of Commerce, etc.

- The Library has a bookshelf of books online, local libraries, national libraries, and that Freedom Shrine we saw back in the Courthouse and Government Center.

The Freedom Shrine contains the Constitution plus pre- and post-Constitution documents, and a historical timeline. For example, post-Constitution documents include the following:

1 1787—The Northwest Ordinance
2 1789—French Declaration of Rights
3 1793—The Proclamation of Neutrality
4 1795—The Treaty of Greenville
5 1796—Washington's farewell address
6 1801—Jefferson's first inaugural address
7 1823—The Monroe Doctrine
8 1862—The Emancipation Proclamation
9 1863—The Gettysburg Address
10 1865—Lincoln's second inaugural address
11 1945—German surrender documents
12 1945—Japanese surrender documents
13 1963—Dr. Martin Luther King, Jr.'s "I Have a
             Dream" speech

- University Circle accesses not only the local colleges, but also the city's Museum of Natural History, the Children's Museum, and the Institute of Music.
- The Teleport has a Terminal Tower for teleporting (telneting) to libraries around the state, nation, and globe.
- The Communications Center is a small Internet hub, with ftp, wais, as well as links to the chat rooms, e-mail, etc.

And it's all free!

That is, it's free for anyone on the Internet who can telnet to it but, more importantly, free for the citizens of Cleveland themselves. They can go there and say, "We did *this*. This is *us!*" as well as "This I can use."

That's empowerment.

Telnet: freenet-in-a.cwru.edu.

Then there are community networks that in some ways are like a subset of a Free-Net, and in some ways, quite different. Blacksburg, Virginia (Montgomery County), is an American community of 36,000 in the Appalachian mountains which has gone online—linking homes, businesses, schools, and government offices to each other and to the world.

Blacksburg Electronic Villagers (BEVs) scan the shelves at the local supermarket, video store, or university library, order groceries or flowers, or pick up a coupon for a local restaurant. The town supports electronic payment of water, sewer, and garbage bills, automobile registration and parking sticker fee payments, as well as filing of complaints.

More than a third of Blacksburg—about 13,000 people—are online. Of a total of three hundred businesses, about half are online, and are reporting noticeable gains in orders. BEV residents discuss issues on the town agenda and review their children's homework assignments. And, from a geographically remote area in the foothills of Appalachia, BEV residents are talking to people around the world.

They are (like ourselves) living history—one of the last generations not to know this new technology and one of the first to adopt it. And so they're documenting the transformation, in an innovative, multimedia history project—recording history while they make it, from multiple points of view.

It originated when local faculty and staff of Virginia Tech approached the campus Information Systems department about extending the campus network into town for those who live off-campus. Then the idea of further extending it to the community took hold. With support of the civic officials, Information Systems put forth a proposal to Bell Atlantic. When they began planning, "the Internet was barely known outside the science and academic community," recalls BEV Director Andrew Michael Cohill. "We bet on the Internet long before it was a household word because we felt it was the only technology that could scale up gracefully to support an entire community."

The town, the telephone company, and the college each contribute staff, support, and expertise. Additionally, college faculty members research and evaluate the use and impact of networking on the lives of citizens, schools, businesses, community groups, and on the community as a whole—starting from Day One. When the project launched, they began by interviewing the developers and key community groups—schools and university, library, government, local merchants, the telephone company, and some of the first 190 users.

Then they documented episodes in the project's development and use. For example, when a contributor to a car-repair forum criticized dealings with a local garage, one of the shop's other customers printed the criticism and gave it to the garage mechanic. The mechanic called the project, to ask how to tell his side of the story. "He was very motivated to join the BEV," says John Carroll, local computer science whiz. "The story is about new consumer empowerment, but it is also an allegory of technology haves and have-nots." Carroll explained further:

> One advantage of an electronic village is it makes services more accessible; but, when some businesses and customers are not able to be online, it can divide a community. It raises an issue of fairness.

Further, all users have been invited to describe an experience they'd like to share, for posting to the web. And anyone can add their notes to anyone else's story. Carroll continues:

> Traditionally, people have gathered around campfires and kitchen tables to listen to a single telling of a tale, perhaps by someone who had directly experienced the events in the tale, or perhaps by someone who had heard the tale and was merely passing it along. But in hypermedia folklore, we will hear (and see and read) many different tellings of a tale by different participants, rather than from a single privileged perspective. This is revolutionary; it democratizes history.
>
> In 1991, I was convinced that taking a historical view of human-computer interaction could provide a better picture of its concepts and practices. Now, I see that the creation of and access to history can be a tool in the design process. It can help ensure that no single view becomes privileged without due process, that the vision of a design project remains accessible and discussible, perhaps even improvable. The BEV HistoryBase is providing a comprehensive documentation system for the residents of the Blacksburg Electronic Village and a dynamic and vivid

model for communities worldwide who want to create their own electronic villages.

Blacksburg: Exit 1 on the Information Superhighway. Http://www.bev.net/

Contrasting the two models, Blacksburg considers itself a global electronic village, providing the community with access to the Internet as well as a local forum. BEV is not free. University accounts are already free, since the university already underwrites access, but home and businesses pay to subscribe. The cost has risen but is still less than an account with, say, America Online. Bell Atlantic of Virginia provided the wiring and telecom links and is using the project to study the values, needs, and interests of an electronic village, and to learn what businesses benefit, and how many users make up the critical mass needed before profitability can be enhanced. The Town of Blacksburg provides grants of up to $500 to help local businesses establish a presence on the world-wide web. Town and university people helped administer the project (with an office located at the university's museum of natural history), and technical staff have now been hired by the project.

Nor is access to the Internet free. Each institution, organization, corporation, or individual with access to the Internet has purchased that access through a service provider. If access has been purchased for an entire organization without the cost being passed along, then the Internet appears to be free. Internet culture was free from the beginning, too, because it was composed of communities of researchers and scholars—who traditionally disseminate knowledge as their profession. How might that translate into civic values, were network access to be made universally available at a local or even statewide level? We're just beginning to see, and the Free-Net Movement's leading the way—entirely bottom-up, of course.

The Internet creates communities of interest that cross boundaries. But in many forums the question has arisen: how can international interest groups discuss locale-specific issues in a global network? Free-Nets demarcate a space wherein local residents can use the Net's possibility to talk about the place where they live. They foster not only a community network but a community of place.

Tom Grundner, the founder of Cleveland Free-Net, states his case quite simply (using an analogy that hearkens back to the beginning of our Internet subject tour):

> The primary analogy we might use for community computing is the development of the free public library. Most people do not realize that in the latter part of the nineteenth century, the free public library did not exist. Eventually, the literacy rate became high enough (and the cost of book production became low enough) that the public library became feasible. People in cities and towns all across the country banded together to make free public access to the printed word a reality. The result was a legacy from which every person reading this . . . has, at one point or another, benefited.
>
> In this century, we believe we have reached the point at which computer "literacy" has gotten high enough (and the cost of equipment low enough) that a similar demand has formed for free, public-access, networked information services—the late-twentieth-century analogue to the circumstances that led to the free public library.

The key to the economics of operating a community computer system is the fact that the system is literally run by the community itself. Everything that appears in a Free-Net is there because there are individuals or organizations in the community who are prepared to contribute their time, effort, and expertise, to place it there and operate it over time. This, of course, is in contrast to the commercial services, which have very high personnel and information-acquisition costs and must pass those costs on to the consumer.

If you couple this volunteerism with the rapidly dropping costs of computing power, the use of inexpensive transmission technology, and the fact that the necessary software to operate Free-Nets is available through a nonprofit organization for $1 a year, then public access computing becomes an economically viable option.

If you're personally interested in seeing a Free-Net in your own community, you well may be able to see it happen. You could begin by locating the key community representatives it might concern: civic leaders, local libraries, schools, universities, medical centers, businesses, phone/cable companies, computer user-groups, media, etc. The Free-Net can offer a start-up association with the other Free-Nets, plus the support of organization, funding, legal issues, and the technology: more importantly, they bring the *process*.

For the future of Free-Nets, Grundner envisions an analog of the Corporation for Public Broadcasting. He'd like to see a permanent fund which would offer a local community an interest-free loan. Estimating the cost of starting up and operating for the first year at $15,000, a community of 625 people charged $1 per month for access could repay the loan in two years. (After that, the only costs of the Free-Net would be for the phone lines and any staff.)

For more information:
National Public Telecomputing Network
30680 Bainbridge Road
Solon, Ohio 44139
Voice: 216-498-4050
E-mail: info@nptn.org
Web: http://www.nptn.org

Virtual communities are not utopian panaceas, nor do they replace real-life communities. Intellectual caution and due prudence are always recommended. As we noted in our Internet map: fit virtual resources in to the overall ecology of your own communication system.

Thus far, an experiential lesson learned from applying the slogan THINK GLOBAL—ACT LOCAL is how important it is to have a local network infrastructure as a base, within which to act, as well as the power of having a maximal horizon within reach from there. When more local and regional communities have their networks, we shall discover new slogans and spatial metaphors, homegrown and universal.

Meanwhile, we might continue to ask how do the dynamics of community life influence networking movements, and how do the emerging networks interact with the communities around them? And how is the emerging network movement changing the nature of social movements and challenging the very concepts of community?

The Net is fostering a broad-based social movement known as network communities. And it fosters, too, the development of community networks, that can facilitate community organizing, local business alliances, and access to community and government information. The two phases—network communities and community networks—can be thought of as a synergy between the social dynamics and technical structures of computer networking. The wide variety of activities the infrastructure can provide is sure to effect substantial changes in our social fabric. And, lest the synergy be disharmonious, a final question we need to continue to ask is: what economic, social, and political consequences will differential access to the technology—haves and have-nots—hold for the emerging Information Society?

▶ *Summing up*

> You have to organize, organize, organize, and build and build, and train and train, so that there is a permanent, vibrant structure of which people can be part.
>
> —RALPH REED, Christian Coalition

In his electronic newsletter, *The Network Observer*, Phil Agre comments on this quote.

> [Reed] is talking about a "structure." He means a membership organization. In his case, of course, it's the Christian Coalition, but the underlying principle applies widely. He's not just talking about getting everyone on the Net. He's not just talking about getting his views out to an abstraction called "the public." He's not just talking about sending out political action alerts to the ether and hoping that someone somewhere will act on them. He's talking about building an organization. What does that mean? It means having chapters and membership lists. It

means giving everyone a chance to discover their own strengths and passions and the support to enact those things within the framework of the organization. It means creating a sense of belonging, productive activity, personal growth, successes, and shared goals. Have you been involved in such an organization? Have you had bad experiences, convincing you that organizations are necessarily boring, static, or oppressive? Have you ever had a chance to learn the skills of working with others democratically within an organization? These questions are good starting points for defining your vision and deciding what you want to be remembered for when you die.

Indeed, much of the Internet's organizing and community-building capabilities quite resemble a function in a church basement. And, like the Gideon Bible, online are the Torah, the King James Bible, the Qur'an, the Book of Mormon, Buddhist precepts and sutras, etc. Each denomination not only has ftp sites, gophers, and web sites, but also its forums gathering together adherents, practitioners, and seekers on the path, worldwide.

Bringing your church group—as well as labor association or business league, literary discussion group or gardening association—online would prove healthy for the group *and* reinforce the health of the Internet. (The Institute for the Study of Civic Values has a good collection of resources on community-building: http://libertynet. org/~edcivic/iscvhome.html.)

You, too, might decide to be a virtual volunteer—either for your favorite charity, or for the Internet, or, best of all, for both. It can be time well-spent!

Paul Evan Peters, Director of the Coalition for Networked Information, has compared the development of the Internet to the Stone Age. To paraphrase: in the Paleolithic Era, hunter-gatherers roamed the forests in search of food; in the Paleo-electronic Era, Internauts roam the networks, looking for bits and bytes. Like their prehistoric ancestors, some have little respect for civilization and engage in rude, predatory activities.

In the Mesolithic, humans began to band together in groups. A few realized some foods were easier to farm than gather wild. And stone tools were made to improve hunting and farming. Today's Meso-electronic information farmers are learning to grow their own data locally, and networkers form coalitions and special-interest groups. Even if they are in competing fields, they share such tools as e-mail, forums, and the world-wide web.

Our Neolithic ancestors refined their tools and farming methods. Populations flourished; social order began . . .

No one knows what the Neolithic will look like, when bandwidth widens to include multimedia and resources converge in a national and global information infrastructure. And there's never a conclusion when talking about the future.

Yet the future is within our reach.

The Internet is literacy for the future . . . today!

APPENDIX

Information Resources

MAIL

There are several "white pages" directories of e-mail addresses. The latest is NetFind. Telnet ds.internic.net, log-in as netfind, or gopher ds.internic.net:4320.

Another e-mail address search is WhoIs. Telnet rs.internic.net, log-in as whois.

Two books, for more on mail: John S. Quarterman's *The E-mail Companion* and Marshall Rose's *The Internet Message*.

MAILING LISTS

Lists of lists

1) Usenet groups such as news.newusers and news.groups sometimes have lists of lists, such as the Publicly Available Mailing Lists (PAML). Here are three:

Gopher://cs1.presby.edu/internet-resources/mailing lists
Http://www.library.ucsb.edu/subjects/internet/paml.
Http://www.tile.net/tile/listserv/index.html

2) There are indexes of lists at a web page maintained by Canadian journalist Michael O'Reilly, in his Cyberspace Shortcuts area: http://publix.empath.on.ca/HelpLink/mo.

3) Each mailing list server will give you a list of all the lists it contains. For example, if you e-mail Listserv@ulkyvm.louis ville.edu, with the message Lists Global, it will send you back a long list of known Listserv mailing lists. Listserv@bitnic.bitnet also has another enormous list of lists.

E-mail Majordomo@acs.ryerson.ca, with the one-word message Lists. And so on for other list software, such as listproc and mailbase.

For more on lists, check out Vivian Neou's book *Internet Mailing List Navigator*.

Usenet Launch Pad

http://sunsite.unc.edu/usenet-i/

List of Usenet newsgroups

http://www.nova.edu/Inter-Links/cgi-bin/newslists.p/

List of Usenet faqs

http://www.cis.ohio-state.edu/hypertext/faq/usenet/FAQ-
List.html
http://www.cs.ruu.nl/cgi-bin/faqwais

About faqs

http://www.cis.ohio-state.edu/hypertext/faq/usenet/faqs/about-
faqs/faq.html

Usenet Info Center

http://sunsite.unc.edu/usenet-b/home.html
ftp.clark.net pub/usenet-b/info/bible-faq

Newsgroup archives

ftp://ftp.neosoft.com/pub/users/claird/news.lists/newsgroup
_archives.html
http://www.dejanews.com

FTP

Archie

Telnet: Archie.sura.net. Log-in as archie. Precede the key
word(s) to search for with the word Prog.

Bsic ftp commands for a text-based interface

cd [directory name]—switches to the directory you want
ls—lists files for that directory

cdup—changes your directories one level up

binary—switches you to binary mode, if you're downloading binary (non-ascii) files; typing ascii will switch you back

get [filename]—transfers the file from remote host to you; (specifying the entire path will save having to navigate directories to get there)

help—lists all the ftp commands

TELNET

Hytelnet is a database of many telnet sites.
Telnet: access.usask.ca. Log-in: hytelnet.
Web: http://library.usask.ca/hytelnet

GOPHER

Where to find it:

Telnet: consultant.micro.umn.edu. Log in: gopher.

Where to find veronica:

Gopher: veronica.scs.unr.edu, and look under Other Gophers & Information Servers.

Moving around gopherspace in a text-based interface

Press return to view a document
Use the arrow keys or vi/emacs equivalent to move around

Up .... :	Move to previous line.
Down .... :	Move to next line.
Right Return .... :	"Enter"/Display current item.
Left, u .... :	"Exit" current item/Go up a level.
>, +, Pgdwn, space ..... :	View next page.
<, −, Pgup, b .... :	View previous page.
0-9 .... :	Go to a specific line.
m .... :	Go back to the main menu.

Bookmarks

a : Add current item to the bookmark list.
A : Add current directory/search to bookmark list.
v : View bookmark list.
d : Delete a bookmark/directory entry.

Other commands

s : Save current item to a file.
D : Download a file.
q : Quit with prompt.
Q : Quit unconditionally.
= : Display url for current item.
O : Change options.
/ : Search for an item in the menu.
n : Find next search item.
o : Open a new gopher server.
! : Shell Escape.

WAIS

Where to find it:

Telnet: wais.com. Log-in: wais.
Web: http://www.wais.com.
   http://www.ai.mit.edu/the-net/wais.html.

WORLD-WIDE WEB

Lynx is low-tech software for accessing world-wide web servers text-based only; no images, videos, or sounds. It's an option if 1) you don't have full Internet connectivity (such as Slip or Ppp) and/or 2) you don't have a super-high-speed connectivity (such as T1 or ISDN) and don't want to wait for images and other media to "fill."

It uses arrow keys, tab, and highlight bars. A very good feature is the command G. Typing this allows you to go from the site's home page to any other you specify.

If Lynx is not installed at the domain you're at, telnet to a site where it is. Telnet:

fatty.law.cornell.edu   Log-in: www
rsl.ox.ac.uk   Log-in: lynx

To obtain the software itself:
    ftp: ftp2.cc.ukans.edu
    path: /pub/lynx/

Three popular web search engines are:

WebSearch	http://www.websearch.com
Lycos	http://www.lycos.com
Inktomi	http://inktomi.berkeley.edu

An excellent repository of web information can be found at the World-Wide Web Consortium, http://www.w3.org.

Bibliography

BOOKS, MAGAZINES, ONLINE MAGAZINES, & ONLINE TUTORIALS

Books

Zen & the Art of Internet by Brendan Kehoe began as an online booklet and was published on paper in 1993, probably the first, major, general Internet book on the shelves. Now there are hundreds.

There are (or will be) books on the Internet in relation to every conceivable subject and human endeavor. And there are tutorials and manuals for every phase of Internet practice, the two most popular (despite their somewhat demeaning names) being the *For Dummies* and *Complete Idiots' Guides*. As an intermediate reference, the *Unleashed* series contains solid, encyclopedic information.

For readers wishing a detailed history of the origins of the Internet, Daniel Comer's *The Internet Book* is the standard in the field. As to its future, we heartily recommend *The New Information Infrastructure: Strategies for U.S. Policy*, edited by William J. Drake, and The National Research Council's *Realizing the Information Future—The Internet and Beyond* (National Academy Press, 800-624-6242). And, somewhere in between past and future, there are quite a number of engaging, resourceful magazines, on paper and online.

Magazines

Boardwatch began way back in March 1987 as the magazine for the BBS world—a professional magazine for amateurs and hobbyists, but has included the Internet in its radar screen of late. Unpretentious, appealing to as diverse an audience as can be, this can be relied upon to have several worthwhile articles every issue. The non-Internet-related articles are of interest as well, as the BBS world continues to thrive. Http://www.boardwatch.com.

The venerable *Internet World* began as a newsletter for commercial and noncommercial uses of the Internet and the National Research and Education Network. Today it is a full, glossy magazine with thematic issues, features, trends, and resources for the average user.

To browse previous articles, point your web browser to http://www.mecklerweb.com—where you'll also find daily updates on the Internet and other information media.

Not an Internet magazine per se, no list would be complete without *Wired*. A trend-setter, *Wired* would be to upscale computer culture what *Rolling Stone* first was to rock and roll in the 1960s, in terms of lifestyle and attitude. Its immediate success upon its debut showed the viability of the market.

Their web site is a completely separate, free, online magazine called *HotWired*. Http://www.hotwired.com.

NetGuide, on the other end of the spectrum, is comparable to *Wired*, as *Seventeen* or *Cosmopolitan* are to *Vanity Fair*. In addition to features and regular departments, new online sites are reviewed each month in various categories. Http://techweb.com/net.

.net: The Internet Magazine, out of Britain, wins the prize for Most Refreshing, Original Perspective. It's available in the U.S. now, but they can be reached at: Future Publishing Ltd., 30 Monmouth Street, Bath, Avon BA1 2BW. Telephone: 01225 442244; Fax: 01225 423212.

Infobahn: The Magazine of Internet Culture debuted in August 1995 with articles about Phil Zimmerman's federal indictment for authoring Pretty Good Privacy e-mail encryption software, the Internet's prime position in the 1996 presidential election, and misinformed myths being spawned by Internet critics. Http://server.postmodern.com.

Having debuted fall 1995, *VirtualCity* advertises itself as "a magazine about cyberspace for those of us who have a life on earth." Http://www.virtcitnow.com.

Having debuted in November 1995, *Websights* is the first magazine devoted to the world-wide web. It makes a good travel magazine to the vast, uncharted web wilderness, featuring recreational and entertaining resources. The online companion is http://web sight.com.

21.C: Scanning the Future, initiated by Australia's Commission for the Future, is a lively magazine of culture, technology, and science. The web sight has a lively, interactive forum: http://www. 21c.com.au.

ConneXions is one of the pioneer trade publications, tracking developments in the computer and communications industry— primarily for technical readers but with occasional gems for the average reader. Http://www.interop.com/#pub.

Plus, there are fine magazines aimed at developers working in interactive multimedia and the online world, such as *New Media* and *Morph's Online*, as well as scholarly journals.

Online magazines

Whether for beginners, intermediate, or advanced, one of the best sources of information about the Internet is . . . through your modem.

The Internet Press is an online guide to electronic journals about the Internet, by Kevin M. Savetz and John M. Higgins, and updated periodically. As with everything else from these intrepid and thorough writers, highly recommended.

To receive a copy, e-mail a message to ipress-request@north coast.com, entitled Archive, which says Send Ipress in the body.

Flash Information is a great weekly news bulletin, a bibliography with abstracts. Http://www.citi.doc.ca.

Edupage is an Internet magazine summarizing information technology news items appearing in leading newspapers and magazines. It's provided three times each week as a service by Educom—a consortium of leading colleges and universities seeking to transform education through the use of information technology. *Edupage* does not talk about education, but it does give one-paragraph summaries of technology stories printed in leading newspapers and magazines.

To receive it, send an e-mail letter to Listproc@educom.edu that SAYS SUB EDUPAGE <YOUR NAME> in the body.

Current Cites is a monthly digest published by Information Age librarians at the University of California, Berkeley. Topics covered include electronic publishing, multimedia and hypermedia, and networks and networking. Citations of articles and books in these fields are accompanied by abstracts and reviews, making it a very useful survey.

To subscribe, send the message "sub cites [your name]" to listserv@library.berkeley.edu, replacing "[your name]" with your name.

New on the Net is an informative collection of news and commentary.

To receive a copy, e-mail: news.on.the.net@reply.net.

CyberWire Dispatch, launched in January 1994, offers commentary, investigations, and hard news relevant to telecommunication issues of the day, including CyberpornGate, the FBI's Digital Wiretap bill, and the National Security Agency's withholding of known flaws in Clipper Chip from the public. Editor/publisher/ writer Brock N. Meeks is a former foreign correspondent, now Washington Bureau Chief for *Inter@ctive Week*. In addition to his unrivaled investigative skills Meeks writes in a "hard-hitting, take-no-prisoners" style that can top the best of Mailer, Didion, Wolfe, and Thompson.

To subscribe: e-mail Cwd-1-Request@Cyberwerks.com with the word subscribe as the first line of your message.

Gopher: Cyberwerks.com.

Http://Www.cyberwerks.com/cyberwire

The Red Rock Eater news service (RRE) is one of the Internet's most respected sources of news and information about the social and political aspects of computing and networking. Now in its third year of operation, with over 3,000 subscribers from fifty countries, RRE is a mailing list that consists of whatever its intrepid editor, Phil Agre, finds interesting: a steady trickle (five or ten messages a week at most) of useful materials filtered from a wide range of different sources. Comparing RRE to more ephemeral electronic communication, one reader attests, ''The difference is like that between white bread bought from a supermarket and a good light rye sourdough bought from a wood-fired bakery. Much chewier, and much healthier!''

How to get it: Send e-mail that looks like this:

To: rre-request@weber.ucsd.edu

Subject: subscribe firstname lastname

For more information about RRE, send a message like so:

To: rre-request@weber.ucsd.edu

Subject: help

On the web: http://communication.ucsd.edu/pagre/rre.html

Interactive Age started out being an industry weekly, somewhat like *Variety*. Then it seemed to shift from being about interactive media in general to focusing on the Internet.

It had launched with a web page, but, within a year of publication, the web site literally devoured the paper version, and now it all exists solely online: http://techweb.cmp.com/ia.

C|net central is a TV-show devoted to computers. It aspires to being a twenty-four-hour station, like the Sci-Fi Channel. Meanwhile, it already does a superb job, and its web site is top-notch and updated weekly: http://www.cnet.com

Web Review covers the people, the technology, and the social dynamics of the web. They don't just talk about technology, they use it in creative ways to tell their stories. The cover story for their launch was *Virtual New Hampshire*, a look at how U.S. presidential candidates use the web to deliver their message. They used RealAudio™ to hold the first-ever political cyber talkshow/roundtable with a member from the GOP, White House, the webmaster for Phil Gramm, and the guy who did the first cyber-political action committee, Newt Watch. Biweekly. Http://gnn.com/wr.

Online Internet tutorials

Last, but not least, tutorials about the Internet are emerging *on* the Internet. Here are some of the best we've seen. For more resources, please look under ''Internet, online aids'' in the index.

Back To School is an Internet beginner's program for information professionals, such as librarians, originating from the University of South Carolina. The thirty lessons are archived and hyperlinked. Http://http://web.csd.sc.edu/bck2skol/bck2skol.html.

BIX, in Ottawa, is in the business of net presence/marketing/net-surfing. Their home page includes a number of online teaching courses, such as the Roadmap mailing list series, and a very fine, hands-on tutorial called ISS-101 (the Internet Survival Series). Http://www.interlog.com/~bxi (select "resources," then "training").

Easy Internet. Cheeky, self-styled "cyber-celebrity" Davey Windey of *net* magazine, tells all about things Internet. Http://www.futurenet.co-uk/netmag/issue1/ewasy/index.html.

Global Village. Accompanying this juicy Internet guide is a beginner's tour which will let you check the stock market, check the latest news, research accounting software, hire a graphic designer, find a government document, and send birthday flowers. Http://www.globalcenter.net/gcweb/tour.html.

Internet Room contains an ample and unique collection of online help for the beginner, including texts by Phil Agre, Patrick Cirspin, Odd de Presno, Martin Raish, Arlene H. Rinaldi, and Roy Tennant. Gopher://lib-gopher.lib.indiana.edu:70/11/research-aid/internet-room.

Mecklerweb's Entry Level, from the publishers of *Internet World.* Http://www.mecklerweb.com/webguide/entry/htm.

Network Training Materials contains aids, guides, and lists, plus a bibliography of online resources. Gopher mailbase.ac.uk.

Newbie's Guide introduces many useful resources, including online manuals. Http://ug.cs.dal.ca:3400/newbie.html.

Understanding the Internet provides over two hundred references for beginners, including links to the latest Internet software, background guides, and several lists of online resources. Http://www.screen.com/understand/explore.html.

Index